Effective Inclusive Schools

Effective Inclusive Schools
Designing Successful Schoolwide Programs

Thomas Hehir with Lauren Katzman

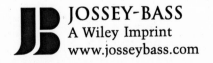

JOSSEY-BASS
A Wiley Imprint
www.josseybass.com

Published by Jossey-Bass

A Wiley Imprint

One Montgomery Street, Suite 1200, San Francisco, CA 94104-4594—www.josseybass.com

Jossey-Bass books and products are available through most bookstores. To contact Jossey-Bass directly call our Customer Care Department within the U.S. at 800-956-7739, outside the U.S. at 317-572-3986, or fax 317-572-4002.

Wiley publishes in a variety of print and electronic formats and by print-on-demand. Some material included with standard print versions of this book may not be included in e-books or in print-on-demand. If this book refers to media such as a CD or DVD that is not included in the version you purchased, you may download this material at http://booksupport.wiley.com. For more information about Wiley products, visit www.wiley.com.

Library of Congress Cataloging-in-Publication Data

Hehir, Thomas.
  Effective inclusive schools : designing successful schoolwide programs / by Thomas Hehir with Lauren I. Katzman.
    p. cm.
  Includes bibliographical references and index.
  ISBN 978-0-470-88014-2 (pbk.), 978-1-118-13363-7 (ebk.), 978-1-118-13364-4 (ebk.), 978-1-118-13365-1 (ebk.)
  1. Inclusive education–United States. 2. School management and organization–United States. 3. Mainstreaming in education–United States. I. Katzman, Lauren I. II. Title.
  LC1201.H44 2012
  371.9'0460973–dc23

                                                                        2011039117

FIRST EDITION

PB Printing 10 9 8 7 6 5 4 3 2

CONTENTS

To Dr. William Henderson: Teacher, mentor, and friend

ABOUT THE AUTHORS

Thomas Hehir, Ed.D., is the Silvana and Christopher Pascucci Professor of Practice in Learning Differences at the Harvard Graduate School of Education. As director of the U.S. Department of Education's Office of Special Education Programs from 1993 to 1999, Hehir was responsible for federal leadership in implementing the Individuals with Disabilities Education Act (IDEA) and played a leading role in developing the Clinton administration's proposal for the 1997 reauthorization of IDEA. In 1990, Hehir was associate superintendent for the Chicago Public Schools, where he implemented major changes in the special education service delivery system, enabling Chicago to reach significantly higher levels of compliance with the IDEA and resulting in the eventual removal of oversight by the U.S. Department of Education's Office for Civil Rights. Hehir served in a variety of positions in the Boston Public Schools from 1978 to 1987, including that of director of special education from 1983 to 1987. An advocate for children with disabilities in the education system, he has written extensively on special education, special education in the reform movement, due process, and least restrictive environment issues.

Lauren I. Katzman, Ed.D., is executive director of special education for the New York City Department of Education. Previously Dr. Katzman served as associate professor of special education at Boston University's School of Education. Prior to earning her doctorate at Harvard's Graduate School of Education, Katzman worked for fourteen years as a special education teacher in New York, New Jersey, and Missouri.

PREFACE: ON ABLEISM

Have you taught people with disabilities like me before?

Will we do math in second grade?

If I find something challenging, what do you request that I do?

—Anthony, a first grader at
the Henderson Inclusion
Elementary School in Boston

Anthony has cerebral palsy and insisted on being part of the process of selecting his new second grade teacher. This young disability activist had previously been successful in advocating for accommodated recess activities for both himself and for a friend with autism.

"If you have a typically developing kid, you have a litany of choices. If you have a specially developing child, then you're presented with an option."

Anthony's parents are pleased with their son's school, having already experienced an unsuccessful placement in another school. "If you have a typically developing kid, you have a litany of choices. If you have a specially developing child, then you're presented with an option," said Anthony's mother, who became emotional speaking about their decision. "And then what happens when you think this school is not a good fit for my child? It's just hard."[1]

The story of Anthony and his parents inspired us to write this book. As two career-long special educators deeply committed to children with disabilities and to improving special education, our experience has taught us that Anthony's story is far too rare. Effective inclusive education is difficult for most parents and caregivers of children with disabilities to obtain for their kids. Finding the right program for a child with a disability often entails inordinate effort.

However, as Anthony's story illustrates, there are schools, like the Henderson, that have been successful in providing effective inclusive special education services. As individuals involved in preparing new teachers and school leaders, we believed the dearth of research on successful practices in inclusive education compromised our ability to prepare future educators. We therefore sought to conduct a study that looked deeply at practices within highly successful inclusive schools.

The failure of the education system to provide more widespread options for children and families undoubtedly has many causes. Schools were designed for average students, not for those with complex needs. However, despite nearly forty years of federal law that seeks to provide greater access to education for students with disabilities, we see the lack of effective inclusive options for parents and children as a reflection of broader, deeply held negative attitudes in society toward people with disabilities—a term we call *ableism*.

Thomas Hehir has written extensively on this subject.[2] The existing definitions of *ableism* share common origins that are rooted in the discrimination and oppression that many disabled people experience in society.[3] *Ableism* was defined by Laura Rauscher and Mary McClintock as "a pervasive system of discrimination and exclusion that oppresses people who have mental, emotional and physical disabilities. . . . Deeply rooted beliefs about health, productivity, beauty, and the value of human life, perpetuated by the public and private media, combine to create an environment that is often hostile to those whose physical, mental, cognitive, and sensory abilities . . . fall out of the scope of what is currently defined as socially acceptable."[4] African American disability activist and talk-show host Greg Smith captures the essence of definitions of ableism in his article "The Brother in the Wheelchair": "I've faced unintentional discrimination, and it's just as damaging as racism. . . . It's called ableism, the devaluation and disregard of people with disabilities."[5]

As Tom Hehir wrote in the *Harvard Educational Review* in Spring 2002: "Applied to schooling and child development, ableist preferences become particularly apparent. From an ableist perspective, the devaluation of disability results in societal attitudes that uncritically assert that it is better for a child to walk than roll, speak than sign, read print than read Braille, spell independently than use a spell-check, and hang out with nondisabled kids as opposed to other disabled kids, etc. In short, in the eyes of many educators and society, it is preferable for disabled students to do things in the same manner as nondisabled kids."[6]

Ableist assumptions cause harm when the . . . services provided to disabled children focus inordinately on the characteristics of their disabilities . . . when changing disability becomes the overriding focus.

Certainly, in a world that has not been designed with the disabled in mind, being able to perform in a manner that is similar to that of nondisabled children gives disabled children distinct advantages. If efficient ambulation is possible, a child who has received the help he needs to walk is at an advantage in a barrier-filled world. Similarly, a child with a mild hearing loss who has been given the amplification and speech therapy she needs may have little difficulty functioning in a regular classroom.

However, ableist assumptions cause harm when the educational and developmental services provided to disabled children focus inordinately on the characteristics of their disabilities to the exclusion of all else—when *changing* disability becomes the overriding focus of service providers and, at times, parents. Narratives of disabled students and their parents or caregivers are replete with examples of how changing disability became the focus of their young lives and how such a focus denied them the opportunities taken for granted by nondisabled people. These narratives speak to the deep cultural prejudices against disability that they had to endure from an early age—an assumption that disability was negative and tragic and that "overcoming" disability was the only desired outcome.[7]

Schools can play a major role in reinforcing the status quo by devaluing disability. How often do individualized education plan (IEP) meetings begin with the question, "What's wrong with this kid?" Indeed, some schools (particularly many charters) appear to actively minimize enrollment of children with disabilities.[8] Some schools inordinately segregate students with disabilities in separate classes or even wings of the building. Lack of access to extracurricular activities is a common complaint of many parents of kids with disabilities. Still other schools hold low expectations for students with disabilities by excessively modifying curriculum. Taken together, these practices keep students away from their nondisabled peers while reinforcing the view that students with disabilities are inferior and undeserving of equal rights. The result is too many students with disabilities leaving school unprepared for employment and full, rewarding adult lives. These practices also do harm to nondisabled peers, who often leave school with negative prejudices about people with disabilities.

There are other, more subtle, examples of ableism in our schools. Children are denied the use of screen readers or taped texts on the grounds that such accommodations are "not reading." This is particularly true for students with dyslexia, whose disability makes reading print a laborious process because their lack of fluency compromises their ability to comprehend and thus their ability to access education through text.

Other examples of ableism involve false impartiality. Schools often require students with behavioral disabilities to "follow the same rules as everyone else" without regard for whether the child needs supports in learning how to behave in school. The high suspension rates of many students with disabilities attest to this.[9]

Schools should approach ableism in the same way they approach other issues of societal equality in relation to race, religion, gender, or sexual orientation, as a matter of diversity.

Thankfully, not all schools engage in ableist practices, and overall, educational outcomes for students with disabilities are improving.[10] As far back as the 1950s, some students with disabilities attended schools that provided effective inclusive education.

Adrienne Asch, a blind woman who is a university professor, described her childhood education:

> In thinking about the writing of disabled adults and reflecting on my own life, I give my parents high marks. They did not deny that I was blind, and did not ask me to pretend that everything about my life was fine. They rarely sheltered. They worked to help me behave and look the way others did without giving me a sense that to be blind—"different"— was shameful. They fought for me, to ensure that I lived as full and rich a life as I could. For them, and consequently for me, my blindness was a fact, not a tragedy. It affected them but did not dominate their lives. Nor did it dominate mine.[11]

Adrienne attended public schools and received instruction in Braille and in orientation and mobility skills. However, most of her education was within the mainstream, with the accommodations she needed as a blind child.

We believe schools should approach ableism in the same way they approach other issues of societal equality in relation to race, religion, gender, or sexual orientation, as a matter of diversity. Further, schools should actively seek to minimize ableism through educational practices that minimize the negative impact of disability, celebrate the positive impact of disability, and maximize opportunities for their students to live full lives.

For the research study on which this book is based, we examined schools that appeared to be actively seeking to confront ableism: schools that valued children with disabilities and sought to provide them with high quality education in inclusive settings. Indeed, Anthony, who is quoted at the beginning of the chapter, attends one of these schools: the Henderson School in Boston. It is our hope that Anthony, like Adrienne Asch, has all the educational opportunities he will need to live a full life. And, as the schools in this book demonstrate, the dreams Anthony's parents hold for his life can become a reality for all children. As you will read in the pages that follow, in providing effective education for students with disabilities, these schools are providing a superior education for all students. We hope this book will serve to promote the proliferation of schools that are equitable and effective for all children. It is our dream that some day ableism will be eliminated in education and that meeting the needs of children with disabilities will be part of the design of all schools. In so doing we will be providing the foundation of a truly equitable society for all.

ACKNOWLEDGMENTS

We first acknowledge some of the many individuals who helped us conduct this study. The principals, teachers, and parents in these remarkable schools have earned our deep appreciation and respect. Carmen Torres, Linda Nathan, Janet Palmer Owens, and Bill Henderson opened up their schools to us and allowed us the unfettered access we needed to conduct this study. We also express our appreciation to Drew Eckelson, the teachers at the Tucker School, and Monica Ng for their work in demonstrating how RTI (response to intervention) works at the Tucker School. Brian Heffernan and his classmates at Newton North have taught us so much about how young people with disabilities persist in their desire to have full adult lives. Walter Lyons, Jen Price, and the parents and teachers at North deserve special recognition for supporting all children in realizing their dreams.

We also thank those who supported us in the production of this book. Our research assistants, Carolyn Glicklich, Jamie LaBillois, Kia Martin, Noora Abdulkerim, and Julia Mayer, did a superb job in collecting the data that undergird this study. My assistant Judy Wasserman also helped so much in compiling the notes.

Finally, we acknowledge the students at their schools whose inclusive embracing of one another gives us great hope for a more equitable and just world.

INTRODUCTION

This book began out of our desire to show what successful inclusion really looks like. We have seen firsthand that—contrary to overwhelming evidence that paints a rather bleak picture of special education—there are individual schools across the country that have been quite successful in providing effective inclusion for kids with disabilities.

Our goal was to find out exactly what the teachers and the leaders were doing at these exemplary schools.

We set out to find schools that were "doing inclusion right," where kids with disabilities, from mild to significant, were enjoying success in general education classrooms alongside their typically developing peers. Our goal was to find out exactly what the teachers and the leaders were doing at these exemplary schools so that we could help inform other schools that are still struggling with how best to set up their own inclusive programs.

The study on which this book is based examined in-depth three effective schools located in Boston, the largest urban district in Massachusetts. To understand how these schools worked, we spent one year speaking with teachers, administrators, and parents, observing classes and examining school data. Using a multiple case study design,[1] we examined the perceptions and activities of these teachers, administrators, and parents within and across the schools. In particular, we focused on the schools' missions, their instructional practices, their leadership structures, and finally, the nature of the relationships among their faculty and staff. We wanted to identify what was behind the success of these schools through in-depth discussions with faculty, staff, and students as well as extensive observations of classrooms.

We have also included mini-cases involving two other suburban Boston schools. These schools were chosen because they exemplify the culture and practices of the three original schools in the study.

Beyond the issue of integration and its potential impact on student outcomes, in this book we view inclusion from the broader lens of societal change and civil rights for people with disabilities. We consider inclusion of children with disabilities in schooling to be an essential element in eliminating the ableism we discussed in the Preface.

> We strongly support educating most students with disabilities—including those with significant disabilities—in general education settings most of the time. In our view, inclusive education is a civil rights imperative integral to the efforts of the disability community to improve the status of disabled people and an educational imperative central to improving educational outcomes for children and youth with disabilities. Research consistently shows that more time in general education classrooms is associated with better outcomes for students,[2] regardless of race, class, gender, and type of disability.

THE NEWS ON INCLUSION IS (MOSTLY) PROMISING

More integration of students with disabilities into general education classrooms is occurring, and there is some evidence that outcomes for many students with disabilities are improving. From 1993 to 2003, major improvements in school completion rates, great enrollment in postsecondary education participation, and gains in employment have occurred.[3] These improvements included:

- Seventy percent of the 2003 cohort youth with disabilities completed high school, an increase of 17 percentage points in graduation and a decrease of 30 percent in the dropout rate.

- Youth with emotional disturbances, a group that averaged more than 65 percent dropout rate, demonstrated a substantial improvement (16 percentage points) in their school completion rate.

- The rate of postsecondary education participation by youth with disabilities more than doubled over time, with 32 percent of the 2003 cohort enrolling in a two- or four-year college or postsecondary school within two years of graduation.

- In 2003, 70 percent of youth with disabilities who had been out of school up to two years had worked for pay at some time since leaving high school, up from 55 percent in 1987.

Most of the gains experienced by students with disabilities are due to improvements in outcomes of children from middle-income and upper-income homes. Unfortunately, the outcomes of students with disabilities from low-income homes are largely flat.[4] Low-income children and children of color are not enjoying the same improvement in outcomes experienced by their White and more affluent counterparts. Further, they are less apt to be integrated into general education settings.[5] From 1987 to 2003, the following findings emerge:

- Youth from households in the lowest-income group did not have a significant improvement in postsecondary education participation, continuing the gap between income groups that existed in 1987.

- Youth from the lowest-income households did not share with their highest-income peers an increase in employment since leaving high school, so that they lagged significantly behind that group on that measure, as well as on their rate of current employment.

- Only White youth with disabilities experienced a significant increase in postsecondary education enrollment overall and in the pursuit of both employment and postsecondary education since high school.[6]

HOW WE IDENTIFIED SUCCESSFUL SCHOOLS

The selection criteria were designed to identify successful schools that were inclusive of students with a range of disabilities and had strong academic outcomes for both students with and without disabilities. We selected schools based on the following criteria:

1. Schools had to have higher large-scale test scores for students with disabilities as well as those without disabilities than what would be predicted by socioeconomic class, race, and disability. These test scores had to have been consistently high for at least three years. We sought schools that, in

> *The selection criteria were designed to identify successful schools that were inclusive of students with a range of disabilities and had strong academic outcomes for both students with and without disabilities.*

the case of high schools, had low dropout rates, and for all levels, schools with low suspension and expulsion rates.

2. The schools had to be inclusive of students with disabilities. Our functional definition of *inclusive* required that schools educated children with disabilities predominately in general education classrooms, with no children placed in separate special education classrooms for the majority of the day. We also sought evidence that the schools were intentionally inclusive through school mission statements and school websites.

3. We sought schools that enrolled a broad range of students with disabilities. A school was considered to be enrolling a broad range of students if it enrolled students with both high-incidence disabilities, like dyslexia, and low-incidence disabilities (those that occur in less than 1 percent of the population), such as deafness, intellectual or developmental disability, or autism.

4. The schools had very low suspension and transfer rates.

Applying these criteria to a broad array of Boston schools initially yielded five schools. One was dropped as a potential site because the principal was new; another, a large comprehensive high school, was dropped because it was divided into three small schools as a part of an overall high school reform initiative in the district. The final sample included two elementary schools, the William T. Henderson[7] (Henderson) and the Samuel Mason (Mason), and one high school, the Boston Arts Academy (BAA), all located in the city of Boston.

> For more detailed information on the schools' academic data, and on how our research study was designed and conducted, please see Appendix B.

HOW THESE SCHOOLS DIFFERED FROM THE NORM

Although these were all public schools located in one urban school district, they differed in some fundamental ways from typical schools. The Henderson was a regular public school designed since 1989 to be inclusive of students with significant disabilities and had a non-naturally occurring population of these students that exceeded 30 percent. BAA and Mason were "pilot schools," charter-like schools within the school district that have autonomy over their budgets, staffing, curricula, and school calendars while adhering to all other guidelines of the school district. BAA was an arts academy that required students to audition to enroll; the auditions were based on artistic potential or ability and did not consider other criteria such as academics or disability.

In all three schools, the desire to provide high-quality education to all students, particularly those with complex needs, spurred innovation.

Though these schools appear very different in many ways, they were similar to each other in culture, classroom practices, and administrative structures. In all three schools, the desire to provide high-quality education to all students, particularly those with complex needs, spurred innovation.

As we began to discuss our finding with colleagues and students, it became clear that the findings of this study were also applicable to non-urban, non-Boston schools as well. All schools must educate students with disabilities, and the issues associated with poverty so prevalent in urban schools exist throughout the nation. We therefore chose to add mini-cases involving three other schools. One, the Tucker, is a suburban elementary school outside of Boston in Milton, Massachusetts. This racially diverse school was challenged with a significant overplacement of students of color within special education and overall poor literacy scores. The school implemented a highly effective response to intervention (RTI) program in the primary grades that not only resulted in a decrease of referrals of children of color to special education but an overall improvement in literacy. This school exemplifies the importance of establishing collaborative, problem-solving cultures, so evident in the three schools in Boston, within a suburban context.

The second mini-case is a large suburban high school, Newton North, in Newton, Massachusetts. We highlight a program within the school that educates students with significant developmental disabilities within an inclusive environment. The students in this program benefit from an inclusive individualized high school experience as well as a highly effective transition program that prepares students to live and work in the community.

HOW THIS BOOK IS ORGANIZED

We believe that these schools can offer lessons for all schools, and we have organized this book to illustrate these lessons. Part One focuses on the schools and their leaders. In Chapter One we provide in-depth descriptions of the schools. We want readers to enter into these schools, to feel their environments, and to get a sense of the adults and kids within them. We have also included in the text some links to YouTube videos to give readers a deeper understanding of what these schools are doing that contributes to their success.

We look in Chapter Two at these schools' leaders, how they do their work, and how they change to meet the needs of their students. We discuss the importance of their leaders establishing a *vision* for these schools. The influence of the school leaders on the culture and effectiveness is so profound that we provide a description of each of the leaders and how they came to value a culture of inclusiveness.

In Part Two we continue the discussion of school culture in the context of organizational literature concerning school change and improvement. Though some readers might find this a bit dense, we believe this is important to a central lesson in this book. For schools to be effective for all students, including those with complex needs, they need to become collaborative problem-solving organizations, as discussed in Chapter Three. Central to this lesson may indeed be that schools may need to question some of the typical traditional practices and structures if they are going to be equitable and effective institutions for all children.

In Chapter Four we focus on how becoming collaborative problem-solving organizations has changed the relationships of the teachers and administrators within these schools. Such changes, while potentially difficult, often lead to greater job satisfaction for both teachers and school leaders. Indeed, these schools have highly stable staffs, with few teachers leaving and many outside applicants applying for vacancies when they become available. The positive relationships that exist within these schools extend to parents and the broader community as well.

Chapter Five deals with the practices these schools engage in that we believe are behind their demonstrable success. We begin with identifying those administrative actions that have laid the foundation for improved teaching and learning at the classroom level. We ground this discussion in the "four frames of leadership" developed by Bolman and Deal in their book *Reframing Organizations*.[8] These frames look at the behavior of leaders in relationship to organizational frames concerning structure, symbols, human resources, and politics. We then move to the classroom and identify strong practices common to all these schools that likely account for their strong results. The lens through which we observed classrooms was rooted in universal design for learning or UDL.[9] Though not all teachers explicitly acknowledged the principles of UDL, their teaching practices exemplified them. UDL is based on three compelling principles:

1. Material should be presented to students in multiple ways, thus allowing the greatest number of children to access the material.

2. Students should have multiple ways to demonstrate what they know and are able to do.

3. Instruction must engage students in multiple ways.

The inclusion of students with diverse needs, particularly those with significant disabilities, within these problem-solving cultures led teachers to these principles naturally.

In Part Three, Chapter Six, we discuss the external policy context that affected these schools. We were frankly surprised at how influential local, state, and federal policies and programs were on the schools we studied. The notion, often promoted by charter advocates, that schools need to become freestanding entrepreneurial entities freed of bureaucracy was not supported by this study. These schools were strongly influenced by external policy in a mostly positive manner. Strong civil rights laws laid the foundation for the inclusiveness these schools exemplified across racial, linguistic, and disability lines. The schools used local, state, and federal grant programs to expand their capacities, particularly in teacher development. This is not to say that the schools did not encounter bureaucratic barriers. They did. However, the influence of policy on these schools was significant and complex and required the significant attention of school leaders and, at times, teachers. In Chapter 8 we end by proposing ways that local, state, and federal policy might be better aligned to promote the development of more schools like the exemplary ones profiled in this book.

We hope that telling the story of these highly effective schools will encourage other teachers and school leaders to begin the difficult, rewarding work of promoting improved educational opportunity for all children. We believe there are lessons in the book for the individual teacher who, though he or she might not be working in an exemplary school, can improve his or her own classroom practice through implementing principles of universal design. Further, it is our hope that that educators might find similarly minded colleagues with whom they may work to promote more collaborative, problem-solving cultures within their schools. We also hope that school principals and district leaders will embrace the example of leadership portrayed in this book and develop schools that are accessible and effective for all children. Finally, we seek a day when district, state, and federal policy makers go beyond simply mandating "adequate yearly progress" to recognizing the importance of developing policies and programs that promote the difficult work of making schools accessible and effective for all students. This can be done.

Effective Inclusive Schools

PART ONE

The Schools and Their Leaders

CHAPTER ONE

The Schools

This book began out of our desire to document successful inclusive education in urban schools. We therefore sought to look deeply at practices within highly successful inclusive schools. We chose three Boston schools that fit our criteria: the Patrick O'Hearn Elementary School (O'Hearn; later renamed the William T. Henderson Elementary Inclusion School), the Samuel Mason Elementary School, and the Boston Arts Academy (BAA), a high school. After we began this study and began presenting our findings to various groups, we were informed by many suburban and rural educators that the lessons learned from these urban schools have applicability to their schools, so we augmented our studies with two suburban schools that appeared very similar in practice to the urban schools. In this chapter we give the reader a detailed picture of the three urban schools studied. We also encourage readers to enhance their understanding of these schools by viewing the YouTube video links provided.

PATRICK O'HEARN ELEMENTARY SCHOOL

A "magical mix of teachers, parents, the students, and Bill Henderson" was how one parent described the William T. Henderson Elementary Inclusion School. The O'Hearn was a school known for educating students so effectively that parents who were eligible to enroll their children in the city's elite exam schools chose rather to stay at the O'Hearn. It was a school known for its inclusive practices. Its principal, Dr. William Henderson, was so well respected that when he retired in 2009, the mayor of Boston proclaimed June 23 William Henderson Day and renamed the school the William T. Henderson Elementary Inclusion School.

We introduce this school by describing its 2007 annual African American history student performance, *Dare to Dream: Sharing African American History Through Storytelling*. The performers and the audience were a racially diverse mix of Black (likely some African American, Caribbean, and South American), Asian, and White. Among students, there was also diversity in disability; some students used wheelchairs, some had visible intellectual disabilities, some had Down syndrome, and there were many students with disabilities that were not visible. Disability at the O'Hearn was as typical an aspect of diversity as racial diversity. A parent of a student without a disability explained, "The children there really end up learning about and caring for others, just the diversity of the world."

The show included students reciting a twenty-minute Langston Hughes poem, students in a traditional African drumming circle, some dancing to the drums, tap dancers, and a performance of a play based on the African folk tale *Why Anansi Has Eight Thin Legs*, complete with the spider, the rabbit, and the monkey. Perhaps the loudest applause came when a student with a significant intellectual disability and limited verbal skills walked across stage, and in a low guttural voice sounding like the real Cab Calloway, belted out the words "Well, hello Dolly!" that Calloway was famous for. Those in the audience knew what an accomplishment this was for the child, and the already enthusiastic applause intensified for him.

The celebration culminated with all students on stage singing two gospel songs, and the audience clapping along with them. In the group, there was a White student with autism, eyes half-closed, shaking her hands in the air as if she were at a traditional Black church service, surrounded by her peers, many of whom are Black. She was belting out the songs, utterly out of tune. Also on stage was another girl with autism who had her fingers in her ears, and although she was not singing, she was standing next to her peers and swaying to the music with her classmates. These children did not stand out in this environment, because students with visible disabilities participate in all school performances. This is a community that appears to know one another and is clearly comfortable across racial, class, and disability lines.

At the end of the show Dr. Henderson spoke to parents about how wonderful their children were and how proud he was of each of them, as well as his talented teachers and staff, calling them out by name. Mary, a teacher at the school, said that "one of the best things about Bill is that he knows the kids that need to be known. . . . On the first day of school, when he was naming specific kids in the school that everybody on the staff has to know and has to be able to help out and be aware of, for me, as a special ed teacher who has worked in a school where the principal doesn't ever come to my classroom because I'm the special ed classroom, to have our principal talk about the kids that I will be teaching and caring about them that much, that's one of my favorite things about him and about being at this school."

> To learn more about the Henderson, view the videos on YouTube, www. youtube.com, by entering William Henderson Inclusion School.

Looking Back with Pride

Dr. Henderson has reason to be proud of his students and teachers. Since 1989, when he became the school's principal, the O'Hearn had grown from an underperforming school with student vacancies to a school with a higher percentage of students with and without disabilities passing the Massachusetts Comprehensive Assessment System (MCAS) in the fourth grade than the overall percentage of the Boston public schools.[1] Instead of vacancies, the school now has a waiting list of parents who want their children, those with and those without disabilities, to attend. Since 1989, the school has evolved from providing special education services in segregated settings, such as special education classes and resources rooms, to providing the overwhelming majority of their special education services in the general education classroom.

Mary, a parent of one child with a disability and one without a disability who both attended the O'Hearn, explained her appreciation for the school: "The children there really end up learning about [and] caring for others, just the diversity of the world. Not everybody's on the same page and same level. And there's been times when . . . my so-called typical [daughter] has gone places and . . . people are really surprised [about] how she doesn't stare when she meets somebody. She can talk to any child, is not afraid. And they go, 'Wow.' And I'm like, 'She goes to the O'Hearn.'"

The O'Hearn is located in Dorchester, a section of Boston with a mix of African American, Irish, and Vietnamese residents. Most students were enrolled at the O'Hearn through a lottery process. Boston has a rather elaborate student assignment process in which parents were given a number of schools they could choose from, and each school is then subject to a lottery. The choice system gave preference to children with siblings who attended the school and whether the school was designated as the child's "walk" school preference.

During the 2004–2005 school year, the O'Hearn enrolled 221 students. Approximately 47 percent were African American, 28 percent White, 8 percent Asian, 6 percent multi-race, and 5 percent were Hispanic or Native American. (See Table B.5 in Appendix B.) Of this population of students, 34 percent received special education services, a percentage high above the national average of approximately 12 percent. The range of student disabilities was vast. The majority of students had milder and high-incidence disabilities, such as learning disabilities. There was also a population of students with more significant and low-incidence disabilities, such as intellectual disabilities, autism, Down syndrome, cerebral palsy, and students who were medically fragile.

Each classroom at the O'Hearn had two teachers, one certified in elementary education and the other in special education. With such a high percentage of students with disabilities in the school, Henderson was able to garner enough resources to make possible this staffing. Though there was also a paraprofessional assigned to each classroom, only one paraprofessional was assigned to work with one student, a boy who had brittle bone syndrome and required individual adult supervision to ensure his physical safety.

The only special education classroom at the O'Hearn was called the Baking Café, a room used collaboratively by the speech and language therapist and occupational therapist to work with students with significant intellectual disabilities to organize and run the school store, to deliver school supplies to classrooms, and to work on functional skills such as cooking. Aside from these activities, speech and language and occupational therapies occurred in the general education classroom.

The classrooms at the O'Hearn were brimming with activity. Teachers were in and out of each other's classes, bringing suggestions, working with students, problem-solving students' needs together. Similarly, students worked collaboratively with their teachers and their peers in the classroom. In one first grade class, students were preparing for a publishing party to which they invited family members and others in the school to show and read from the books they had created. Students were asked to choose one of their stories from the stack that they had written, go through the story to see if they could add more sentences, make sure that each sentence had a period, and make sure that their illustrations matched their words. Conversations between students about their books were serious. These first graders were asking each other detailed questions about their illustrations and how what they drew was in their story. They listened to each other read and asked specific questions about their stories. These six-year-olds took great pride in their work.

In another first grade class, students were read part of a story and were asked to turn to their partners to talk about how one of the characters was feeling. The teacher called this activity "accountable talk" because students were working to explain or to be accountable for their ideas. Once the story was completed, students broke into small groups to work on their reader's workshop activities. "Letter Blocks" was an activity in which students were asked to use four letters on blocks to "mix it, fix it, check it." Another activity was to work on a computer program that supplemented phonetic instruction. The third activity was to work in their guided reading groups run by each of the two teachers. In one of these groups, students were asked to write their names on a piece of paper. For the student in the group who could not write his name, there was a name stamp ready for his use. Accommodations like this were typical at the O'Hearn, and the school was a pilot school for the use of Kurzweil technology, a text-to-speech hardware, as an accommodation eligible for use with the MCAS.

A Parent Influences Federal Policy

In 1994 I (Tom Hehir) visited the O'Hearn with then-Secretary of Education Richard Riley and Assistant Secretary Judy Heumann. Secretary Riley wanted to see an inclusive school because inclusion was such a controversial issue. I told him about the O'Hearn and to my astonishment he said, "Let's go visit it."

After visiting classrooms we met with several parents of children with disabilities, who spoke about how their children had thrived in inclusive classrooms, developing communication skills, making friends, and achieving academically. One mother whose three non-disabled children attended the O'Hearn told us her oldest daughter had "tested for advanced classes" (referring to Boston's gifted program). When she and her husband visited the program that was housed in another school, they found that the students in the gifted program were doing lower-level work than her daughter was doing in her inclusive class. They decided to keep her at the O'Hearn, where "every child has an individualized program." She went on to say that even more important to her and husband was their kindergartner's experience: the little girl had asked for a wheelchair for Christmas because "some of her friends had them and she thought they were cool." Mom concluded, "That's exactly the kind of values we want our children to have!" Given that Secretary Riley mentioned this visit many times in subsequent years, I believe the experience contributed to his becoming such a powerful supporter of inclusive education.

We spoke to a parent at O'Hearn who had chosen the school for his children after learning that he and his wife were expecting a child with Down syndrome. He had transferred his older children without disabilities from a local Catholic school to the O'Hearn so that all his children would attend the same school. This anecdote not only illustrates how the assignment process works but also demonstrates the desire of many parents in Boston to have their children attend an effective inclusive school. One parent explained that she wanted her daughter there because she "wanted the fact that she had Down syndrome not to be such a big deal." The school was so highly regarded by parents that Bill Henderson has received the annual Martha Ziegler Founder's Award from the Federation for Children with Special Needs, the largest parent organization in the state. The demand for placement at the O'Hearn is so great that the central special education office assigns students to the school as a means of avoiding due process hearings. For instance, there are children at the Henderson whose parents have not been able to obtain satisfactory inclusive placements in other schools and have exercised their rights under federal law to challenge the school district's proposed placement. In these instances the Boston Public Schools have offered the Henderson as a means to settle the dispute. Anthony, the child portrayed in the Preface, is an example of such a child.

The O'Hearn began changing from an underperforming school to what it is now in the spring of 1989, when, according to Bill Henderson, "there was a group of parents, led by the special needs parent advisory council, who demanded that there be an inclusive option for the system. And the system did develop a taskforce with central office folks, existing teachers, and parents." Henderson was a member of this group. As he explained, he was "involved in a lot of parent groups." He was also becoming blind, and he had been "promoting disability awareness in Boston." Henderson was hired August 19, "a few days after school had started for principals," to take over this school and develop inclusive practices for its September opening.

That first year, the O'Hearn enrolled eight students with significant disabilities in its two kindergarten classes, with four new teachers: two special education and two general education. The remaining teachers had the choice to stay or transfer out. Three people left. One who left was a special education resource room teacher. When asked by Henderson why he was leaving he said, "Well, you know, all the handicapped are coming." Henderson remembers saying to himself that he was glad he was leaving and explained that it went to "my premise that sometimes the biggest resistance for inclusion is not necessarily the general education educators. It's the special ed teachers who have been used to doing things in their own way, in their own room, not having to worry about the curriculum, not having to worry about, you know, following the same kind of schedule, and doing their own thing." The O'Hearn is now a school where teachers do not leave unless they are retiring, and getting a job there is close to impossible.

The O'Hearn is a school where teachers do not leave unless they are retiring, and getting a job there is close to impossible.

SAMUEL W. MASON ELEMENTARY SCHOOL

The Samuel W. Mason Elementary School was, in the truest sense, a laboratory for learning. Evidence of student learning was everywhere. There was student work sitting on the table outside of the main office; it covered the walls that went up the stairs from the basement to the third floor. Teachers displayed student work on the walls in every classroom. Improving instructional practices was the theme at staff meetings. The Mason, named in 1990 by the *Boston Herald* as "the least chosen school in the city," was, in 2005, a school that *Boston* magazine called one of the top elementary schools in Massachusetts.[2]

One way to introduce the Mason is to describe an observation in a classroom and another at a teachers' instructional leadership team (ILT) meeting. In a fourth grade classroom, the walls were packed with student work, handwritten posters explaining many different academic and behavioral processes, a carpet, a beanbag chair, and many, many books. Students in the class were quietly working on personal letters. When students talked, they whispered. This quiet whispering did not appear tense or unusual, but rather evidence of intense work. Their teacher Karen walked around the class helping students, as did the full-time intern from the Boston Teacher Residency (BTR) program. At one point, a boy walked to the sample personal letter on the white board. He was obviously frustrated and was crying quietly. Karen walked to him and stood with him looking over his paper. She said, "I don't think that you've followed directions." They moved closer to the example, looked at it together, and then looked back at his paper. She said to him kindly, but firmly, "This isn't worth crying over." She stayed with him and they began to work at the whiteboard. Together, they sat, and she stayed with him until he was able to continue independently. When she left his side, he was deep in the work.

The walls were packed with student work, handwritten posters explaining many different academic and behavioral processes, a carpet, a beanbag chair, and many, many books.

Moving and looking over the shoulders of students working, Karen again walked around the room until she noticed a girl in need of support. She took a stool, put it down next to the girl, and worked with her for a full ten minutes while all but one student in the class appeared to be on task. After some time, the BTR resident clapped his hands to gain students' attention. Most students clapped after him, but not all. Seriously, but with a bit of a smile, he said, "Let's do it again." All students followed this time. "Let's clean up and get ready for reading." Several kids moaned, but these students were moaning at being asked to stop doing their work. The observation was a full period, and students were steeped completely in their work.

Teachers at the Mason, in fact at all three schools, spent a great deal of time developing their craft together. Weekly, teachers at the Mason met for two hours after school in meetings focused on literacy, the achievement gap, and assistive technology, and once a month, the ILT worked with staff on a variety of topics. This week, the agenda listed the meeting's "desired outcomes" as "discuss[ing] concrete dilemmas we face in raising the level of accountable talk in our classrooms, following the Consultancy Protocol," and "review[ing] math end-of-year assessment and MCAS data."

What was most impressive about this staff meeting was the professionalism of the presenters, the sophistication of their activities, and the relevance of the work to the teachers and to the students. A fifth grade teacher facilitated one section with a review of math end-of-year assessments and MCAS data for the third through fifth grades. Bear in mind, in all three grades, the Mason outscored the district, and in the third and fourth grades, they outscored the state. Although there was acknowledgment of a job done well, this presentation focused on improving their practice. Their analysis of the school's data revealed issues with their use of mathematical language. The facilitator builds this argument by providing example test items and an analysis that shows that the language on the assessment is different from the language in the mathematics program the district has adopted. This conclusion draws sighs of acknowledgment from the audience, but what draws sighs of relief is that the facilitator has developed a solution to address the issue. There are materials that have been developed at the district that help teachers align the language of the curriculum with the language of the state assessment. They decided that all math teachers will use these for ten minutes every day. This section of the meeting concluded with a discussion about setting up a workshop for parents on mathematics to better help them help their children at home. Teresa explained, "It's not even [just] holding high standards for the students, but we hold high standards for ourselves. . . . Most teachers are doing something, whether they're leading workshops or attending workshops, some are in other certification programs." Said one parent, "You can see the amount of work they do with their students. Hopefully there's an award or something out there for them."

A Gem Among the Warehouses

The Mason is located in a desolate industrial area bordering Boston's hospital areas and the more residential but poor section of Roxbury. During the 2004–2005 school year, the Mason enrolled 208 students. As shown in Table B.5, more than 63 percent were African American, more than 25 percent Hispanic, nearly 8 percent White, and approximately 2 percent were classified as multi-race. Of this population of students, 20 percent received special education services, a percentage high above the national average of approximately 12 percent. The range of student disabilities was expansive. The majority had milder and high-incidence disabilities, such as learning disabilities. There was also a population of students with more significant and low-incidence disabilities, such as intellectual disabilities, autism, and developmental delays.

Student achievement, as measured by the MCAS, was impressive. The students at the Mason as a whole and the subgroup of students with disabilities who passed[3] the MCAS in English language arts and mathematics in the fourth grade was higher at the Mason than for the Boston public school district as a whole[4] and for the state of Massachusetts. (See Tables B.3 and B.4.)

Meera, a parent of a student without a disability, explained to us that she wanted her son at the Mason because it was inclusive, or what she called "integrated." She explained, "Of the good schools that he would be eligible for, it was one that had integrated ed. . . . I heard [a] parent, actually the one I was telling you about, whose daughter goes to the O'Hearn, gave a very compelling argument for why integrated ed is . . . really great for a kid in a more holistic way. . . . Not just their learning, but . . . their humanity." Each classroom teacher at the Mason carried both elementary and special education certifications. Each student at the Mason was enrolled in a general education classroom. There were certain special education services, such as speech and language and occupational therapy; however, the dually certified teacher in the general education class provided the bulk of special education services.

BOSTON ARTS ACADEMY

The Boston Arts Academy is a public high school for the visual and performing arts. BAA opened in 1998 as a partnership between the Boston public schools and the ProArts Consortium, a collaboration of six Boston area higher learning institutions.[5] Students at BAA must audition in dance, visual arts, theatre, or music, and they are enrolled based on their proficiency or

their potential in one of these areas. Students' academic records are not taken into consideration during the auditions. As Linda Nathan explained, academically, "we don't know anything about the kids before they come." BAA consults academic records only after the school accepts the student. Given this, their 97 percent graduation record is even more impressive.

In addition to what is offered at the school by teachers fully immersed in the arts in all areas, opportunities from the art world at large find their way into BAA. Students have studied dance with highly acclaimed choreographer Bill T. Jones and members of the Alvin Ailey American Dance Theatre, and they have hosted guest artists such as Yo-Yo Ma, Hugh Masekela, and Quincy Jones.

From 2004 to 2005, BAA enrolled 389 students. As shown in Table B.5, more than 40 percent were African American, approximately 30 percent were Hispanic, 20 percent White, and approximately 3 percent were classified as Asian or multi-race. BAA enrolled 12 percent students with disabilities, close to the national percentage. The range of students' disabilities was vast. There were students with high-incidence disabilities, such as learning disabilities. There were students who were deaf, students with emotional disturbance, and some with intellectual disabilities. As Tables B.1 and B.2 show, at BAA, the percentage of students with and without disabilities who passed the MCAS in English language arts and mathematics in the tenth grade was higher than they were for the Boston Public School District. Their scores, with the exception of students without disabilities' math scores, were also higher than those of the state of Massachusetts.

At BAA, there was a mixture of staffing configurations; in some classes there were two teachers, one special and one general education certified; in some classes there were general education teachers who co-taught; in some classes there was a teacher certified in both a general education subject and special education. The majority of general education staff at BAA were working toward special education certification in addition to their general education licenses in special education. They were so committed to this that they offered the classes on-site. BAA had two co-headmasters, Linda Nathan and Carmen Torres, who shared the responsibilities for the school.

To learn more about BAA, go to www.youtube.com and search Boston Arts Academy for numerous videos of the school.

A walk through the hallways of BAA is a good place to begin to understand this school. BAA and Fenway High School share the same building that sits directly across the street from Fenway Park, home of the Boston Red Sox. (Linda Nathan and Carmen Torres, the founders of BAA, also founded Fenway High School.) Students were talking, they were hugging, and their laughter was loud and infectious. The two security guards at the entrance were on a first-name basis with students and were equally as boisterous. Also in this mix was Linda Nathan. She greeted students, addressed them by name, asked them personal questions.

During the day and in between classes, the hallways continued to be places where students talked, hugged, and laughed. Students were not out of control, but rather extremely engaged. The hallways were a powerful indicator for many. One parent who had sent his child to a private school for elementary and high school and was willing to do so for high school explained that his experience with students in the hallway at BAA convinced him to send his son there: "What impressed me the most is the fact that kids, when you talk to them in the hallway . . . for a few moments, [they] say, 'I'd really love to continue talking to you, but I really, really need to get to my next class.' And it was their commitment, not that they were afraid, like, of being late, but that they wanted to get there to learn something. They were afraid to miss anything. It really convinced me that, hey, you know, this is a place that kids are dedicated. It's not like most high schools I'd seen. So that for me was the deciding factor."

Christa, a teacher in the music department, explains, "The energy . . . the loud [noise] in the hallway is about people wanting to get to each other, to share with each other, to be in each other's space. . . . The dominant thing is, 'I haven't seen that person in fifteen minutes, and I want to give them a hug.'"

Students are required to pass vocal juries each year in order to be promoted and remain at BAA. In these juries, students must perform and be evaluated in front of their teachers. The first semester jury counts for 10 percent of the final technique grade, and the final jury counts for 40 percent. Outside the room of the final jury, there was a schedule, each student receiving fifteen minutes. Three students were waiting outside the door. One was reading, one explained to us that she was nervous, and one other talked excitedly but in a hushed tone to those walking by. All three young women were dressed in formal attire. Inside the jury room, students were rated as novice, competent, proficient, or artist in areas of tone quality, intonation, rhythm, technique, interpretation, diction, stage habits, and sight reading. Each student was assessed singing two songs, one memorized and one piece that was read.

A young woman, Sonia, walked into the jury room wearing a very fancy dress with very high-heeled shoes that had fur around the ankles. Her memorized piece was "Amazing Grace"; her piece to read, a song in Italian. Sonia exuded confidence. Her voice was deep and strong, but she did have a difficult time in some places. During the Italian song, her voice cracked in places. Christa, her teacher, says to her, "You know it's because you're not breathing." And next, "What are your plans this summer?" Sonia tells her that she's going to be doing some work and she is looking to take classes to improve her singing. Christa says without question or hesitation, "You're going to study with me this summer. It's $25 for the summer and $5 every time you don't come." The girl at first looks perplexed and then understatedly excited. Christa goes on, "You're fearless with your shoes; you need to be fearless with your singing. You had the best rhythm of anybody today." Sonia leaves, looking a bit proud, with her summer planned differently than it had been ten minutes ago when she walked into the room.

The teachers at BAA worked in-depth with their students. Heather, a humanities teacher, explained how she had individual check-ins with each of her fifty students twice a week, for 10–15 minutes each. She explains, "It's my job to learn how to teach all of my students." Her check-ins ranged from working with students on comprehension to fluency to word attack skills. She credited her ability to understand these skills to the professional development at the school.

The teachers and administration at BAA are committed to working with all students, as their high graduation rate indicates. As Noel expressed, there is a tone in the school that "all kids can learn, and that if they're not doing well we have to ask why." Heather explained that they work hard to meet all of their students' needs. "I think every year we get closer and closer at coming to the kind of services and the ways that we want to provide education to all of our kids. We get closer to that every year."

"It's my job to learn how to teach all of my students."

INCLUSION AS A CENTRAL MISSION

These schools were committed to a mission of educating all students to high academic standards in inclusive settings. They were deeply driven by this mission. While each school's statement was unique in its wording, each contained an inclusive message. O'Hearn stated, "Our students are from diverse ethnic, linguistic, and ability backgrounds. We are inclusive. . . . Our goal is to help students work at or above grade level or to achieve the objectives stipulated in individual education programs." Mason's written statement said that their school was a place where "students are taught in fully inclusive classrooms" with teachers "determined to present rigorous academics." BAA stated that they were "proud to be the first Boston Public School that has been named an inclusion high school," and "while all BAA students must pass the MCAS exam in language arts and mathematics, the staff sees their performance on this exam as only one very narrow measure of their academic achievement and growth." We wanted to understand their successes more deeply and understand whether these statements were merely text or were reflective of the schools' cultures and practices.

Teachers Support Inclusive Mission

Teacher interviews quickly led us to understand the significant depth of commitment to the mission of teaching all students to high academic standards in inclusive settings. Teresa from the Mason explained, "Teachers as well as the administration hold really high standards for the kids, and understand that even though we do have special needs kids, standards shouldn't be lowered for them." At the O'Hearn, Samantha said that the "mantra" at her school "that's been inspired by [our principal was] . . . everyone accessing the curriculum at grade level. . . . So, everybody [is] participating in grade-level activities . . . to the best of their ability."

In addition to holding high academic standards, teachers deeply embraced the concept of an inclusive environment, welcoming students with disabilities in their classes but further understanding inclusive education in a broader sense than the traditional definition of students simply placed in a general education class. Participants described the inclusion of students with disabilities in their schools in the same terms that they described the inclusion of students from various racial, ethnic, and linguistic backgrounds. Students with disabilities were valued as an important and positive aspect of a diverse "democratic" institution. Karen explained, "We, the collective we, value diversity in everything; not just cultural diversity or racial diversity, but diversity in how we learn and diversity in economic factors." Heather, inspired by critical pedagogy theorist Paulo Freire, described working to create a microcosm of the world that she wanted her students to experience. She said that within such a microcosm, students needed to find ways to embrace the differences in each other. She said, "It's one of the Paulo Freire things. . . . Your classrooms are these microcosms of the world. . . . So . . . the point is what kind of world are we trying to create and that's what you are going to create in your classroom. . . . If you somehow are creating a classroom

Students with disabilities were valued as an important and positive aspect of a diverse "democratic" institution.

where you said well, some people don't belong in our classroom because they don't have this kind of skill, or they're not quote unquote normal in this way, then you're saying . . . that's how we should treat them in the world . . . and that's not the message you want to say. What I want to say is that we are a society that . . . fully embraces . . . everyone."

Mission Driven Leaders

To the administration, their schools' missions were a driving force that evolved as the schools matured. For Dr. William Henderson at the O'Hearn, the early focus on the mission had been on staff selection and developing school culture. He explained, "[We] fought very hard, select [ed] our teachers and our paras, and [made] sure we had people who bought into that commitment to inclusion, that vision. [We had] not totally defined what it was, because we [were] still evolving, but at least people were excited and enthusiastic and hopefully with some experience, too, and some ideas about wanting to be in a place where kids with disabilities [were] throughout the school. That was very important." Henderson said that currently he believed that his school had successfully "committed to helping all kids," but that no matter how far you have come, "you never arrive. You're on the journey."

Dr. Linda Nathan, co-headmaster of BAA, explained how her school had always embraced the concept of teaching high academic standards to all students in inclusive settings. In the beginning, their focus was "about moving from my kids, [to] your kids, to our kids." Teachers worked to erase the separation between special and general educators' responsibility for students with and without disabilities. Michelle, a school-level special education leader, explained that as BAA developed, the focus of their mission deepened to examining questions of a "common vision of teaching and learning" that included students with disabilities. She explained that they had evolved to focusing on how to "direct skill support well within every content area," what she now thought of as "the real struggle of inclusion." In fact, all the administrators understood that their missions required continual fine-tuning as their schools developed. Michelle explained, "Part of doing inclusion well is constantly asking, 'What could we be doing better? Is this kid really being served? Is this structure really working? How could we take our resources and use them?'"

The missions focused clearly on providing an education for all students based on high academic standards in inclusive settings. In these schools, disability was considered a strength, a difference that served to benefit the school. Further, these educators thought of the students with disabilities as the "backbone of the school," because if they attended to their needs effectively, "just think of how well everybody else is going to do who don't need quite that much."

The leaders, teachers, and parents in these schools moved toward this vision in a number of ways, one of which was through symbolic changes. For example, at the O'Hearn, there was a clay sculpture attached to the outside of the building that shows three students, one of whom used a wheelchair. Under this was written, "We Are All Special." Publicly, the Mason announced that they only hired teachers who held dual certification in both elementary and special education. At BAA, virtually all written documents we read and many interviews we heard called attention to the fact that they were the "first inclusive high school in Boston." One parent was exposed to this when she visited the school. "When I got there, I did see a girl in a wheelchair participating in dance classes. So yeah, [it] became very obvious to me very quickly that this was a school that if the kid has a passion for dance and they [could] somehow perform in it, let them perform." These symbols were important to creating the schools' cultures. They said to those in and outside of the school that all students were included.

TO SUM UP

- The schools highlighted in this study are all schools that serve highly diverse, primarily low-income students of color.
- The schools enroll students with a broad array of disabilities and educate them in mainstream environments.
- The schools are mission-driven environments in which the inclusion of students with disabilities is central.
- Students with disabilities are not only included but educators have created cultures in which meeting their needs has a broader impact on all students' learning.

However, a focus on culture, no matter how essential, does not translate into an effective school where students learn and exhibit positive behaviors. The factors undergirding the success of these schools were much more complex than this. First among these was the extraordinary leadership provided by principals and teacher leaders in these buildings. These individuals were not only central to establishing the vision for these schools but also provided the conditions under which all children and families were welcomed and in which teachers could be successful providing challenging instruction to highly diverse groups of students. Chapter Two gives a profile of each of these leaders and details the actions they engaged in that appear most important to the schools' success.

CHAPTER TWO

The Leaders

The formal leaders of these schools—the principals and, for the Boston Arts Academy (BAA), the co-headmasters—were very different in many ways. They came from different educational backgrounds, from diverse racial and economic backgrounds, and held different views on policy issues. All, however, were driven leaders whose personal and professional backgrounds had a profound influence on their leadership.

The leadership they provided to these schools was essential to their success. Major factors in their success were the traits that drove them as people to provide the extraordinary effort required to transform these schools. We provide brief descriptions of their backgrounds and their motivations as leaders.

BILL HENDERSON AT THE O'HEARN

Bill Henderson, the principal of the O'Hearn, had a general education background, having taught and been an assistant principal in a Boston middle school as well as in a dual-language elementary school where students spoke English and Spanish. Bill became fluent in Spanish while working for a church group in Latin America in the early 1970s. He began losing his vision during his thirties due to retinitis pigmentosa and was advised to "go out on disability" by a physician. Bill responded negatively to this suggestion and instead expressed his desire to be a principal. Ultimately, Bill was assigned to a then underperforming elementary school, the Patrick O'Hearn.

Prior to becoming a principal, Bill could be described as a teacher leader. He served on various committees in his school and for the district. He was well known and well thought of throughout the district. Bill's experience of "coming out as a blind person," gradually admitting to himself and the world that he had a disability, was a lengthy process due to the progressive nature of his disability. As Bill began to lose his vision, he became aware of the disability community and the disability rights movement. While still a teacher, he served on a districtwide committee that sought ways to promote greater integration of students with disabilities throughout the district. (Thomas Hehir chaired the committee at the time.)

This experience brought Bill into contact with several parent activists who were seeking the establishment of a school within the city where children with significant disabilities could be integrated. They approached Bill, and he responded with a plan to make the O'Hearn an integrated school for students with significant disabilities. (The term *inclusion* was not widely used at the time.) His proposal was based on the premise that if he had access to the money currently being used to serve those with the most significant disabilities in the area, he could provide two teachers in each classroom. This proposal assumed that approximately 20 percent of the students enrolled would have moderate to significant disabilities, mostly cognitively disabilities.

"You don't know what kids are capable of until you include them."

Bill's personal experience with disability informs how he leads the school in many ways. First, Bill had experienced what unites so many in the disability community: discrimination.[1] He therefore was conscious of developing a school that did not discriminate and taking to heart the concept that "all means all." Though many administrators claim to run inclusive schools today, many of these schools fail to enroll the most significantly disabled students. This is not the case with Bill. "You don't know what kids are capable of until you include them." Bill points to Mary, a young girl with significant disabilities and numerous highly pessimistic reports. Bill had a video of a successful Mary, who was beginning to read using an alternative communication system.

From a policy perspective, Bill was a strong supporter of firm civil rights protections in federal law and was a supporter, broadly speaking, of standards-based reform. He did, however, argue passionately for robust accommodations in testing to make sure students with disabilities could demonstrate what they know and were able to do with the means that are most efficient for them. This at times puts Bill in conflict with state and federal policy makers. Bill has testified in Congress on these issues and led a successful fight by advocates in Massachusetts to turn back efforts by the state to limit accommodations. Bill's experience teaching students in general education in urban settings has led him to support standards-based reform as a vehicle to overcome historic practices based on low expectations. In his article titled "Champions of Inclusion," Bill writes, "There are still many who do not act like students with disabilities can succeed. They do not expose students who have disabilities to high levels of teaching and learning. They do not promote students' independence, and they do not hold students to high standards." He said that "champions of inclusion challenge students with disabilities to work their best towards high standards."[2]

A parent called Bill a "rock star" of a principal because, she said, "He's good at it. He's got a formula. . . . He works it." Another parent explained, "He can balance it all. He's doing everything like he's supposed to do. . . . He takes care of the teachers, the parents, [and] the students."

JANET PALMER OWENS AT THE MASON

Janet Palmer Owens was a high school guidance counselor prior to assuming the elementary school principalship. She did not seek the position, and, when the superintendent offered her the job, she questioned whether she was qualified. Though she had taught elementary schools many years before, she felt that she needed to spend her first year as principal primarily observing in classrooms to reacquaint herself with the curriculum and to build credibility among the teachers.

Janet was driven to improve educational outcomes, particularly among African American children. "As an African American myself," she said, "I know that education was the route to a better life for me. I grew up in one of the projects that many of my kids come from." Her views concerning the failure of the education system were reinforced during her experience as a high school guidance counselor. "I was appalled at the low skill levels of so many of the kids." Indeed it was this experience that ultimately made

> "I knew you had to get to the kids early. High school was too late."

leading an elementary school in a predominately African American community appealing. "I knew you had to get to the kids early. High school was too late."

Janet's desire to improve educational outcomes for students in urban schools led her to be an early and enthusiastic supporter of standards-based reform. She stated that the MCAS (Massachusetts Comprehensive Assessment System), reinforced by No Child Left Behind (NCLB), was the "best thing" that had happened for urban students in her career. Like Bill Henderson, she viewed these policies as countering the low expectations common in urban schools. Though she acknowledged some shortcomings in the NCLB approach, by and large she strongly supported the fundamental principles behind standards-based reform: clarifying what children should know and be able to do, assessing students to determine mastery, and holding schools and teachers responsible for producing results.

In the area of special education, Janet had some ambivalence. She clearly supported the desire of many of the parents of students with disabilities to have effective integrated education. Indeed, many parents and caregivers of students with disabilities from other parts of the city opted to have their children attend the Mason. However, she viewed traditional special education as a source of educational inequity for African Americans, particularly males. "Look who is in those classrooms and tell me if you think that's right," she told us. It wasn't only the segregation that bothered Janet, but also the lack of accountability for outcomes associated with traditional special education practices. Janet viewed inclusive education as a potential antidote to these inequities both for students who had disabilities and those who may have been inappropriately placed in special education.

CARMEN TORRES AND LINDA NATHAN AT BOSTON ARTS ACADEMY

Boston Arts Academy was co-led by two headmasters (the Boston title for high school principal), Carmen Torres and Linda Nathan. They served very different roles in running the school in a way that clearly complemented one another. Each refers to the other in terms of role, liberally giving her credit for the school's success. One teacher describing them said, "They're two parts . . . like the mind and the soul and the spirit. They just are that one entity, but different parts of it complementing the other."

One admirer aptly referred to Linda as an "education warrior."

Linda Nathan began her career as a Title I teacher in San Juan, Puerto Rico. She eventually became a bilingual teacher in a large middle school in Boston where she and her students were "segregated in the basement." She described how her students would return to her class after venturing out for the little integration they had at lunch or art with bruises inflicted on them by the other children. This was occurring during Boston's court-ordered integration when, she said, "we should have been seeking racial healing." Linda described herself as driven by "questions of access and equity." One admirer aptly referred to her as an "education warrior."

During her time at the middle school, Linda began an after-school theatre program as a means to promote integration for her students and to promote relationships across racial and disability lines. The program was designed as trilingual: Spanish, English, and American Sign Language. Soon friendships developed where animosity had previously reigned, reinforcing for Linda the power of the arts.

Linda's role at BAA was both visionary and entrepreneurial. She was the one dealing with the external political environment, she was the primary spokesperson for the school, and she was its principal fundraiser. She had received numerous awards and has recently published a well-acclaimed book about the school, *The Hardest Questions Aren't on the Test: Lessons from an Innovative Urban School.*[3] Linda also took an active role in the day-to-day management of the school, greeting every student and teacher as they entered the school in the morning and being actively engaged with teachers on issues of curriculum and instruction.

Politically, Linda described herself as "left" and was a fierce critic of standards-based reform. She said she was "very, very scared" of the current milieu with its focus on testing, which she said was "making creativity and play obsolete." However, she did support providing students with access to demanding academic curriculum, and, like the other schools in the study, students at BAA had high test scores. She was a vocal supporter of inclusion for students with disabilities and eloquently connected issues of disability access and equity with issues involving other minority groups. Describing Linda, one of the teachers at BAA explained, "She brings brilliance, but not headiness. She brings nurturing, but not pandering. She's brilliant in that she supports people in very different ways. She's also like a political machine, she's a political beast, and she knows what she wants, she has her agenda, and she believes in democratic schools, and she tries her best to be democratic, and it works, and she loves to give the staff authority and voice. We have a lot of voice in our school. But she definitely is going to exact her vision."

Carmen Torres was a thirty-year education veteran who had been educated in the New York City Public Schools. She came to Boston to attend Brandeis University as an undergraduate and pursued an additional degree there in human service management. She moved on to found the Health Careers program at Brighton High School in Boston, and she was among only three employees of the Boston Public Schools to have national board certification in high school science. At BAA, Carmen focused her efforts more on internal operations, particularly in the area of student support services. A teacher at BAA described Carmen this way:

"A lot of us look at Carmen as the heart. . . . She's able to wrap the arms and the warmth around the culture."

> Carmen, a lot of us kind of look at her as the heart, you know, where Linda's kind of like all in the head. Carmen is the one who is the humanity of the administration, that team. And so, she's able to kind of help put—wrap the arms and the warmth around the culture so when the change is happening, Linda's like, "This is what we're doing, this is what we're becoming," Carmen is like, "And this is why we feel good about it. And this is why it's going to make things better for you, and it's okay. You'll be okay." And it's really kind of great to have both of those people.

One incident captured both Carmen's role in the school as well as her values. One of the teachers related that they had not been successful with all students, particularly students with emotional disturbance. We asked Carmen about two children with emotional disturbance who had dropped out. She clearly was upset and emotional. She stated, "We failed them." Her knowledge of the specifics of these two cases was impressive, as were the lengths that both she and the school had gone to meet the needs of these students. Carmen and the school had reached out to community organizations for supports, provided mental health services, and coordinated with the other agencies involved. In fact, Carmen played an active role in coordinating efforts to involve the communities that the students came from with the school. Given the fact that students come from all over Boston, this was a daunting task. Yet Carmen viewed it as central to the school's mission and success. The two students did not graduate; however, the lengths that Carmen and the school went in addressing the needs of these kids were impressive.

Neither Linda nor Carmen described children as deficient; rather they situated the problem of access with the school.

From a policy perspective, Carmen's views were similar to Linda's. She viewed the provision of high-quality education from an access perspective. She too linked disability access to language access. For Carmen, access to demanding material was an issue that required continual attention from the institution. Neither Linda nor Carmen described children as deficient; rather they situated the problem of access with the school and searched for what they could do to educate all of their students. The same can be said for Janet and Bill.

HOW THEY LED THEIR SCHOOLS

The personal histories of these leaders speak to their motivation and values. Such qualities, important as they are, may exist in many leaders who fail. A compelling personal narrative is not enough to provide effective leadership. Ultimately it is what leaders *do* in leading their schools that makes the difference. And, on this level, though these school leaders differed in many ways, there were striking similarities in how they led their organizations. All attended to change through multiple but similar pathways.

To analyze these pathways we used the "four frames of leadership" framework developed by Lee Bolman and Terrence Deal in their book *Reframing Organizations.*[4]

Lee Bolman and Terrence Deal, authors of *Reframing Organizations,* contend that effective and sustainable change occurs only when leaders address several fronts—or frames—concurrently: the symbolic frame, the structural frame, the political frame, and the human resource frame.

1. The *symbolic frame* addresses the values and culture of the organization.
2. The *structural frame* attends to the organization of the institution, its resources, and policies.
3. The *political frame* addresses how the organization deals with power.
4. The *human resource frame* deals with how individuals within the organization are treated, supported, and developed.

These schools' principals attended to all four frames, and they developed school-level teacher leaders who also attended to the four frames. Though they used widely varying strategies, each frame received considerable attention by leaders and teachers in these exemplary schools.

The Symbolic Frame

Organizational theorists who emphasize the symbolic frame in their work see organizations as places where values and culture are the driving forces of change. Symbolic leaders appeal to people's values and greater sense of purpose. They celebrate organizational success, tell stories that exemplify the organization's purpose, and look for opportunities to demonstrate values in action.

The schools' missions were deeply internalized among teachers and parents. Many schools go through a process of determining their missions and values. However, what matters is the degree to which the school community embraces this vision. It's not uncommon to find teachers in some schools who consider inclusion only for students who are "doing grade-level work." This is not the case in any of the schools profiled. Though all the leaders acknowledge that some children may need more restrictive environments, they begin with the assumption that children should be included regardless of type or severity of disabilities.

> *The schools' missions were deeply internalized among teachers and parents.*

This inclusive orientation came clearly from the leadership, who have used the symbolic frame in part to develop staff who can focus on educating all students to high academic standards in inclusive environments. The missions did not "bubble up from below." On the contrary, these leaders were clear about their schools' fundamental mission and actively imposed them on their organizations through a variety of symbolic actions. To them, inclusion was a non-negotiable grounded in civil rights.

At the O'Hearn, Henderson made it clear that all teachers would at times have to assist children in the toilets. He believed there was no other practical alternative, but he also believed that teachers' willingness to assist children with significant disabilities with toileting was symbolic of their willingness to accept these children and do what was necessary to provide an inclusive education. According to Bill, "If they didn't like this, they were free to leave, and one did." At the Mason, Palmer-Owens resisted the advocacy of some teachers to seek to limit the number of students with intellectual disabilities enrolled in the school when these students appeared to be negatively affecting test scores. Recalling the incident, no matter what the schools' scores would be, she said, "I refused to do that. Inclusion is at the core of who we are." Symbolically, aside from the arts, BAA was known for this distinction.

While the priority for these leaders was that their own school embraced the culture that they were creating, they also placed the work in the context of a larger change effort to remake schooling to be more equitable and inclusive. These leaders looked beyond their schools to the broader society. They viewed their schools as examples of how the overall education system could promote social equity through education. Bill, who has now retired from the O'Hearn, works in Latin America bringing education to children who are blind and who have other disabilities. Janet speaks throughout the country about how schools can be successful with low-income kids, particularly African Americans. Linda spoke throughout the country on the importance of the arts in education, emphasizing its power to bring children together across racial, economic, and disability lines while at the same time increasing academic skills.

Another example of her symbolic leadership occured when, after a lengthy process, the parent representatives on the school council did not reflect the diversity of the school. She simply could not accept this and even risked a lawsuit for overturning the process, insisting on a new process that resulted in a more representative body. Carmen traveled with a group of students to Australia to do an exchange between an arts-centered program there and at BAA. Collectively these leaders have spoken to governors, Congress, and the media about their work. However, though they advocate for change using their schools as examples, they do not do this in a self-aggrandizing way. They readily admitted they still had work to do, yet they never compromised the broader agenda they sought to promote. The term *burnt out* would never apply to these leaders. They burn with passion for their work and clearly delight in it. Though the leaders of these schools were assertive concerning mission and values, we remind readers of teachers' remarkable commitment to the mission and values discussed in Chapter One.

Each School Took Their Own Path to Inclusion

While they all sought high achievement for diverse populations of students with disabilities, each school took a unique path to get there. The focus on an inclusive education started at the O'Hearn about twenty years ago by a group of parents of students with significant disabilities who "demanded that there be an inclusive option for the system." Bill explained, "It was a political movement. We demand our civil rights to have inclusion for our kids with significant disabilities." Bill recalled his role in the taskforce developed by the district to study the question and explained that the district wanted to do what was right but believed that they needed to study the topic first. The parents, however, frustrated with the idea of studying how to develop this school, threatened to go to the media and say, "You don't care about handicapped kids." The district acquiesced, and Bill became the principal. He explained that to develop the culture at his school, he had to work with an already existing staff to help them embrace the idea of including students with disabilities. "We fought very hard . . . [to] make sure we had people who bought into that . . . commitment to inclusion, that vision, not totally defined what it was, because we were still evolving, but at least people were excited and enthusiastic and hopefully with some experience, too, and some ideas about wanting to be in a place where kids with disabilities are throughout the school. That was very important, establishing that culture, and having the expectation, if you work in the school, this is what you have to believe."

Bill defined the culture in his school with three attributes: "I talk about beliefs, attitudes, and behaviors. Beliefs, you have to talk about the strengths about the kids with disabilities, and not about all the deficits. Attitudes, you have to be enthusiastic and you have to make the kids feel comfortable. . . . And then the behaviors, not only do you have to welcome them, but you have to challenge them."

Janet inherited a school well along the path toward inclusive education. She embraced that direction and moved the school forward by welcoming a more diverse population of students with disabilities and by ensuring the inclusion of students with disabilities in the testing program. "They [students with disabilities] were already in general education classrooms but we had no idea what they were learning. When we included them in the testing, our scores went way down. We had to establish a baseline. We had to be accountable for their learning too." Janet says that the culture in her school is "incredible. . . . This is the real world, this is the success of this building, is that we celebrate all types of differences, and kids celebrate those."

The administration of BAA started their school with a public commitment to be the first inclusive high school in the district. Their path began with a focus on including students who were deaf. Linda had worked with students who were deaf, and several deaf students had auditioned into the school. BAA learned quickly that the deaf community had a strong culture with a clear focus on civil rights. BAA's special education director explained that by beginning their "inclusion conversation" with an eye toward students who were deaf, they were "[thrown] to level ten right away." She said, "We had to prove ourselves to the deaf community from the beginning that we were going to do right by these kids. And, God bless them, that's exactly the way it should be. And so our vision started with some very core conversations about . . . when is the right to be separate? When is the right to be included? Meaning, what services do the deaf students get that maybe other students do not, definitely other students do not, and what—how—what do we need to do to ensure that they'll be included?" Their education on deaf culture took them on a unique path toward developing their inclusive practices. Linda described how enrolling these students influenced her and Carmen's thinking about inclusion: "Carmen and I thought we knew everything about special ed because we had been bilingual teachers. How wrong were we? We opened this school with deaf students. And we thought we knew everything about bilingualism, [so] what was different? Deaf kids are the same, they're just bilingual. We were really wrong. So that's when we began thinking about, what does it mean to be an inclusive school?" She hired a teacher from the Horace Mann, a school for the deaf that they relied upon heavily to help them create an inclusive environment for their students who were deaf, and then from there, to their students with other disabilities.

Symbolic Actions Large and Small

We saw evidence of symbolic markers highlighting schools' culture in ways large and small. At the O'Hearn, a small symbolic gesture that was very powerful was a rule that forbade disparaging remarks concerning students or their families in the teachers' lounge. We never heard disparaging remarks about students or their families in this or any of the schools.

Another aspect of the symbolic frame concerns ceremonies and rituals. All of these schools had frequent events that celebrated their successes and provided opportunities to reinforce their values. For instance, at the O'Hearn there were frequent performances that involved all students. In one production, a student with significant disabilities who was nonverbal had his wheelchair converted into an armored vehicle that shot across the stage in *The Sound of Music*. All three schools embrace the arts as both a vehicle to reinforce academic skills and as an outward means to manifest their values.

The leaders themselves at times serve to reinforce core values. They are all values-driven people who view education as a vehicle to promote civil rights. Janet grew up in one of the projects that feed her school. She was open about this fact and used it to emphasize to the students that education was her route to success. She related how she informed one boy that he was living in the apartment in which she grew up. Bill is blind and was clear that his perspective as a person with a disability underscored the importance of inclusive education as a vehicle for social equity. Carmen as a Latina shared the experience of being an immigrant with many of her students. The fact that BAA was co-led by a white woman and a Latina was viewed by some as a positive statement concerning equity and power. Linda explained that while her goal had always been to create heterogeneous classes in her school, "Why this was all so important to us," she explained, was "the subtext. . . . What does it mean to create success for all students, taking into account, not regardless of, race, gender, socioeconomic background, language background, disability, artistic background, family, cultural background, you name it."

The Structural Frame

The structural frame focuses on how leaders organize their schools, including their policies, their resources, and other structures that support the goals of the school. Within the structural frame, leaders pay particular attention to differentiation and coordination. These principals had developed organizational structures and used their resources in ways that supported their schools' missions.

The structures at these schools were in many ways nontraditional. For example, the staff placement did not follow the traditional one general education teacher to one general education class, with special education as a separate entity. In these schools, teachers co-taught, held certification in both general and special education, or both. In each school, there were also paraprofessionals, most of whom were attached to whole classes rather than to individual students. The leaders of these schools generally rejected the concept of one-on-one paraprofessionals, as they believed such supports could foster dependence and also result in an inefficient allocation of resources. Paraprofessionals tended to assist any student who needed help under the direction of the teacher. Each of these schools employed student teachers and interns liberally and actively recruited the most talented into their ranks. These administrators worked to provide adequate and appropriate supports for all students within all classrooms.

Providing supports within classrooms for both students with disabilities and those who needed extra support because they were struggling or were advanced meant that in these schools teaching was not an independent, isolating activity. Teachers worked collaboratively, and it was common to see more than one adult in a room. These schools, therefore, were not, as Jennifer O'Day terms, "egg crate" structures in which teachers work largely independently of each other.[5] This structural aspect of these schools was one of the foundations that allowed these schools to become collaborative problem-solving cultures (discussed further in Chapter Three).

Another structural support to the schools' culture of collaborative work and focus on problem solving was a great deal of planning time and staff development created and supported by the school leadership. Time is a scarce commodity in schools, and these administrators relegated significant amounts of time to their teachers in order for them to develop their relationships and work together and to engage in professional development activities. This dedicated time was perhaps the most important structural resource that administrators used to support teachers' work. Linda explained, "We always have thought of ourselves as having a rich, professional learning community. And in order to have a rich, professional learning community, you need some things in place. Obviously you need time." Yet, time is costly. Michelle explained, "The adults who are having that dedicated common planning time are able to do that because some other adults are doing direct work with the kids. . . . Time in a school context equals money." Each of these schools has found ways to schedule a significant amount of time for teachers to work together to find ways to better deliver the curriculum to students.

A structural element that helped promote high student performance was that each of these schools had found ways to extend the time available for learning. Bill stated, "The school day is simply too short. We can't do all we need to do within the time allotted." The Mason developed an after-school program when parents identified this as a priority. Many parents and caregivers felt compelled to keep their children inside due to the dangerous nature of the neighborhood and felt that their children were spending too much time watching television after school. The after-school program was well developed and had a direct connection to classroom academics as well as providing the students with other enrichment activities. BAA had both after-school and summer programs. One special education teacher stated that these options were critical to providing extended literacy options for those struggling most with reading. "We are able to provide both intensive remedial interventions without having to pull the kids out of English class through our after-school and summer options." As noted in the Introduction to this book, Mason and BAA were pilot schools and thus could have longer days due to the flexibility this status provided under the teachers' contract.

Entrepreneurial Activities Strengthening Structures

These structural features of these schools cost money, and these principals were able to provide them by being exceptionally entrepreneurial. They were skillful in garnering resources in addition to those provided by the district. The schools had numerous grants, partnerships with local universities and nonprofit agencies, as well as state and city services. The leaders also strategically integrated community resources in their schools. Examples of entrepreneurial behavior abounded. BAA asked Ray Kurzweil to donate access to his advanced Kurzweil screen-reading software to every student in the school. Linda taught a course at Harvard Graduate School of Education and donated her payment to BAA. Bill had developed a strong relationship with the VSA (formerly Very Special Arts) program that enabled the school to infuse art throughout the curriculum and to produce top-quality shows. Bill also secured "respite care" money from the State Department of Mental Retardation to help support the after-school program. The Mason has integrated the South End Community Health Center into the school in an effort to expand students' access to mental health services. All three schools used various federal programs in an integrated manner to support staff development and to provide support to students who were struggling. (See Chapter Six.)

These schools exhibit a wealth of technologies, literature, and supplies, most obtained through the entrepreneurship of the leaders. When people visit these schools, they often notice the level of available resources and conclude that this is the result of these schools being exceptionally resourced. This at times plays into what Elmore referred to as the "default culture" too prevalent in education.[6] We have frequently heard other educators in Boston express this belief. A leader in another school stated, "We can't possibly do what the O'Hearn or Mason is doing; we do not have the resources they do." Yet the O'Hearn, the Mason, and BAA each started out with the standard budget provided by the school district. The leaders in these schools have been able to secure additional resources through a number of means. They did not accept the "default" but rather established a strong inclusive direction and found the resources to make that happen.

These entrepreneurial leaders at times turned down resources or did not apply for some grants if they believed they would detract from the central focus of the school. Janet spent a good deal of time early in her tenure winnowing down the

The leaders . . . did not accept the "default" but rather established a strong inclusive direction and found the resources to make that happen.

number of grants coming to the school or renegotiating them because she felt they were pulling the school in too many directions. "The grants are only useful if they can be directed to our needs. Otherwise, they can be a distraction."

The Political Frame

The political frame addresses how leaders deal with power, both within their schools and in the external environment. Theorists who write about the political frame view organizations as political arenas in which individual and group interests play out. Conflict is inevitable in organizations where resources are scarce and interests vary, such as in schools. Effective managers within this frame do not bemoan politics but rather view political conflict as a given and use various means to extend their positional power to promote their goals. They do this through agenda setting, developing coalitions both within the school and out, personal persuasion and power, and effectively using rewards and sanctions.

These leaders worked skillfully within the political frame. Though it is easy in urban schools to "blame the system," these leaders were more apt to use the system and were quick to praise those within the bureaucracy who had helped them. Even though our interviews revealed frustrations with various aspects of the bureaucracy, there were many instances where these leaders were effective in using the bureaucracy toward their ends.

When Tom Hehir congratulated Bill on an article written about the successes in his school,[7] Bill's response was a bit less sanguine. He said, "The piece looks like I am putting down the central office. That's not the way it was. I had my conflicts but by and large they have been great." He was concerned that the piece might damage these important relationships and thus undermine the school. The praise from the *Boston Globe* was secondary. Bill's point was indeed valid, albeit subtle. Tom had read it as positive journalism; Bill believed that he needed to do political damage control.

Janet invited several people from the central office to a celebration of the centennial anniversary of the Mason. She heaped praise on them for all they had done to "make the Mason the school it is today." Particular praise went to a worker in the facilities department who had gone out of his way to help with renovations. In an interview Janet commented extensively on the help she had received from one of the deputy superintendents of the district: "I don't know what I would have done without her during those years."

Janet, Bill, and Linda praised then superintendent Tom Payzant, who presided over the district during the time of the study. They credited him with changes that they felt were essential to their schools' successes. Among these was the establishment of pilot schools, the standardization of the curriculum, and the support he gave to innovative principals to experiment. These schools seem to have benefited from stability within the superintendency, which was held by Payzant for ten years. An interview with Payzant revealed his deep respect for the principals of these schools.

The Politics of District Office

An interesting political frame story emerged concerning the district's central special education department. It is ironic that special education seemed to be the only department these leaders were wary of and actively had to problem-solve around. The belief that the special education department "did not support inclusion" was common among them. Indeed, Boston has higher rates of identifying students for special education and of segregating special education students than both the nation and the state. (See Chapter One.) Further, members of the central special education department had been witnessed speaking in a disparaging or dismissive manner concerning these schools, even though their results were far superior to those of the overall system. One was quoted as saying, "Of course the O'Hearn can do inclusion. It has all those resources. It's just not replicable."

At the time of this study, Boston had a highly centralized, bureaucratized, special system in which school placement for many students with disabilities was in the hands of both school-based and citywide evaluation team facilitators (ETFs).

In each school, the principal had brought the school-based ETFs into the leadership structure. Interviews with these facilitators revealed a deep commitment to the schools' missions and approaches, and the principals considered these people key components of their schools' success. The ETF at BAA was seen as the special education leader and as a third leader of the school, after Linda and Carmen. She explained inclusion worked well in her school:

I think part of it is just because we were first at the high school level. And I think first counts for a lot. . . . In my experience one of the roadblocks to inclusion is willingness. And so by being first, you demonstrate you're really interested and committed. And that counts for a lot. I think also . . . it's hand in hand with being a pilot school. Because we're a pilot school, and particularly because we're an arts school, we are, by definition, committed to thinking creatively and complexly about students. And inclusion fits naturally into that, not just having easy categories or boxes for students or for curriculum or for schedule.

The ETF at the Mason was also a principal in residence. One teacher at the Mason explained that Leigh had "taken very much a leadership role, more than any other ETF we have, in terms of things like lesson planning, specific needs being met, the needs of English language learners, and the relationship of all that to professional development we're doing at the school." The ETF at the O'Hearn, which was not as integrated as in the other schools, had a similar level of commitment to the school. She described the school this way:

At the risk of sounding a little corny, there's a real community feeling in this building, and part of it is the leadership. . . . Why does [the O'Hearn] have a good reputation? Because we get the job done. Children are succeeding. Children are accessing the curriculum. Anything you would expect in a general education school is happening here, and it's happening by virtue of the fact that the kids aren't separated because they present with disabilities. They are a part of the community and they participate in everything.

These leaders also realized that they needed to strategize around what they understood to be problems created by central district staff. Janet recalled that a central special education staff person had come to an individualized education plan (IEP) meeting in her school concerning a student. Janet was perplexed as she felt the child was doing well and knew the parent was happy. It appeared that the child had a disability designation in the computer system that in the eyes of the central office was incompatible with the Mason. The central staff person insisted that the child be transferred to the O'Hearn.

Janet said that as long as the parent was okay with it, "I was not going to fight it." In an effort to look further into this incident, we inquired Bill about this student. He said, "None of us could understand why this child was sent from the Mason but he is doing fine here."

In another incident, Bill was upset that a high-level central office staff person associated with special education supported curtailing accommodations for students with disabilities in large-scale state testing. At issue was whether students could use screen readers (text-to-speech technology, specifically Kurzweil) as an accommodation for subject area testing. The administrator opposed its use, because in her view they were not "reading." Bill's position was that they were not being assessed in reading, but rather the subject matter, such as mathematics, and the accommodation allowed these students, particularly students with dyslexia, to actively demonstrate what they knew and were able to do. Bill's view ultimately prevailed with the state department board of education because of the political base he had developed outside the district's special education bureaucracy. Now, all MCAS tests are available in a Kurzweil format for students throughout the state and may be selected as an accommodation.

The relationship of these schools to the central special education department revealed several aspects of how these leaders handled the political frame. First, neither Bill nor Janet was willing to take on the department over the reassignment of individual children. However, these leaders had been able to work around the special education department because they had power sources elsewhere. The general education leadership of the school system seemed to go out of its way to support the schools. This more powerful support system checked the ability of the district special education office to interfere with these schools through relationships that were at times was tense. However, whenever appropriate, these leaders praised individuals from the central special education office. Linda spoke of her relationship with a particularly effective special education central office staffer: "She's really been for us, like, a touchstone. You know, when she retires, I think we'll all die. But she comes in, kind of once or twice a year, and we do a case study with her. And we do a tune-up. We call it a tune-up with her. And we'll present something that we're really worried about and that we're thinking about. And she just kind of listens."

Linda went on to say how important her insights had been to the development of the school. Bill also spoke of similar relationships.

An Inclusive Network Emerges

The relationships that developed between these three schools and two others known for their special education work formed another interesting power base. One of these schools was another inclusive school (one of the schools we had identified for this study that had decided not to participate), and the other, Horace Mann, the school for the deaf mentioned previously. Both teacher leaders and the principals spoke to each other around common concerns and identified teachers who had taught at more than one of the schools. One who had worked at two of the schools stated, "I could only work in an inclusive school and there are only four in the city." BAA collaborated a great deal with the fourth inclusive school in Boston. This informal network yielded benefits for these schools. In a sense, these schools had established an inclusive enclave in a system where segregation predominated.

Other external coalitions and collaborations were important to these leaders. For Bill, connections with disability advocacy groups were critical. He involved various disability groups and advocates (including Tom Hehir) to appeal successfully to the state board of education on behalf of keeping robust accommodations in MCAS testing. Particularly important to Janet was the South Bay Business Association, an organization that was instrumental in providing funds and other supports to the school. Boston Arts Academy was closely linked to many arts organizations and to a local arts college that provided various supports to the school and offered students classes as well as internship sites. Recently a coalition of these groups presented a report to the superintendent on the need to increase arts education in the schools. This report received extensive coverage in the media, with BAA held out as the model. Indicative of the esteem with which she is held, Linda appeared with the superintendent and several other leaders from the arts community on a PBS special addressing the need to expand arts education in the city.

The Power of Teacher Leaders

Each of these principals clearly had established a power base within their schools. Teachers and parents deeply respected the principals and appreciated their leadership. Maricel said of Bill that the reason teachers respected him was that "he is so in tune with us and so encouraging and knows what's going on and trusts us as professionals to make good decisions. . . . We respect him. And I see it all over." Teachers generally felt they were fortunate to teach in schools with good working conditions and collaborative opportunities. They also commented on the work ethic of their leaders and colleagues and respected the effort they exerted to improve their schools. Blair explained that at BAA, "People have massaged me and worked with me into really expanding my professional development . . . [and] making sure that we get what we need to stay here, to be here, and to grow while we're here, and to be better people for these students."

Teachers in these schools seem to have a clear idea of how their leaders approached their work. Melissa, a teacher at the Mason, explained that Janet was "very dedicated to the school" and "had this general love for all the kids that are here, all the families." She was particularly "impressed at her ability to outreach to get funds to bring in partnerships for the building" in order to get the specialists they needed to support the work of the school. A parent at the Mason was initially concerned about whether her child who had a disability would be able to keep up academically. The parent explained, "There are really high expectations" at the Mason. She said that initially, she was "a little nervous about these high expectations." Janet quelled her concerns and told her that the school would provide her child the support she needed. This parent said, "I feel like [my daughter] has, by and large, been supported the way she needs to be supported."

Teachers and parents wept at Bill's retirement party. Janet was able to get three-fourths of her teachers to vote to become a pilot school even though such a vote reduced some of their contractual rights and benefits. The union representative at BAA was one of the teacher leaders in the school overseeing the special education services and enjoyed a close relationship with Linda and Carmen. None of these leaders spoke disparagingly of the Boston Teachers Union in any of our interviews, and union officials have spoken positively about these schools. There was none of the anti-teacher rhetoric prevalent in many policy circles today in any of these interviews. On the contrary, these leaders praised the hard work of their teachers and actively strove to create environments in which teachers could be successful in the classroom.

However, each of these leaders actively sought to remove teachers they did not feel were competent.

These principals were well known and respected and had garnered a great deal of political support in the community as well as within the school district. Some of this respect had clearly come from the recognition the schools had received for being high performing under NCLB. The district and even the state have held up these schools as exemplars. All three have developed national reputations. Leaders have spoken at conferences, with one receiving a visit from the Secretary of Education and another receiving an award from Hilary Clinton. One principal served as an advisor to the governor, and another received frequent visits from the mayor, who delighted in the student performances. Though these schools enjoyed the political benefits brought by success, they had to earn this respect.

> *Each of these leaders was significantly counter-cultural.*

In many ways, each of these leaders was significantly counter-cultural. The O'Hearn and Mason schools began their transformation toward inclusion in the late 1980s, long before inclusion became a national trend. BAA was Boston's first arts school in the oldest public school system in the country.

Each leader was seeking to challenge the status quo of the Boston public schools. These leaders all had to dance a very delicate political dance of being counter-cultural while being part of a large tradition-bound school system. It is doubtful that these leaders' success would have been possible without their highly developed political skills. One gets the clear impression that any one of these leaders could have had a successful career in politics.

The Human Resource Frame

Leaders who are skillful within the human resource frame focus a good deal of attention on the fit between human needs and organizational goals. These leaders recognize that individuals come to their work lives seeking meaningful and satisfying work. They further recognize the importance of developing the skills employees need to feel competent. In the traditional school context, where individuals work relatively independently in O'Day's egg crate structures, the ability of leaders to promote the interdependency needed to improve organizational performance is daunting.

In these schools, however, the fact that these leaders created collaborative structures, connected to a deeply internalized mission, created the conditions upon which the teachers and other staff were more likely to have their human needs met. Further, these leaders used their entrepreneurial and political abilities to garner resources needed to develop the skills of the personnel who worked in these schools. Looking through the lens of the human resources frame, we noticed the inter-relatedness of mission, collaborative work, and professional development. Teachers were deeply connected to the missions of these schools. They had time to work collaboratively and had extensive professional development available to them. This resulted in workplaces where teachers had strong relationships with one another, focused on a common purpose. The attention by these leaders to the human resource frame was extensive and critical to the success of these schools.

Parents and teachers understood Bill to be a person who would champion for the best education for all of his students. They believed that he knew what that would look like and he knew how to make it happen. Samantha, a special education teacher at the O'Hearn, explained, [Bill] "has access to very current information . . . in terms of inclusion, and this philosophy that we're working under. And he shares that information so that you always feel that you're ahead of the curve. If he hears something that's out there that's going to help students, he's the first one to offer. He finds ways to make it available. . . . I always feel that every year I've learned something new. It's like you're getting a master's degree, renewed every year."

The depth and breadth of professional development in these three schools was significant. Professional development activities took many forms, all dedicated to the mission of providing an education based on high academic standards to all students in inclusive settings. Schools examined a wide range of topics, most focused on instruction and behavior, some also focused on the larger political view of education and society at large. Professional development activities were not self-contained in one time period, but rather occurred before, during, and after the school day, during the school year, and over the summer. Professional development happened in the school building and off-site, in large and small groups, as well as in individual study. School staff and experts from outside the school facilitated professional development activities.

Professional Development Defined

Defining professional development in these schools is not a simple task. First, each school addressed a number of specific topics. Mason's professional development activities focused on closing the achievement gap, assistive technology, race, and culture, and they continued their professional development on literacy. At the O'Hearn, they were examining assistive technology, math accommodations, and stamina reading. At BAA, teachers focused on "dominant ideologies" in terms of "race, class, gender, and looking at boys of color." Teachers at BAA were also involved in a special education certification program through ongoing courses offered at the school and were beginning to focus on electronic portfolios.

Professional development took many forms. One of the more intensive professional development activities was the study group. Study groups consisted of teachers working in small groups to study in-depth and report to their colleagues on a topic. Groups would research the topic and report to the full faculty on their findings. Delphine explained, "We look at a particular subject, and then end up with a product, which we present . . . to the faculty. So it's not just a—what's the word—[a] theoretical type of thing. We have to present an actual product. So we have to come up with math accommodations for MCAS questions for the first, second, and third grade in my particular group."

Another quite intensive form of professional development was peer observations. Here, teachers formally observed each other on a particular school-wide focus or individual professional goal. Teresa explained the process at the Mason:

> What we do is at the beginning of our cycle, usually in our initial
> meeting, we'll set up our agenda, which states our focus. And then
> different teachers will set up an agenda for who's going to demo each
> week for those four weeks. And we pick a specific focus so ahead of
> time, they know what they're coming in to watch a teacher do. So,
> we usually do a quick pre-meeting, just to kind of run through the

lesson. And then following the lesson, we debrief about it and kind of shoot ideas back and forth.

Delphine at the O'Hearn explained how teachers there visited each other's classes in order to strengthen their practices, particularly in literacy and mathematics. "We go and visit another classroom and talk about it. . . . Really looking at classrooms . . . looking at effective practices, very nitty gritty, hands-on." These structured observations were powerful learning tools for teachers.

There were, to a lesser degree, one-session workshops. Delphine described a speaker, a young man of color with a disability who had come to the school to talk with students and teachers. Delphine said that this speaker "talked to the faculty . . . telling about his experiences, sharing some of his poetry, and giving his view for what would make a better school." While teachers appreciated this speaker, what they called "one-shot workshops" were not the norm in any of the schools. Karen from the Mason explained, "There's not a lot of going to these one-shot workshops." She said that professional development needed to be more substantive so that it could address such questions as "How does this satisfy the standards? How is this related to what kids need to know? How is this related to how they come to understand math? You know, how is the world language related to how kids learn to read and write?"

Another form of professional development activity was book discussions, where school personnel all read and discussed the same book together. Teachers at the Mason had read *Courageous Conversations About Race: A Field Guide for Achieving Equity in Schools* by Glenn Eric Singleton and Curtis Linton[8] and teachers at BAA were planning to read Jonathan Kozol's book, *The Shame of the Nation: The Restoration of Apartheid Schooling in America.*[9]

In addition, teachers attended and presented at local and national conferences, provided professional development to other schools and for the district on a variety of topics, taught in the district's alternative certification program, mentored interns and student teachers, and took graduate courses at local universities or online. This was Alice's fourth year as a teacher, her first year at the O'Hearn. She said of all of this professional development: "[It] is very helpful to me, and I feel like, as a special ed teacher . . . I'm learning more than I've ever learned in a school before, just because it's stuff that makes sense for what I'm doing."

Teachers' Commitment to Professional Development

Teachers were committed to engaging in professional development. Teachers in all three schools went significantly beyond the eighteen hours of professional development required by the school district. John explained that at BAA, "professional development opportunities are awesome. . . . And they provide a lot. . . . It happens a week before [school], a week after, on retreats, there's so much professional development. I think two years ago we had 250 hours!"

Teachers were also under no illusion that they were not working long hours; however, the culture at these schools was such that a commitment to ongoing professional development was the norm. Delphine at the O'Hearn explained, "The culture in the school is that this is what's required. And it's just standard, and everybody gets into it." Teachers, paraprofessionals, and at one school, the secretary all participated in the professional development activities. Delphine laughed as she told of a teacher who had retired the previous year after many years of teaching, "thirty-five years of teaching and fifteen years here . . . and honestly, in May, she was still going to workshops about technology. . . . And that's just totally standard." According to Teresa at the Mason, "Most teachers are doing something, whether they're leading workshops or attending workshops, some are in other certification programs. I think the teachers here hold a lot of high standards for themselves." Heather explained that all teachers at BAA had participated in their literacy professional development, and they all used what they learned in their classes, no matter their subject. "The school had us have professional development in reading skills writ large, regardless whether you're a math teacher, a music teacher, or whatever. And then we take that in to our practice." Teachers understood that their commitment to their professional development was significant. Melissa explained the professional development activities as "opportunities." She said, "It's interesting, when I talk to other teachers, even other teachers I know within [the district] that don't have those opportunities at their school, you can tell the difference."

Teachers' Relationships Supporting Professional Development

Professional development activities in these schools were most often carried out in groups or pairs, and as such, were dependent upon teachers working together. In these schools, strong teacher relationships supported teachers' abilities to engage in strong professional development.

Professional Development Activities Chosen with Teacher Input

In each school, teachers had input into the focus for the year's professional development. At BAA, Noel explained that the school came up with their topics from examining teachers' mid- and end-of-year reflections. From these, according to Heather, "the school sets goals for itself." Once these schoolwide goals were developed, individual teachers "make goals based on that." At the O'Hearn, Delphine explained that "each of the staff . . . chooses at the beginning of the year one subject that they're going to look at. We look at a particular subject, and then end up with a product." Teachers at the Mason had decided eight years prior to focus as a school on a particular literacy model. According to Karen, "The staff looked at and evaluated the program. Went to team training to explore it where a team of teachers all went to [a local university] for, I think, three days and decided. There was a vote. The faculty agreed, voted, decided that this was a program that we were going to try. Mostly because it's not a product, it's a framework for teaching literacy and the program for professional development for teachers." To be sure, teachers were intricately involved in what they studied each year.

Professional Development Activities Dependent upon Teacher Collaboration

The bulk of professional development rested on teachers working together. In study groups, teachers and other staff researched a topic together and then presented their information to the rest of the faculty, as well, at times, to parents, other schools, and organizations. Maricel saw benefit in these types of working relationships. She explained, "I think it really, really makes a big difference, having the study groups, because you can choose what you're interested in or what you really feel you need to learn more about and . . . you're really given a chance to get into the material and to try things out, and you have a group to come back to and kind of play ideas off of [others]."

Peer observations also required teachers to form relationships with each other. Heather describes the model that she called the "professional development [PD] partner":

> *Every year you have a professional development partner. . . and you're matched with them for the year to both observe their teaching and learn skills and strategies from them, and also to give them feedback so they learn strategies from you and also observe you. . . . But then twice a year formally you have to do a professional development observation that you write up based on a research question that that person is looking to figure out for themselves. And you write that up and you send that to [the headmasters] and your PD partner. And then at Friday meeting, you bring that right up and—maybe a triad or a group of four people sit together and discuss the PD.*

When asked how she felt if a peer observation did not go well, Teresa said, "I've had lessons that just didn't go the way I expected. But I mean, that's the reality of the field. . . . I think [my colleagues] just understood that this is a reality, it happens in their classroom as well."

Professional development activities were also based on teachers problem-solving with each other. Talking about how their literacy professional development had evolved over the years, Karen explained the experience:

> *[The professional development] gave us this forum of we were going to sit together . . . for two hours every week and we were going to talk. And we were going to develop this, sort of, shared system of beliefs around how kids learn to read and write and learn about language. And I don't think that's responsible for everything, but I think that got the ball rolling. And then people started to look at math, and, "Oh, we're going to do this professional development around math together." And then it became . . . "There's this new model for something called ILT [Instructional Leadership Team] in Boston." And so we eventually, over time, rolled everything into those two hours every week that became shared, common, professional development experience.*

Blair expressed his understanding of professional development at BAA: "We're taught to think about things in a really deep and thorough way. . . . We have a synergy. I feel like our professional development is ongoing, because we problem-solve everything in the moment." Teachers engaged in this work together; however, once again, they did not embark on this work for pleasure. Teachers focused on a mission to educate all students to high academic standards.

TO SUM UP

- Though these leaders are very different people, their actions were remarkably similar when viewed from Bolman and Deal's four frames.
- Symbolically they provided strong moral leadership concerning issues of inclusion and diversity, frequently "telling the story" of their schools and continually celebrating success.
- Structurally, each provided opportunities for teachers to work together and problem-solve.
- Politically, they mustered support within both their schools and communities that enabled them to move their schools' missions forward.
- They devoted enormous resources to develop the skills of the teachers and staff within their schools.

These schools have become what the organizational literature refers to as *collaborative problem-solving organizations* where the school community is continually confronting new challenges and innovating. This is an important distinguishing characteristic of all three schools and we believe is central to their success. Chapter Three is devoted to this concept, one that we believe is central to improving schools for all children.

PART TWO

What They Do Differently

CHAPTER THREE

Collaborative Problem-Solving Organizations

There is no cookbook. You can't mandate this. You have to figure it out kid by kid. Sometimes the teachers who work with the kid can do that themselves. Sometimes you have to get some specialized help from the outside. But, you've got to figure it out.

—Bill Henderson

I'll think about a young boy and how much he's struggling, and it's really great here, because you can think along with someone else.

—Nancy, teacher at Samuel Mason Elementary

We're taught to think about things in a really deep and thorough way. . . . Our professional development is ongoing, because we problem-solve everything in the moment.

—Blair, teacher at Boston Arts Academy

These quotes, along with many other statements from educators at the schools we studied, sum up what makes these schools distinctively different from most. The inclusive vision established by school leaders—in which there is a clear expectation that all students will be educated together to high levels of achievement—have resulted in schools that are structurally and culturally different from the norm. Structurally, teachers work together a good deal both within and outside the classroom on delivering the curriculum to highly diverse groups of students and on ways in which their schools can improve practice. And, it appears that the children who most deviate from the norm have promoted this change. In short, from an organizational perspective, these schools have become *collaborative problem-solving organizations.*

The work of various organizational thinkers provides an informative frame through which to look at schools. Increasingly, school leadership programs incorporate curriculum traditionally taught in business schools. The job of leading and improving schools is considered by many to be as complex as running corporations; the lessons from that literature are applicable to much that school leaders do.[1] In our role preparing future leaders in education, we have found this literature to be valuable. Central among this literature is the work of Tom Skrtic.

We were greatly influenced by Skrtic's work in structuring this study. His work in synthesizing a huge body of organizational and political theory and applying that to the issue of school equity as it relates to the education of students with disabilities is in our view a tour de force. (In the interest of full disclosure both of us have included his work in edited books we have published, with Hehir having originally solicited Skrtic's article for the *Harvard Educational Review.*[2]) In the research we conducted for this book, we used Skrtic's theoretical framework to help analyze our data, and indeed we found much support for his theory within the practices of these schools. However, though we admire Skrtic's work, we have found using his articles in courses to be challenging due to the academic nature of his writing and the prior knowledge required of the reader to understand the text. Here we attempt to "deconstruct" Skrtic's work to make it accessible to our readers. We begin by summarizing the main argument Skrtic developed in his 1991 seminal piece.[3] (We discuss Skrtic's work and its influences on our research in more detail in Appendix B.)

Skrtic captures the dilemma that all good teachers face: "Teachers, whether in regular or special class environments, cannot escape the necessary choice between higher means [that is, maximizing mean performance by concentrating resources on the most able learners] and narrower variances—[that is, minimizing group variance by concentrating resources on the least able learners] as long as resources are scarce and students differ."[4]

Good teachers lose sleep struggling with this dilemma. "How can I possibly give him the help he needs when I have twenty-five others who have a claim on my time?" "I just don't know why she is not learning to read." "I don't object to her being in my class but I've never taught a blind child." These are the types of statements we hear frequently from teachers in traditional schools. Some might view these as indications that these teachers are not accepting of inclusion. We do not. These teachers are expressing the reality of the traditionally organized school. They are struggling with the dilemma. That is, there is only so much you can expect a teacher to do by herself within the grade and subject structure of most schools.

PROFESSIONAL BUREAUCRACIES

Skrtic goes into a deep and scholarly analysis drawing on a wide variety of organizational theorists to examine the fundamental question of how schools might become more equitable and excellent. He asserts that school systems are fundamentally professional bureaucracies. This reflects an organizational pattern developed in the early twentieth century that served the needs of efficiently providing a basic education to a rapidly expanding population.

Unlike a machine bureaucracy like manufacturing, where work is relatively certain, the work of educating children is complex and uncertain. Students vary from one another, and the composition of a given grade may vary from year to year. Teachers are thus given a great deal of discretion over how they run their classrooms. Teachers are trained and credentialed to serve roles as professionals in this structure. The third grade teacher, for example, is a specialist in educating eight-year-olds in the third grade curriculum. The special education teacher is an expert in educating children with a particular type of disability who may have difficulty fitting into the standard program. As a result, traditional schools are organized into professional bureaucracies, where work is divided among specialists, grade level teachers, and support staff who are trained to do their jobs for a group of assigned students. These professionals are overseen by a bureaucracy that seeks to standardize the preparation of these professionals and to supervise the fidelity with which they deliver their assigned roles.

Unlike a machine bureaucracy like manufacturing, where work is relatively certain, the work of educating children is complex and uncertain.

PERFORMANCE ORGANIZATIONS

According to Skrtic, schools are thus "performance organizations" in which specialists execute their "standard programs." The math teacher delivers the algebra curriculum to the freshmen, while the special educator might assist the students with strategy instruction in the resource room. This type of organization is inherently nonadaptive for students who struggle as well as those who excel.

The resulting grade-level elementary structure and subject-oriented structures of most high schools and many middle schools are pervasive in American education and speak to what David Tyack refers to as the "grammar of schooling."[5] In other words we have come to expect our schools to be organized this way because they always have been.

This structure may persist because it serves many children efficiently and well. However, for students with disabilities and other students who do not prosper in the standard programs, problems arise because professionals have a finite repertoire within their standard programs. There is a room for some adjustment but not enough for students who fall outside the margins. Without this room for adjustment, there are limited and inadequate choices for both the child and the school.

Skrtic goes on to posit that the creation of special programs reflects organizational failure that reinforces inequity for the student. His thesis is that if schools do not address the fundamental questions about schools as organizations, they will continue to perpetuate inequity: "Given the inevitability of human diversity, a professional bureaucracy can do nothing but create students who do not fit the system. In a professional bureaucracy all forms of tracking—curriculum tracking and in-class ability grouping in general education, as well as self-contained and resource classrooms in special, compensatory, remedial, and gifted education—are organizational pathologies created by specialization and professionalization and compounded by rationalization and formalization."[6]

In other words, there is only so much diversity the traditionally organized school can handle. The "solution" of sending children who don't fit in to specialists has proven inadequate. The failure of Title I over the years to improve the educational status of low-income children and the inadequacies of segregated special education approaches are well documented.[7] No Child Left Behind (NCLB) has shed light on the poor performance of most schools in bringing these "subgroups" to proficiency. The widespread discontent with the American education system and the continual chorus for reform we believe reflect the failure of the traditional professional bureaucracy.

Skrtic went on to critique the Individuals with Disabilities Education Act (IDEA) approach to reforming education for children with disabilities:

> From an organizational perspective, the basic problem with the EHA is that it attempts to force an adhocratic value orientation on a professional bureaucracy by treating it as if it were a machine bureaucracy. The EHA's ends are adhocratic because it seeks a problem-solving organization in which interdisciplinary teams of professionals and parents collaborate to invent personalized programs, or, in the language of the EHA, individualized education plans (IEPs). But this orientation contradicts the value orientation of the professional bureaucracy in every way, given that it is a performance organization in which individual professionals work alone to perfect standard programs.[8]

In different words and style, the principals and teachers of the schools we profile and Tom Skrtic may be saying the same thing. That is, in order to educate students with significant disabilities in mainstream environments, you cannot just offer the standard program. The students don't fit in due to the nature of their disabilities. You have to offer a customized program for each child that has to be "invented" on the site, and this program must be developed by knowledgeable professionals, parents, and caregivers working together in an adhocratic manner.

The establishment of special programs in traditional schools is consistent with the fundamental structure of the professional bureaucracy and thus, according to Skrtic, buffers the organization from change. However, this response fails to meet the needs of many children with disabilities in that the programs tend not to be truly individualized and do not promote integration. Students who do not fit must be removed rather than adjusting the program to meet the child's needs.

The framers of IDEA did envision the need to create custom individualized program for students with disabilities through requirements for individualized education programs. Further they recognized the desirability of integration through the incorporation of the "Least Restrictive Environment" provisions. Added to this was the force to spur implementation through the due process options given to parents and caregivers, allowing them to look to the law to uphold these standards. However, Skrtic would contend that this bureaucratic approach, using rules and pressure, was inadequate to promote true equity for students with disabilities and failed because it was naive in its inability to recognize the organizational reality of traditional schools. Indeed the ubiquity and growth of resource rooms and special classes in response to the passage of the original IDEA, P.L. 94142, lends considerable credence to Skrtic's theoretical framework.

ADHOCRATIC PROBLEM-SOLVING SCHOOLS

Skrtic proposes that schools evolve into problem-solving organizations where the fundamental structure of the classroom is replaced with more flexible structures that are more adhocratic in nature or focused on problem solving—organizations in which educators customize programs for individual students. For Skrtic, in a problem-solving school, disability becomes an opportunity to innovate and improve. "Regardless of its causes and its extent, student

In a problem-solving school, disability becomes an opportunity to innovate and improve.

diversity is not a liability in a problem-solving organization; it is an asset, an enduring uncertainty, and thus the driving force behind innovation, growth of knowledge, and progress."[9]

These schools have evolved in ways that reinforce Skrtic's analysis. They have moved away from "egg crate" approaches and have found ways teachers can work together to address the dilemmas all teachers face in meeting the diverse needs children bring to school. Further, these schools by and large do not segregate students within specialized programs while educating children in regular education classrooms. There is ample evidence that the teachers and leaders in these schools are continually problem-solving, resulting in innovative organizations that are continually improving. Most important from our perspective is that the presence of students with significant disabilities with the expectation that all will be educated to high levels of achievement has become an organizational asset spurring innovation that is beneficial for all.

Mary, a teacher at the O'Hearn, says, [the O'Hearn is] "a place where people are always thinking of another way to do things, rather than saying 'But this is the curriculum. That's how we have to do it.' . . . The teachers [here] are being more creative."

Linda spoke of the early years at Boston Arts Academy (BAA): "None of us knew how complicated it was to have so many kids who weren't programmatically the same. . . . It wasn't like we had all L4s [students with learning disabilities assigned to separate classes]. . . . We had one of this, one of this." The crowning moment was when one of her math teachers said that he was going to teach a separate class for some of his students with disabilities, something that worried Linda.

> "I'm going to teach another math section for the deaf kids, [he said], because I just can't do it with them in the room with everyone else." And I was, like, "Oh, I don't think that's a good idea. I think we really have to think about this integration stuff." He said, "No. I'd like to put in all the ADD [attention deficit disorder] kids with the deaf kids, and let's see what happens." So it was just this bizarre experiment where he said, "I'm going to take the ones like Jack who literally can't sit still, because the whole way I'm going to do this class with the interpreter's gonna slow the whole thing down, and

those ADHD [attention deficit/hyperactive disorder] kids are going to be fine." And so they were actually. It was this very interesting experimental class.

So somewhere around year two or three, probably year three, as we actually hired a second special educator, Carmen and I again had come from a place in terms of Fenway where we said, "We want our kids to be included. We're not going to do this other track, because we don't have the staff to do it. So everyone's going to be in mainstream classes. We'll have this learning center support. Now, we really need to think about what all this means for us."

She went on to describe how they hired a university professor to teach a Friday afternoon class to all the faculty, what she called, "Special Ed 101." She credits this activity with increasing their "learning curve" and bringing them to a "new level."

As this story indicates, these schools all struggled with what inclusion entailed, and they did so within cultures that allowed for experimentation and respected teacher advocacy. However, the temporary solution of a special math class not only reinforced Skrtic's view that the standard class is limited in its ability to address the needs of diverse learners but highlights the inherent inequity of this solution. Linda and Carmen knew they had to pursue an alternative because it violated their core values. The result today is universally designed inclusive classrooms in which both teachers and students are supported and produce higher levels of learning for all.

FROM THEORY TO PRACTICE

There is considerable evidence in this study that supports Skrtic's theoretical arguments. Linda's story illustrates his contention that children with disabilities represent an opportunity for organizational growth and innovation for schools that are problem-solving organizations. Many of the comments from teachers and administrators quoted thus far show clearly that these educators view the challenges presented by students with disabilities as opportunities to improve their practices and that benefit others as well. As seen from the words of the three teachers at the beginning of this chapter, all schools focused their work on problem solving and experimentation.

All three schools have had to devise school discipline approaches with students with behavioral disabilities in mind, as described in Chapter Five, resulting in low suspension rates. All three schools have had to problem-solve around children who have various communication issues, which required them to adopt various technologies that have benefited others as well. All three schools have had to face the failure of traditional approaches in literacy and math for many of their students and have implemented strategies that have resulted in higher performance in these areas. Each school has had to face the needs of students with mental health issues, and all three have integrated resources to deal with these issues within their schools that have been used by other students as needed.

The examples of innovations being spurred by issues facing students with disabilities are resplendent in our data with virtually all interviewees. Granted, our interview protocols sought such data, but teachers and administrators could offer them readily and enthusiastically. We did not get any responses that were negative about students with disabilities or any other groups of students. In addition to positive attitudes toward disabilities, the interviewees were reluctant to situate the problems of educating students with disabilities within the child. Students with disabilities were spoken about positively and the tenets of special education were perceived as good for all students, as exemplified in Samantha's statement about her work: "It's just a matter of how do I accommodate everybody when they're walking in the door here."

This is not to say, however, that these schools were successful with every student. They were not. We specifically looked for children who had dropped out or had to be transferred to another program. However, in every instance when we followed up on such a child, we found that a great deal of effort had been expended to try to figure out how to serve the child. As Bill Henderson said, "Yes we have been unable to serve some very complicated kids. Inclusion is not the right setting for a small number of kids. But, you do not know until you try everything to serve him." Further, failure to be able to serve a child provided an opportunity to examine current practices and to develop capacity where none previously existed. For instance, the O'Hearn integrated outside expertise to improve its ability to serve students with significant autism. BAA is currently working to increase its mental health services.

In addition to supporting Skrtic's contention that students with disabilities have assisted these schools in growing and innovating, these schools were not schools where teachers taught in isolation. These teachers had time built into their day to collaborate and problem-solve and to engage in professional development. But, these schools still retained the traditional classroom structures of most schools. There are age-level grades and subject-oriented classrooms that retain the "grammar of schooling."[10] However, within these traditional structures these schools have developed adhocratic practices that appear to serve most students very well.

Improving High School Literacy at BAA

A detailed example of how BAA structured its literacy approach exemplifies how all three of these schools have become more effective problem-solving organizations. One of the administrators related that, when BAA opened, many of the students who were enrolled thought they would "dance and sing their way to graduation, kind of like *Fame*. We had to disabuse them of that notion right away." The opening of BAA was accompanied by the Massachusetts school reform act that would eventually require students to pass exit exams in literacy and math. Further, as one of the leaders said, "We needed to impress on the kids the fact that many if not most of the kids would not be getting jobs in the arts. They all needed to excel academically as well. We did not want the arts to replace academics but rather to enhance academics."

When the first class appeared, composed of students who were chosen only on arts ability, the teachers and administrators were appalled at the low literacy of many of their students. Further, as one special education teacher related, there appeared to be a disproportionate number of students with dyslexia. This may conform to the emerging understanding of dyslexia that appears to support the likelihood that dyslexics are more apt to exhibit more talent in the arts.[11] The teacher stated, "We had these talented students entering who were barely literate."

The school was faced with the challenge of how to get all the students to the level where they could read at grade level and could pass the Massachusetts Comprehensive Assessment System (MCAS). A group of teachers across the school grappled with this issue, and what ultimately emerged was a comprehensive approach to improving literacy levels for all students. This approach was developed over years of study and experimentation among faculty and leaders within the school. Linda described how the challenge of educating talented arts students who were functionally illiterate provided the impetus to change their approach to literacy:

> So I think it's [their current literacy program] just been fabulous for us. And I know what the—kind of the root of it has been, having these just brilliant kids artistically, and seeing Andres—I'll never forget. He was one of those first kids, could draw his ass off. You couldn't get him to talk or write, you know, for all the tea in China. You just couldn't get him to do it. But if you said, "I'm thinking about this conflict," you know, like, he actually illustrated a Holocaust survivors little book. I mean, imagine that. Imagine listening to this man talk, and then being able to do that. That's what Andres could do. But we couldn't figure out how to translate that to success in academic skills. And that happened again and again. Simon, I can remember him, you know, banging his head against the table. But then you'd see him perform on his guitar and you'd go, "Wait a minute—how can I not be able to teach that kid writing? He's brilliant. . . . When you can see kids down the hall be beautiful, brilliant, successful, and they're not doing that in your classroom, then there's something that you as the classroom teacher aren't doing. And so that was the other place that this came from, is, we just know our kids are brilliant. It's just that one part of their brain's been developed. And then how do we as teachers of some other content area latch onto that developed part of the brain and figure out, how do you transfer that? And that led us to say, well, we obviously don't have the skills to do that. We don't know this world.

As one special education teacher leader described the current approach, "It's about all kids, some kids, and a few kids." The approach as it has evolved over time incorporates several key elements that have resulted in a comprehensive approach to literacy instruction, rare in secondary schools.

All entering freshmen are given a comprehensive diagnostic reading assessment early in the school year. The results of these assessments are analyzed by staff to determine which students may need extra support and interventions.

Students who do not meet a certain criteria on the assessment are provided supports in a class called "Support & Enrichment" and are required to attend an intensive summer program until their scores rise. This is based on an individual assessment, not a large-scale state assessment.

These results are shared with student faculty advisors. BAA has designed a system whereby each student is assigned a faculty advisor. This role is a central one in the way in which BAA operates. The advisor serves to keep track of their advisee's needs. As Blair explained, "My role . . . is more of the front person, the main contact person to link between home and school and between student and the other teachers. . . . I advocate for them." The centrality of this role to the operation of the school is evident in our data as every teacher interviewed discussed the advisory.

All students, including incoming freshmen, are required to read and write a great deal.[12] The importance of reading high-level literature is underscored by the fact that all students must read at least two books every summer and write about them. This is non-negotiable; students who fail to meet this requirement must attend Saturday sessions. Seniors are required to write a grant proposal to an arts agency or foundation as a capstone project.

This standard is never modified; however, the way in which students access text may vary. For instance, students are allowed to use screen readers or audiobooks to access books that might be well above their current reading levels. So a student who might have fluency issues due to dyslexia might be able to compensate for his slow reading rate or the fact that he has to stop frequently to sound out words by using a screen reader. Both BAA and the O'Hearn used the Kurzweil text-to-speech software throughout their classes. Another student, who may lack English proficiency, might be able to highlight words that she does not know and have the computer read and define the words in Spanish. We asked an English teacher if dyslexic students were allowed to use screen readers. "Yes, they all are." To which we responded, "All dyslexic students?" The teacher clarified, "No, I mean all the students. They all can use the Kurzweil if they want

> *"They all can use the Kurzweil if they want to. I don't care how they read Shakespeare. I only care that they read Shakespeare."*

how they read Shakespeare. I only care *that* [emphasis added] they read Shakespeare." The point is that all students are expected to read a great deal, and the school has devised ways to accommodate a broad array of learners. The teacher added, "By the way, Shakespeare was intended to be listened to. They are plays."

To support students in reading and writing at high levels, all teachers are expected to be teachers of reading and writing. The work group that originally dealt with the issue of literacy recommended that reading and writing improvement be done across the curriculum. As one science teacher put it, "We are all teachers of reading." He went on to explain that fluency problems can be a barrier to accessing science given the reading levels of the texts and that it was his responsibility to give struggling readers the same level of access to science as facile readers. Indeed the school has invested significant resources in developing the capacity of all teachers to improve literacy levels of students while also connecting these efforts to writing improvement across the curriculum. The school's website is explicit about this in its Web statement about the academic program. "Throughout the curriculum a special emphasis is put on writing."

Some students may come to the school with relatively good skills in literacy but still need to improve to handle the level of curriculum offered at the school. Based on their initial and ongoing assessments, some students may need specific help in comprehension. Others may have difficulty going from American Sign Language to standard English. Still others may be struggling in learning to read in English. In general there is an attempt to give students the help they need. Their advisors work with them so that they develop a good understanding of themselves as readers, their strengths and weaknesses. They then problem-solve around what types of support they might need to become more proficient readers or writers. They then discuss the help available that would be most appropriate for the student, either through accommodations within classrooms or through tutoring and other services. The students' support team at BAA includes twelve professional support staff.

For students with the lowest level of literacy, generally grade 5 skills and below, the school goes into what we describe as "triage." These students are at risk of not being able to pass the exit exams as well as dropping out. First, the student is made aware of how serious the situation is and that he or she will have to do a great deal of hard work to become a literate adult. Then a multiyear plan is developed with the student that is likely to include intensive tutoring, usually from a learning disability specialist, during the school year and during the summer. The student is also shown how he will be able to access the curriculum while his reading and writing skills are being developed. For many of these students, who have grown used to lowered expectations and restricted access to higher-level curriculum, this is an entirely new approach that requires them to adjust their views of themselves as learners. This emphasis on metacognition or understanding the self is increasingly viewed by researchers as an essential component in improving outcomes for struggling learners, particularly adolescents.[13]

This comprehensive, elegant approach to improving literacy levels at BAA was the result of years of study and experimentation at the school. The work is ongoing. The original work was prompted by students with the most challenges concerning literacy, students with dyslexia and, deaf students, but resulted in practices that have benefited the whole school. The work involved teachers working together to study potential approaches and implementing them schoolwide, reinforcing Skrtic's theory concerning the value students bring to schools that are organized as problem-solving adhocratic entities.

The other two schools have functioned in much the same way as BAA; they have approached challenges brought about by including students with disabilities. The Mason's approach to improving elementary literacy instruction has marked similarities to that of BAA. Teachers at the O'Hearn conducted a study of the effect of using screen readers on comprehension for students with dyslexia. This study, which showed marked gains in comprehension, was used by teachers to promote access to more text-to-speech technology but also to refute those outside officials who were reluctant to allow their use. It would be a mistake however, to interpret the approaches toward literacy instruction developed by each of these schools as emphasizing accommodation over reading instruction. Each of these schools offers students intensive intervention in learning to read print and considers print reading essential to overall literacy. The point is all three schools consider access to text as so important to literacy development that learning how to read print, or struggling with fluency, or learning to speak English is not allowed to prevent students from accessing text. All three schools adopted remarkably similar and apparently effective approaches for addressing the need to vastly improve literacy levels among diverse learners, including students with complex disabilities. In this and other areas they have demonstrated the benefit of inclusion and the power of establishing problem-solving cultures and structures among teachers who are competent and mission driven.

Gifted Students: The Unexpected Story

Another interesting theme that emerged was the frequency with which teachers brought up the issues involved in educating students who were considered gifted. Even though we were not specifically asking questions about these children, issues involving children who were progressing rapidly in the curriculum surfaced in both our interviews and observations. Teachers spoke about the need to individualize and customize programs for these students. We observed one grade-level team at the Mason that was discussing individual students and how to best serve their needs. The first child they discussed was a child with cognitive impairment who was writing his first words, and they were considering how best to continue his progress. The second child was already a brilliant writer who was advancing at a rapid rate. The teachers wanted to make sure they continued to challenge this child so that she could eventually qualify for one of Boston's prestigious exam high schools. The children could not have been more different, yet they were in the same grade and they were both benefiting from the problem-solving culture and structures in the school as well as the supportive classrooms. At the O'Hearn, we met a parent whose daughter had "tested into an advanced work class" (Boston's gifted program). After she and her husband visited the proposed class, she decided to keep her daughter at O'Hearn because the students in the advanced work class were doing lower-level work than her daughter was doing in the inclusive classroom.

The attention to the needs of gifted students again reinforces Skrtic's theory in that these children, like many students with disabilities, are not served well by traditional professional bureaucratic schools because they fall out of the repertoire of grade and subject level teachers. Like students with disabilities, their needs are sometimes addressed by placing these students in special programs. Though there are few parents who object to this treatment, as it generally carries with it a degree of prestige and does indeed provide these children with more advanced curricula, these programs are often criticized for failure to enroll diverse populations of students and for the use of culturally biased tests to determine admission.

An article in the *New York Times* concerning Hunter College High School, a highly regarded and sought-after selective school for gifted students, highlights these tensions.[14] The school, which uses a single test to determine admission, has been under pressure for failure to enroll significant numbers of Black and Hispanic students. The entering seventh grade class is 3 percent Black and 1 percent Hispanic. In a faculty-approved graduation address, an African American student shocked his audience.

"More than anything else, I feel guilty," Mr. Hudson, who is Black and Hispanic, told his 183 fellow graduates. "I don't deserve any of this. And neither do you."

They had been labeled "gifted," he told them, based on a test they passed "due to luck and circumstance." Beneficiaries of advantages, they were disproportionately from middle-class Asian and White neighborhoods known for good schools and the prevalence of tutoring. "If you truly believe that the demographics of Hunter represent the distribution of intelligence in this city," he said, "then you must believe that the Upper West Side, Bayside and Flushing are intrinsically more intelligent than the South Bronx, Bedford-Stuyvesant and Washington Heights. And I refuse to accept that."[15]

The faculty and the principal, seeking a more robust multifaceted admissions procedure, have come into conflict with the president of Hunter College, who advocates the continuing the use of a single test. Mr. Hudson's comments underscore the contention of many advocates for students who are gifted that decries the lack of options for these children, particularly those from low-income backgrounds. And, unlike students with disabilities, there is no federal mandate requiring school districts to address the needs of these students.

These three profiled schools have found ways to challenge students who are gifted without the need to develop special programs that employ controversial admissions procedures. Interviews with teachers and administrators indicate that the needs of these students are taken as seriously as those who are far below age-level curriculum.

A Henderson teacher summed up this concern for all children including those who are gifted: "Just that this school values all children: children who are gifted, children with disabilities, all children. They all learn from each other. And that there's such high expectations here for all children, and that all children are valued in what they can offer each other. You know, a child who's gifted can learn from a child with a disability, and vice versa. Kids who are considered normally developing or typically developing can learn things from both groups. They can all learn from each other. So I think that's a value."

The problem-solving culture and structures that have been established in these schools are being used to serve these students as well. It appears that in these schools the need to continually challenge all students to grow and to provide them with the necessary opportunities to do so are deeply internalized values.

TO SUM UP

These schools have all developed independently, yet they are remarkably similar when viewed from the perspective of organizational theory developed by Thomas Skrtic. Specifically:

- They have developed adhocratic cultures and structures that have enabled them to better educate highly diverse populations.
- The presence of students with disabilities who diverge significantly from their age-level peers in academic performance, communication mode, or behavior has made it necessary for these schools to fundamentally question assumptions inherent in the traditional professional bureaucracies of schools.
- These students have provided opportunities to develop new approaches that benefit all children.
- Most important, these schools have become problem-solving organizations with the ability to adjust to the changing needs of their student populations and to continually innovate and improve. The result is three schools in

which most students perform considerably above comparable children in other schools.

These schools, however, are more than highly performing organizations. They are places where adults and children work and learn; they each have their own culture where a myriad of human needs are played out daily. The human side of these schools is the subject of Chapter Four.

CHAPTER FOUR

Relationships, School Culture, and Accountability

Alone we can do so little. Together we can do so much.

—Helen Keller

In the previous chapters we described three schools that evolved from performance organizations into problem-solving organizations. The visions developed by leaders and largely embraced by teachers in all three schools were remarkably similar in their values of inclusion and high expectations. Though these schools' faculties differ in many ways, there are striking similarities in school culture, pedagogical approaches, and administrative support. Teachers, like their administrators, considered the education of students with disabilities central to their mission of welcoming a diverse population of students. Most teachers understood how to meet the needs of those students with the greatest challenges, and teachers found that these practices benefited all students. Students in these schools succeeded academically, as evidenced by state assessment scores. They exhibited positive behaviors, as evidenced by low suspension rates and, at the high school, low dropout rates.

> *Teachers, like their administrators, considered the education of students with disabilities central to their mission of welcoming a diverse population of students.*

As described in Chapter Three, teachers in these schools were able to accomplish this, in part, because of their investment in a mission that *all students could reach high academic standards in inclusive settings.* A BAA teacher described this well. "I think we do really well because that mission, we picked up this mission of representing the whole population of the city of Boston and not being an elitist school and not being some place that, you know, if you're together, you can get in."

However, investment in a mission alone does not guarantee the kind of results these schools enjoyed. Even low-performing schools often prominently display mission statements.

Structurally, each of the leaders had created opportunities for teachers to work together to solve problems of instruction on both the individual and group levels as well as to address other schoolwide issues such as discipline. Providing this structural change, though central to the success of these schools, was probably not sufficient to promote the successful practices these school employ. Many schools provide these opportunities without such powerful effects.

The literature on improving schools, particularly the work of Richard Elmore, supports much of what we witnessed at these schools concerning teacher attitudes and behavior. Professor Elmore's work over the past two decades has centered on the intersection of policy, research, and practice, focusing on building the capacity of low-performing schools. A colleague of Tom Hehir at Harvard, Elmore continues to spend a day a week working directly in schools and classrooms. He has been outspoken in his opposition to the accountability structure in No Child Left Behind (NCLB); his research indicates that schools do not improve in the linear manner envisioned in the law. Rather, even under the best of circumstances, schools that innovate and develop more effective practices also experience plateaus. He has also shown that less effective schools under NCLB sanctions may even regress, emphasizing practices that have little chance of improving student performance, such as "drill and kill" remedial approaches or "teaching to the test" as opposed to robust improvement in instructional practice.[1]

RELATIONSHIPS: THAT'S IT!

The schools depicted here go far beyond the concept of people having strong relationships with each other; these relationships are a necessary condition upon which effective practices are developed. In short, the relationships are around the work.

When we asked teachers how they thought they accomplished their schools' missions, many of them talked about the relationships they had within their schools. Dr. Bill Henderson, principal at the O'Hearn, in speaking about what made his school effective, said, "The bottom line is that it is all about relationships."

Prior to working at Boston Arts Academy (BAA), Blair taught at a school where he witnessed what he saw as "staff that worked really, really hard . . . the soldiers on the front lines, just really loving kids and working with kids and working really hard, and I just saw a system that didn't support them." As a result, he said, "I was done," and he planned to leave teaching after just one year. When we interviewed him, Blair was in his eighth year of teaching, the past seven at BAA. He explained to us that what had made the difference—and why he decided to stay in teaching—were the people. "BAA is an amazing place because of the people. I think—no, I don't think; I know—that if we see any success, if we see anything that other places don't, it's purely because of the staff. . . people who will pretty much put it all on the line for students and work, and we support one another."

At the end of the second of two hour-long interviews, Blair declared, "This could've been a two-second interview. Four syllables: *Re-la-tion-ships*. That's it." In fact, all the special and general education teachers we interviewed explained that, in some manner, relationships were at the core of their schools' successes.

Teachers in these schools respected and worked well with their colleagues. Professionals working together within classrooms was the norm in each of the schools. The administrators had structured this into the schedule and had laid out clear directions on how this precious time should be used.

Christa described the sheer joy she had working at BAA: "[It's] just amazing! And when you're working with the kind of people that we work with, you can't wait. You just can't wait." Similarly, at the Mason, Nancy described her colleagues as people who cared about their work and enjoyed each other's company, even on the weekends. She explained, "People really care. They really care. And you can tell because they're thinking about it all the time. If we get together on a weekend, that's what you're going to talk about. Not always the latest movie, but why is so-and-so not doing so well? What do you think? . . . I don't know how that happens, whether people are just attracted to this place because they see someone else who cares."

Bev at the O'Hearn expressed a similar sentiment: "At lunchtime, sometimes teachers will bounce ideas off about students, but a lot of times we talk about movies, and we talk about what's going in our families, so people get to know each other. So they'll say, 'How was your weekend?' 'How was this?' People will know it's your birthday. And you might not see them all the time, but they'll come and give you hug."

What was the meaning of these relationships? Did these teachers simply have the good fortune to be working with colleagues who were likable? Did their relationships extend beyond the personal?

Much More Than Friends: Supporting a Mission

Though teachers and administrators spoke frequently about the importance of relationships, these strong bonds were more than just friendships among colleagues; they were directly related to the work of the schools. Teachers were clear that the importance of these relationships centered on their professional priorities, they saw that their work was to educate all students to high academic standards in inclusive settings, and their professional relationships supported this work. The personal took a back seat to professional responsibilities. Maricel explained, "Even if teachers have personal issues or whatever with another teacher, they don't allow that to come into a professional setting. And I think that that really, really shows [the] character of people and I think that it shows that teachers are here for the students."

> "Even if teachers have personal issues or whatever with another teacher, they don't allow that to come into a professional setting. That really shows that teachers are here for the students."

As we discussed in Chapter One, each of these schools had language in its mission statement concerning high academic expectations and inclusiveness. But were their missions lived missions? If so, how did teachers do this work? Further, how did teachers' relationships affect this work?

Teacher interviews suggested a significant depth of commitment to teach all students to high academic standards. Teresa explained, "Teachers as well as the administration hold really high standards for the kids, and understand that even though we do have special needs kids, standards shouldn't be lowered for them. . . . It's part of our contract that we hold high standards and we will make sure the kids meet these standards." At the BAA John described how all students were asked to reach these high academic standards. "Teachers at BAA hold really high standards for all kids. And so even if a special education kid can't achieve what someone with 130 IQ can, they can still have a high limit, a high bar set for them. They are . . . challenged."

In addition to high academic standards, teachers embraced inclusive environments. Their understanding of inclusion, however, was broader than the traditional definition of students with disabilities physically placed in a general education class. Their understanding was focused on the value of diversity. Teachers spoke of building a diverse community in their schools, one that included race, ethnicity, class, and ability. A BAA teacher explained how this value undergirded her efforts as a teacher: "And for me it's such a simple lesson, but it's very hard to do. So I think that that's—You're trying to say to the world, 'Here, let's create a world where everyone is part of that and valued to us.'" Bev, who taught at the O'Hearn, described the positive nature of a diverse student body as a "value": "This school values all children—children who are gifted, children with disabilities, all children."

Teachers embraced inclusion as a means of creating a microcosm of the world that they wanted their students to experience. Heather explained that within such a microcosm, students needed to find ways to embrace the differences between them. As Blair said succinctly, "We live in a diverse world. We need to learn how to live in a diverse world well."

> "We live in a diverse world. We need to learn how to live in a diverse world well."

Teachers were aware that the relationships they experienced with their colleagues were not the norm in most schools. This awareness was clearest to those who had taught elsewhere, such as Maricel, who said, "It's imperative that you have colleagues that work together. . . . [At the O'Hearn] I'm just—I'm healthier, I'm happier. I have [a] more sound mind." She attributed her improved internal state to her relationships specifically because she had a clear sense of how challenging the work can be in isolation. As she explained, "It's really, really hard making inclusion work when it's only you."

We believe the strength of relationships among teachers has enabled teachers to address complicated issues in a nondefensive and productive manner. It is not easy to get negative feedback on your instruction or to address issues on which people hold deep beliefs, such as school discipline. Yet, teachers were open to each other's feedback and approached difficult issues in an open and honest manner, seeking solutions.

SCHOOL CULTURE: COLLABORATION AND COHERENCE

Teachers described a collaborative culture infused throughout these schools that ensured that no teacher was solely responsible for any one student, but rather, together all teachers were responsible for the education of all students. The schools' culture supported reliance on each other, and, as described previously, teachers ascribed a value to this interdependence. Heather explained, "We are a talking, teaming faculty. And by that what I mean is that we value conversations with each other, and we value time to spend with each other talking about kids, talking about practice, talking about ourselves as people." According to Karen, "It's one of the things that I value the most about this school. . . . I think you feel like you are not here working in a void. When there is a problem, there are people who support you."

Samantha, who was currently working with another colleague to help a local middle school develop practices that were more inclusive, tried to explain what she called the "roadblock" to collaborative work. "When I go to places and talk about inclusion, that's the biggest roadblock. . . . Teachers are so used to being evaluated on closing that door, you're in charge, and you're in charge of that classroom, behavior, and academics, and you're so used to being evaluated on being the teacher in charge. But to open that door and to share your students and share your curriculum, and to hear or to allow other people's ideas to come in, and that there may be other ways to approach this—I think that's been the hardest thing to get through to people."

Teachers explained that their instruction was far-reaching in part because they did not guard their teaching practices or consider them the sole property of individual teachers, but rather they shared their ideas and materials with each other without hesitation. According to Maricel, "People are not afraid to say, 'Oh, come into my classroom, watch me teaching. Yeah? You like that lesson? Sure, you can come see it. . . . Oh, you want to borrow this? Take it. Go ahead. Don't reinvent the wheel.'" Similarly, Karen said, "There's not much going in your room and shutting the door here. There's really not much at all of that." Teachers expressed concern for their

> *Teachers' instruction was far-reaching in part because they did not guard their teaching practices or consider them the sole property of individual teachers, but rather they shared their ideas and materials with each other without hesitation.*

colleagues in other schools who worked on their own. "So many teachers teach in isolation," bemoaned Bev, "and I just would not like that at all. I love to be able to bounce ideas off of other adults."

Teachers said that the relationships they had with each other gave them the opportunity to problem-solve with their colleagues to better meet their students' academic needs. As Nancy described, "I'll think about a young boy and how much he's struggling, and it's really great here, because you can think along with someone else." Noel explained that at her school, "I think we're really good at . . . identifying what the problem is, and trying to get some really smart people around a table, brainstorming, very open-endedly." A Henderson teacher explained how teachers worked together. "We're all working on something together. So that you can see that even with differences, we come out with the same product or we come out with a similar product, or we get darned close. And I think that's what we're trying to do in here, is make it a cohesive class where everybody's working together and we come out with something that's similar, but we're accessing it at different levels." As Karen explained, when faced with a dilemma concerning how to help students achieve, they might have to rely on someone other than themselves and "find the person to solve it."

Together, teachers developed a comprehensive understanding of their curriculum that allowed them to provide more consistent and more connected instruction. At the Mason, Karen explained that they had developed a "shared system of beliefs around how kids learn to read and write and learn about language" that stemmed in part from a whole-school study on the development of reading and writing and how to implement effective practices in their classes. At BAA, all teachers, whether certified in academic subject areas, the arts, special education, or some combination of these, had been involved in literacy professional development activities. Christa, a music teacher, described incorporating literacy training into her work: "Most of [the] work that I do is about reading comprehension through the song text that we're working on." Blair, a visual arts teacher, described using a technique called "BDA . . . before, during and then after techniques—like pre-reading, skimming. We've done a lot of professional development around that. We try to do chunking, things like that, using graphic organizers to help kids read things." Through a schoolwide focus on literacy, BAA had added a supplemental reading and writing class that was required for all students and that was taught by pairs of teachers from different disciplines across the schools. The range of topics studied together was vast. At the O'Hearn, during the 2006–2007 school year, teachers studied in small groups and then systematically shared what they learned with their peers on three topics: teaching with technology, developing mathematics accommodations, and effective practices for English language learners (ELL). By studying together, teachers were able to develop an understanding of curricular concepts that spanned the school and were embedded in all classes.

How Coherent Effective School Cultures Evolved

Highly desirable, coherent effective school cultures cannot be willed or mandated. The emergence of these highly coherent school cultures took years to develop. Though these schools each have a distinct culture, their common strong cohesiveness of individual responsibility and collective accountability around issues of inclusiveness and high expectations appear to have taken years to evolve. We believe the emergence of these strong cultures were initially highly influenced by leadership behavior. In the case of BAA, the only school that was a startup, Linda and Carmen had the opportunity to assemble a staff who shared their values. Further, they brought some staff from the previous school they'd led who were like minded. They paid a good deal of attention to the hiring process. In discussing their hiring of a teacher for the deaf when they opened the school, they were clear with interviewees that the school would be inclusive. In the resultant discussion with the applicant, they also made it clear they did not know how they would implement inclusion for deaf students and that her input would be critical. The successful applicant provided some informative perspectives that impressed Linda and Carmen and influenced the manner in which deaf children would be included in the school. They were demonstrating not only the values they expected teachers to embrace but also the collaborative problem-solving culture they hoped would evolve when they opened their school.

Indeed all of the leaders in these schools take hiring staff very seriously. They actively recruit teachers who share their values and have reputations for being effective within collaborative inclusive schools. As mentioned in the Preface, filling a vacancy at the O'Hearn is a big deal. Bill feels the importance of this extends to all people who work in the building. Bill emphasized, "The people in the lunch room are just as important as everyone else. They have to buy into the vision." In one of our meetings with Janet, she showed us a stack of résumés for one position. "You know how important this is Tom. However, I know already whom I'm hiring. She's been an intern here and she's terrific. She'll fit right in."

The importance placed on assembling a staff that shares the vision and mission of the school that can also deliver high-quality instruction in a collaborative culture is so strongly felt among these leaders that some people might label them "control freaks." Bill, for instance, anticipating his retirement, took three years to find a person he considered a suitable replacement. When he identified the person he wanted, he resisted requests by the parents to "do a national search" or by other administrators in the district who wanted to "transfer in." He was ultimately successful in naming his successor. All of these leaders actively control the hiring process in a large urban school district where there are many pressures to accept transfers and teachers who are "excessed" from other schools. And, they succeed.

Further, it appears that many teachers who apply to these schools appear to be attracted to them because of their values and operating philosophies. A special education teacher at BAA who had taught previously at a highly successful inclusive elementary school described how she was drawn to BAA, having witnessed how successful her former students had been at the school. She recounted, "I could only work in an inclusive school." She was also attracted to the school because teachers had such a strong voice in the school's direction. Active in the teacher's union, she had a major role in designing and implementing the literacy program.

These leaders "walk their talk," continually reinforcing the schools' values and operating principles. Linda's refusal to accept an advisory council that was not sufficiently diverse, Janet's insistence on including students with intellectual disabilities, and Bill's insistence that everybody in school assist children in toileting are three of many examples of how these leaders actively live the schools' visions through their actions. Also, these leaders actively seek to remove teachers who are not performing.

Last, and possibly most important, the cultures of these schools are so strong that teachers and staff consistently reinforce the inclusive vision and collaborative problem solving of these schools. An O'Hearn teacher said, "What are these kids going to learn being segregated? You need to assume integration and then figure it out." This self-enforcing culture is strongly evident in all our interviews and observations. Another BAA teacher stated that someone who did not support the values of inclusion and high expectations would be "very uncomfortable here."

Christa described what might have been difficult, but in her opinion the necessary pressure teachers placed on one another in order to stay focused. "We are in each other's business, professionally, as much as we can be. Because we know that that's good for kids, and we know that that's good for us because it pushes our practice and pushes our beings."

ACCOUNTABILITY

During two-plus decades of work, Richard Elmore has sought to examine how policy plays out at the classroom and school levels. His years of research and thinking on this fundamental problem of educational policy are summarized in his book, *School Reform from the Inside Out: Policy, Practice and Performance.* His thesis is best expressed, "The problems of the system are the problems of the smallest unit."[2] The guiding principle is that for school reform to work it must happen from the "inside out." Elmore's work on school-level interpretations of accountability helped us analyze how these schools all met the standards of the Massachusetts Comprehensive Assessment System (MCAS) and NCLB. Though the topic of external testing and accountability came up frequently in our interviews, none of our interviewees seemed to put the testing programs at the forefront of their work. Teachers and administrators did not appear to be driven by state and federal accountability systems. These professionals appear to be primarily driven by both a strong sense of individual responsibility as well as collective accountability toward one another.

In their essay, "When Accountability Knocks, Will Anyone Answer?," Elmore and his colleagues interviewed educators in twenty diverse schools (traditional public, charter, and parochial) in two metropolitan areas (one on the west coast, the other on the east) to ascertain how accountability influenced their daily work.[3] They used as their conceptual framework a theory drawn from the work of Wagner that posited that a school would react to external accountability requirements by examining a set of relationships among three factors: "individual conceptions of responsibility; shared expectations among school participants and stakeholders; and internal and external accountability mechanisms."[4] As Elmore and colleagues explained, "An individual school's conception of accountability, in our view, grows from the relationship among these three factors."[5] We found much support for this assertion in all three schools.

Elmore and colleagues define *accountability mechanisms* as the ways, both formal and informal, by which educators give account for their actions to someone in a position of authority inside or outside the school.[6] An example of internal accountability may be a principal requiring teachers to provide copies of lesson plans or to display examples of student work on a bulletin board. External accountability increasingly involves assessment of student progress through district- or state-administered standardized tests. Other examples include external oversight of curriculum and dropout rates as well as state monitoring of regulatory compliance. Accountability mechanisms vary in consequences; some have relatively low stakes, such as principal disapproval, and others have high stakes, such as teachers and principals losing their jobs due to the failure of their schools to make adequate yearly progress under NCLB. (A detailed discussion of the policy implications of this study appears in Chapter Seven.)

Putting this all together, Elmore and colleagues describe their working theory: "Responsibility, expectations, and accountability operate in a close mutual reciprocal relationship with each other, and this relationship takes a variety of forms in different schools. This relationship is captured in Figure 1. Individual conceptions of responsibility may influence collective expectations or, alternatively, collective expectations influence individual conceptions of responsibility. Similarly, individual conceptions of collective expectations may influence formal or informal accountability mechanisms, or vice versa."[7] They contend that the power of internal accountability mechanisms is greatly enhanced when they are aligned with individual responsibility and collective expectations, as they clearly are in these schools. They go on further to assert that the efficacy of external accountability mechanisms are mediated by internal alignment. The schools' responses to an external mechanism would, they

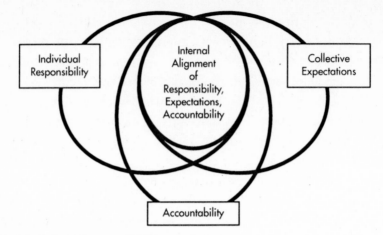

Figure 4.1 Interactions and Alignment

Source: Elmore, "School Reform from the Inside Out." p. 141

assume, depend on the degree of alignment between the purposes of the external mechanism and the internal norms of the school.

Elmore and colleagues present a series of case studies that place schools within the Venn diagram shown in Figure 4.1. One school, for instance, had teachers with a strong sense of individual responsibility, with very few collective expectations and with weak internal accountability mechanisms. Such a school is "atomized"; that is, teachers work largely in isolation from one another, and would likely respond to external accountability in a number of ways, largely determined by individualized reactions and not by collective action. In such a school, external policy mechanisms such as NCLB would unlikely produce their intended effects.

Turtle Haven

One school described by Elmore, a pilot school like BAA and Mason, is presented as an organization in which individual responsibility, collective expectations, and internal accountability are well aligned. This school, "Turtle Haven," has a principal who has made her expectations clear to teachers concerning classroom appearance, frequency of meetings with parents, and high expectations for children academically and behaviorally. Interviews with teachers indicate that they have bought into these expectations. Turtle Haven was a new school, and the principal had the opportunity to hire teachers who reflected her beliefs and expectations. Teachers, like the principal, resisted what Elmore refers to as the "default culture" common in many urban schools, where teachers characterize children's families and communities as the source of the problem of poor academic performance. At Turtle Haven, expectations influence responsibility. As one teacher stated, "Not that we're trying to prove something to keep Mary pleased, but we really believe and buy into the practice that all children can and will learn if you set the stage, and set high expectations. And, if these are your ideals that you believe in, you have a place here."[8] The case goes on to describe the consequences for a teacher who did not buy into this internal accountability system. The teacher agreed to leave the school after a "meeting of the minds" with the principal.

Schools like Turtle Haven are described by Elmore and colleagues as having a high level of coherence across individual responsibility, shared expectations, and internal and external accountability. "In these schools, collective expectations have gelled into highly interactive, relatively coherent, informal and formal systems, by which teachers and administrators held each other accountable for their action vis-a-vis students."[9] This the type of school is best positioned to deal with an external accountability mechanism, and that mechanism is going to be most effective if it is aligned with the school's internal normative environment.

All three schools studied are clearly tightly coherent on all three dimensions of this model. Teachers and administrators had a deep sense of responsibility for providing high-quality education for all students. Teachers had remarkably similar values as they related to their students, their rights, and their capabilities. The default culture described by Elmore of externalizing the problems of educating a diverse population of largely low-income students to their background and communities was not evident in any of our interviews or our observations. We believe this finding is exceptional and represents one of the factors most important to the success of these schools.

The attitudes and dispositions of staff toward children with disabilities and their families exemplify this. Disability, like family background or poverty, was never cited as a reason that children could not learn; quite the opposite. The degree to which positive attitudes toward disability are internalized by the teachers and administrators of these schools was impressive. By and large the teachers in all three schools consider it their responsibility to respect the value of inclusive education and to provide the opportunities and accommodations needed by students to succeed. As Samantha from the O'Hearn stated, her job was to work with all students. "It's just a matter of how do I accommodate everybody when they're walking in the door here." We observed students with autism at both the Mason and O'Hearn who were singled out for their advanced math skills. The disabilities of these children were turned into assets. At O'Hearn, a student's wheelchair is converted to a tank in *The Sound of Music*. At BAA deafness is viewed as another form of diversity where the native language, American Sign Language (ASL), of some of the students is incorporated into arts performances in much the same way Spanish might be. Teachers at BAA acknowledge that dyslexia may be an asset in an arts environment. Bill Henderson speaks openly to teachers about how being blind has made him a better administrator. These educators do not carry the negative or ableist attitudes that characterize so many schools. Far from a default excuse for poor academic performance, the teachers in all three schools recognize their responsibility to minimize the negative impact of disability while providing children with opportunities to fully participate in school activities as do children without disabilities.

Individual Responsibility

A special education teacher at BAA said, "It's my job to make sure these kids are all competent readers by the time they graduate."

Responsibility in this framework is individual and refers to the educators' sense of personal responsibility for their work. Teachers' beliefs about their work, about the capacity of their students and their responsibility toward parents and toward one another, stem largely from personal values and experience and are likely influenced by their experience with other educators. Assuming that teachers largely work in isolation, Elmore posits, "We assume that organizational and external influences may play a part in teachers' perception of role, but that individual values are certainly influential."[10]

Clearly the teachers in these schools hold themselves to high standards and hold remarkably similar values concerning inclusion and diversity. These values are deeply internalized; we found relatively little difference among the teachers on these dimensions. Further, we observed no instances in which teachers "externalized," as so often happens in urban schools where poverty, race, culture, and disabilities are often attributed to the difficulties students might have. Quite the contrary, teachers and administrators approached the real issues these students might bring to school as a challenge for the school to address. The problem-solving time structured into the teachers' schedules provided the opportunity for these like-minded teachers to explore improved practice.

The schools, of course, had different cultures and missions. BAA teachers and administrators obviously spoke frequently about the importance of the arts. Educators at the Mason were apt to talk more frequently about the importance of high-quality education to the African American community. Many individuals at the O'Hearn are proud of their role in promoting disability equity. Though these schools are different, the values of inclusive education and high academic expectations are common. These are schools where individual responsibility and collective expectations are well aligned.

The sense of responsibility held by teachers extended beyond the issue of inclusive education in all three schools and included a remarkably similar attitude toward high expectations for all children and the value of rigorous academic curriculum. As Bill Henderson said, "Having positive attitudes toward disability is not enough. First and foremost you have to have a strong academic program to include kids in."

> "Having positive attitudes toward disability is not enough. First and foremost you have to have a strong academic program to include kids in."

Collective Accountability

Discussing an academically gifted student, a Mason teacher said in a meeting with fellow grade-level teachers, "We have to figure out how we can keep challenging this girl, to make sure she is prepared for [a competitive exam school]."

Expectations in Elmore's framework are collective in nature and are characterized by "shared norms and values of school participants developed in order to get the work of the school done."[11] Examples of collective expectations include the responsibility of teachers at one grade level to prepare students for successive grade levels, student discipline, and school values. The important aspect of expectations is that they constitute beliefs about the behavior of others, though individuals may include themselves. These expectations may be held by all parties or by groups within the school, such as teachers who teach the same grade or subject. The degree of consensus around shared values and norms, coupled with a strong sense of responsibility to one another, was impressive among the teachers and leaders in these schools.

Internal Accountability

As Elmore would predict, the internal accountability structures of these schools reflected these twin values of inclusiveness and high academic expectations, and the internal accountability structures reinforced personal responsibility and collective accountability. The way in which teachers problem-solved around individual children reinforced the personal responsibility of teachers to meet the needs of all children while emphasizing the collective expectations of the school. School discipline was not strictly the realm of individual teachers but was also addressed on a collective level, with clear expectations for students and teachers across the schools.

All three of the schools spent a good deal of time analyzing and acting on student data concerning academic progress. They are, as Dick Murnane would call, "data wise."[12] The example of how BAA revised its literacy approach was a demonstration of this. The O'Hearn had recently revised its approach to math instruction based on less than satisfactory test results. One year the Mason reacted to a drop in fourth grade scores by looking at each child's scores to determine which students needed the most attention. The culture of these schools were ones in which educators accepted the responsibility to reach all children and to meet high expectations, but that responsibility was viewed as both individual and collective. In these schools, ongoing assessment of student progress is part of the culture. They do not wait for state testing data to act.

External Accountability

Each of these schools had experienced the impact of NCLB to varying degrees. And, as Elmore would predict, the level of coherence of these schools around responsibility, expectations, and internal accountability had positioned them well to deal with this external presence. The fact that these schools valued and produced high academic performance has also aligned them with the goals of NCLB, thus minimizing its potentially disruptive effect.

The most potentially disruptive influence of NCLB occurred at the Mason one year when their fourth grade aggregate scores put them in the "needs improvement" category. (Given its small size, the Mason could not dis-aggregate disability data every year.) As we described in Chapter Two, some of the teachers attributed the drop to the impact of students with intellectual disabilities on the aggregate scores and advocated that Janet curb the enroll-ment of such children. The teachers were correct in their assessment of the influence of these children on the aggregate scores. Given their habit of being data driven and that they took collective responsibility for student outcomes, they were well aware of the profile of the fourth grade cohort. Janet resisted limiting enrollment of students with intellectual disabilities, appealing to the values of inclusiveness and high expectations. They responded to the central office by showing that the aggregate scores changed when the students with intellectual disability were taken out of the calculation. The Mason was taken off the list. This incident underscores the degree of cohesiveness within the school and the importance of their values. A leader in a less cohesive and less values-driven school might have succumbed to the teachers' request, to the detriment of the students. Such an action would also contradict the intent of NCLB, which is to promote higher achievement for all students, including students with disabilities.

Though NCLB was a subject of the interviews of all the leaders, with the exception of the Mason we saw relatively little influence of its effects. As we discussed Chapter Two, the principals vary in their views on NCLB, with Linda Nathan at BAA adamantly opposed and Janet at the Mason a strong proponent. Given their cohesiveness and that their cohesiveness is strongly focused on academic attainment, the high academic performance of these schools has meant that they are not the targets of NCLB interventions. However, at both the Mason and O'Hearn, the school leaders used the threat of NCLB to help spur continual innovation.

Special education regulations and enforcement appear to have had an impact on these schools. Special education is frequently criticized as being excessively compliance driven.[13] Central office and state staff routinely conduct audits of schools' paperwork and programs and require schools to take "corrective action." This external accountability presence may at times be needed to safeguard the rights of children and parents, but at times they may divert efforts of educators from teaching and learning by focusing inordinately on paperwork. Though, as we described in Chapter Two, these leaders have had to at times deal with less than supportive central office special education leaders, we observed little negative effect of external special education monitoring. This may be due to the schools' strong results and popularity with parents and general education leadership. It would be hard to argue that these schools have not complied with the spirit of the Individuals with Disabilities Education Act (IDEA); outside regulators recognize that and act accordingly.

However, another potentially more powerful external mechanism, special education law, with its individual due process rights, emerged in our study, particularly at the O'Hearn. As described in Chapter One, the O'Hearn was created as a result of parent advocacy of an inclusive education option in Boston. It is unlikely that these parents would have had the power to force the school board to engage in this bold experiment without such extraordinary legal leverage. Bill Henderson agrees with this assertion. However, given the large number of students with significant disabilities at the O'Hearn, Bill has had to deal with parents who have used the due process system in order to get their child into the O'Hearn or to leverage the O'Hearn for services the school might not otherwise provide. The presence of due process protections has both enabled the school to offer its innovative program and at the same time has created challenges to ways of operating—a potential double-edged sword. One challenge has come in the form of requests for one-on-one paraprofessionals. To date the school has resisted these requests for all but one student who needs special medical attention. Bill states his view on this issue: "We explain to the parents that we support all children in classrooms with teachers and paraprofessionals, not individual kids full time. Further, one-on-one paras can lead to dependency, where we stress independence. We have gotten to the point with some parents to suggest that they might want to find another placement for their child. They rarely do." None of the teachers we interviewed at O'Hearn advocated for individual aides, supporting Bill's view on the subject. Again, a cohesive school that has demonstrated success has been able to resist this external pressure. And, given the degree to which the O'Hearn's goals are aligned with IDEA, it is doubtful a parent could prevail in a hearing against them.

TO SUM UP

- Teachers in these schools have deeply internalized the individual responsibility concerning their roles to assure that all children learn to high levels.
- Teachers are accountable to one another for student learning with these collaborative problem-solving schools.
- The influence of external accountability systems is far less important to the success of these schools than the individual and collective responsibility teachers and leaders in these schools hold for themselves.

These highly coherent schools in which teachers enjoy deep and effective relationships with one another within a problem solving environment, we believe, undergirds much of the success of these schools. We feel it is important here to go into greater detail concerning the types of innovative practices that were produced by these strong school cultures. In the next chapter we detail many of these practices from the lens of universal design for learning.

CHAPTER FIVE

Universally Designed Schools

As we demonstrated in the previous chapter, the schools profiled in this book show a high-level of coherence with closely aligned responsibility, expectations, and internal accountability. The values of high expectations and inclusive education are deep in each school and are shared among them. The superior results these schools achieve are evidence that this level of coherence has had a strong effect. In this chapter we share specific examples of how teachers and administrators have innovated at both the classroom and school levels to provide improved education for all children in these schools.

UNIVERSAL DESIGN FOR LEARNING

Universal design for learning (UDL) requires that teachers reach a wide array of students by providing access to the curriculum and to the myriad ways that students learn. This is by no means an easy task. Taken with the fact that these schools educate students with and without disabilities together, some might call it a daunting task. Yet, we found that these teachers worked to make the curriculum accessible to a diverse array of learners. Reflecting the coherent culture of these schools, teachers explained that in no way did they do this work in isolation but rather they relied on each other to make their instructional practices effective, and this interdependence broadened their professional capabilities. Teachers were committed to UDL, and their relationships supported their abilities to provide this universally designed instruction.

First applied to architecture, the principle of universal design called for designing buildings with the assumption that people with disabilities would be using them. With the legal backing of the Americans with Disabilities Act, these principles are applied increasingly to new construction and to the renovation of public buildings. Ramps, automatic door-opening devices, accessible toilets, and fire alarm systems with lights activated for the deaf are examples of universal design features that are incorporated into contemporary buildings. Other examples extend to technologies. Captioning devices are required features on all televisions, and digital text can be read from computers with screen readers. Universal design allows for access without extraordinary means and is based on the assumption that disabled people are numerous and should be able to lead regular lives.

Universal Design and Schooling

Simply put, universal design applied to the school context seeks to develop curriculum, strategies, and school administrative practices that assume that children with disabilities will be participating in all aspects of schooling. For instance, we should universally design our reading programs assuming that children with dyslexia will be in virtually every school and classroom. Given that dyslexia directly affects learning to read, different approaches and interventions are needed to design reading and literacy programs that will be effective for these children.[1] Researchers have demonstrated that schools that design reading programs with these students in mind can have more effective reading programs for all students while preventing unnecessary referrals to special education.[2] The current efforts in schools to implement response to intervention (RTI) reading approaches in the primary grades is an example of universal design.

We should universally design our reading programs assuming that children with dyslexia will be in virtually every school and classroom.

Another area where universal design concepts are increasingly being applied is behavior and discipline approaches. Researchers have long recognized that in order to integrate students with the most challenging behaviors, such as children with autism, schools must have consistent approaches to behavior management and must explicitly teach appropriate school behaviors to some students.[3] However, when these effective approaches are implemented schoolwide, researchers have shown there are marked declines in suspensions and expulsions across the board.

Though these common innovations are examples of successful universally designed approaches, some educators and parents are advocating that this way of thinking be applied to all aspects of schooling, from the design and delivery of curriculum to school organization and administrative practice. In contrast to traditional approaches, where "categorical" programs like special education and bilingual education operate as separate from each other or from the regular education program, powerful universally designed approaches are developed to meet the needs of both individuals and groups within the mainstream.[4]

In regard to design and delivery of curriculum, a comprehensive approach to UDL has been developed by David Rose and Anne Meyer. This work unites the recent insights derived from brain research with the opportunities provided by the digital age.

From brain research Rose and Meyer derive two central principles:

1. Learning is distributed across three interconnected networks: the recognition networks are specialized to receive and analyze information (the "what" of learning); the strategic networks are specialized to plan and execute actions (the "how" of learning): and the affective networks are specialized to evaluate and set priorities (the "why" of learning).

2. Learners cannot be reduced to simple categories such as "disabled" or "bright." They differ within and across networks, showing shades of strength and weakness that make them each unique.[5]

These understandings have been greatly influenced by remarkable new technologies such as PET scans and functional MRIs that enable researchers to view the working brain.

The advances in technology brought about by the digital age have enabled Rose and Meyer to develop new multimedia approaches that can help remove barriers inherent in traditional teaching methods and curriculum materials. Originally they worked on developing individually tailored devices to enable students with disabilities to increase their access to print-based curriculum. Providing assistive technology to students with disabilities demonstrated how access to curriculum could be accomplished for many students who previously were unable to access curriculum.. However over time they evolved into a new role, "the use of technology to transform the nature of the curriculum itself."[6] One of their early products, Wiggle Works, demonstrated that an electronic book could allow for features that enable all kinds of students to access the material. For instance, students with physical disabilities can turn pages and access controls with a touch of a key or a switch. Students with visual disabilities can expand the size of the print. Students with learning disabilities can have words they are having difficulty decoding read to them. Various scaffolds can be individually built into the program that call students attention to important details or concepts.

These technologies, many of which are free or at low cost, have advanced considerably in recent years. Teachers can digitally scaffold books through Book Builder (http://bookbuilder.cast.org/resources/). Teachers who have students with print disabilities have access to hundreds of digitized texts through Book Share (www.bookshare.org). Many computers now have screen readers built into them, and other readers can be downloaded for free. An excellent free site that teachers, administrators, and parents and caregivers can use to find many additional tools and keep up on developments in the field is provided by the federally funded National Center on Universal Learning (www.udlcenter.org/).

Combining these technologies with neuroscience, Rose and Meyer have developed UDL based on the following principles:

1. *To support recognition learning, provide multiple, flexible, methods of presentation*
2. *To support strategic learning, provide flexible methods of expression and apprenticeship*
3. *To support affective learning, provide multiple, flexible options for engagement*[7]

UDL is a giant step away from the classic retrofitting model of education experienced by many students with disabilities with traditional special education practices. Students do not have to wait for materials to be put on tape or settle for low-level text because they have inadequate decoding skills. All students can deal with the same text, tailored to their needs. As in the case with architecture, UDL has demonstrated that it is much more desirable and efficient to design our curricula assuming the participation of students with disabilities. Such design allows for full participation and access for students with disabilities while providing individualized options for all.

Universally Designed Instruction

Though not always explicit in referencing the term "UDL," teachers were clear about the importance of using principles of UDL to reach all students. They focused their efforts widely, from students who struggled to those who grasped concepts quickly, rarely expressing a need to identify who were students with and without disabilities. Karen said, "It's very hard for me to tease out what I do that's different for the kids with special needs. Because it's not so much what I do for the kids with special needs, but it's what I need to do for each learner. . . . That's the thing, to ensure that every kid learns. . . . And so, it's teasing out what you need to do for each kid."

Teachers worked to ensure that each student, whether he or she had a disability or not, was provided with effective instruction. Noel from BAA explained, "I think we try to do a lot of things hands-on when we can, as much as we can, so that students have more than one mode in which to take in information. So there'll be an experiment, and a reading, and a lecture, so that students have different ways."

Disability status was not a presumed barrier; rather, each student's needs were taken into account as teachers worked to provide them all with a quality education. That said, teachers found benefit in developing instruction that could reach those students with the most need. Teachers explained that working specifically to meet the unique needs of individual students who were often, but not always, those with disabilities helped them to develop lessons broad enough to meet the needs of a large array of students. By focusing on reaching those who were potentially most difficult to reach, these teachers found that their planning served to benefit the larger population of students. Delphine explained how she and her co-teacher had developed supports for several first grade students who specifically struggled with organization and found that their methods benefited the whole class. "Instead of singling out—you know, there are five that have serious [organizational] problems," Delphine explained, "[now] everybody keeps [their] desk clean. Everybody learns to put the crayons on the right side, starts with a clean slate. And we just do that for every single person." Bev said that students who might not be identified as having a disability could "benefit from some of the accommodations and some of the strategies that I'm using." Mary described the practice at her school of focusing on the students with disabilities first, calling these students "the backbone of the school": "The way I've always looked at it is that I

> By focusing on reaching those who were potentially most difficult to reach, these teachers found that their planning served to benefit the larger population of students.

know the O'Hearn was set up . . . it's thinking of the children with disabilities first. So, because they're placed at the center of what's going to happen here, everything else has to be built around that. So it's almost like thinking, if the kids who need the most support and the most help and have the hardest time are going to succeed here, then just think of how well everybody else is going to do who don't need quite that much."

In order to develop and implement instructional practices that could meet such a diversity of learning needs, teachers explained that they needed each other. As Chapter Four described, teachers in these schools perceived that their relationships improved their ability to provide universally designed instructional practices. The results of this work are evident in each of these schools. At BAA a group of students and a math teacher developed an animation that uses no words to illustrate quadratics which is accessible to both hearing and deaf students; another video uses dance to illustrate trigonomic functions. (See YouTube: search "Boston Arts Academy.") Henderson teachers have demonstrated that using text-to-speech technology can greatly improve comprehension of text for students in the intermediate grades. Teachers at the Mason have used the arts to enhance the academic program. The same can be said about their approach to developing universally designed behavior management.

Tucker Elementary: A Suburban RTI Success

Only a few blocks away from busy Mattapan Square, just as Blue Hill Avenue turns into Blue Hills Parkway, sat the Tucker Elementary School, the smallest elementary school in the Milton Public School District. Wide sidewalks, tree-lined streets, and attractive landscaping surrounded the compact, three-story brick school building, adjacent to single family homes.

Of the four elementary schools in Milton, the Tucker's school population was the most racially, economically, and linguistically diverse. Students were assigned to schools based on the street where they lived, and most students at the Tucker lived in the densely populated northwest corner of Milton. Nearly 60 percent of the student population was identified as Black or African American, Latino, Asian, or multi-racial. Mattapan was home to a large number of Haitian immigrants, and Tucker Elementary was the only school in Milton to qualify for Title I targeted funding to support the academic achievement scores of its low-income students.

In 2004 the Tucker's scores on the Massachusetts Comprehensive Assessment System (MCAS) made it the only low-performing school in the otherwise high-performing, affluent, and predominately White district. When district lines were redrawn, Milton received local and national attention when a few parents threatened to sue if their children were placed at the Tucker. Only 42 percent of students at the Tucker scored "proficient" on the English language arts (ELA) portion of the MCAS, and it was identified by the Massachusetts Department of Education as a "needs improvement" school.

The New Principal

In 2005, Drew Echelson was hired to serve as the new principal at the Tucker. A recent graduate of the Harvard Graduate School of Education, the twenty-eight-year-old Echelson had never led a school before; he had served previously as an assistant principal in Boston. The Tucker would be his first principalship. He was immediately drawn to the racial, ethnic, linguistic, and economic diversity of the school. Although the district leadership and parents seemed excited about Drew's leadership, teachers seemed more concerned. "People thought I could talk about the work and intellectualize it, but they weren't as sure I had the leadership skills to deliver," admits Drew. As a result he developed a strong entry plan, and that summer before school started he began meeting with all the families from the school, both at school and in their homes.

As school opened, Drew worked to deliver on the "technical pieces" that seemed to be the top concerns of teachers and families. He created and implemented a new discipline plan, improved routines around arrival and dismissal, and developed a working bus plan. Immediately, teachers began to notice the improvements. "People felt like their job was easier to do because there were far fewer discipline issues," Drew noted. "Those first few months I worked like a horse to make sure everything was tight because we needed to get to the instructional piece."

Moving Toward Instructional Leadership

Starting in September, Drew began taking learning walks around the school to observe instruction. At the time, the district was using a basal reading program for literacy instruction, and Drew was immediately struck by "teachers, who I thought could have an amazing amount of talent, hugging their basal books like if I pulled them away they'd have no idea what to do." At his previous school, teachers had successfully employed a Readers and Writers Workshop model, so Drew hired three teachers from another school to begin professional development. "I had to create an argument that we could put the basal books down, and so we focused there." Drew began offering his teacher three-hour optional workshops outside of regular school hours. He credited the dedication of his teachers: "Nearly 100 percent of teachers participated and that continued throughout the school year."

As part of their professional development, teachers began watching videotaped lessons, using descriptive protocols, and eventually volunteered to have their own classrooms videotaped for analysis. "Through this process we ended up with a good vision and clear expectations about what good teaching was going to look like at the Tucker. It was developed collaboratively in leadership teams and finally brought to the full faculty. It gave me a good sense as an administrator that people knew the things I was looking for and had agreed upon as a whole school."

Special Education

The Milton School District had a decades-old program that allowed parents to choose a French language immersion program or a regular instructional program in English for grades 1–5. For a small school like the Tucker, with only two sections at each grade level, it meant that children were with the same classmates through their entire elementary school experience, as there was no option to transfer into French after the first grade. Drew felt that bringing the co-taught model that had been attempted at a neighboring school would allow them more flexibility in class placement and help the school transition to more inclusive instruction. Drew felt that the community at the Tucker would be more supportive of the model than the other parents in the district had been. "There's a feeling within the school community. Teachers and parents embrace the diversity and talk about it. I felt like it was an easy sell."

With the co-taught model in place, Drew and the Tucker guidance counselor began to address the special education teachers who worked with students with individualized education plans (IEPs), who represented one-third of all the students in the school. In his audit of the files, Drew had quickly recognized that many students were being identified simply because they were struggling to meet grade-level expectations, not because they met the qualifications for special education based on the discrepancy model. He offered one student, "Angelique," as an example. "Angelique had come from Haiti a year earlier and was not proficient in English; neither were her parents. She had been identified with a disability in the first grade, but it was inconsistent with the reauthorized version of IDEA [Individuals with Disabilities Education Act]. She hadn't had time to have explicit English instruction. I felt there were a lot of people worried about her, genuinely so. As I walked into classrooms I saw lots of adults doing different things with her. And so as I began to reflect what it might be like to be a student who comes into another country where you don't know the language and you have six adults, hovering over you, each of whom is doing something very different, might not be the best instructional strategy."

When Drew and the school's guidance counselor met with the special education teachers, Drew had the data from the files to support his claim that students were being inappropriately identified. He described to them the ways in which attempts to support students like Angelique pulled them in "ten different directions" and weren't ultimately supporting their academic improvement. He asked specialists to begin spending as much time in the general education classrooms as possible to deliver services. "I told the occupational therapist [OT], you need to be in the classroom during Writers Workshop, doing OT while writing is happening. And speech therapists should be working on articulation issues during reading time. There was a lot of pushback," Drew recalls. "They did it reluctantly. But that was how we were able to start the process."

The guidance counselor supported the model, saying, "When you only deal with special education students in your room, you're couldn't really see what was being expected or what students were being challenged with in the classroom. And it reduced the idea that special education was a mystery thing where we fixed kids. It became more collaborative with teachers asking more questions and special education teachers sharing their specialized knowledge, making it more accessible to teachers." In implementing the Readers and Writers Workshop model, special education staff was able to support small group instructional needs, working with students with IEPs and those without.

Response to Intervention
Based on public health models of disease prevention, RTI calls for universal screening of children beginning in the early grades, with frequent monitoring of students who were determined to be at risk for academic difficulties. After reading research on RTI, teachers developed interventions to ameliorate difficulties, which increase in intensity based on children's responses to preliminary interventions. Students who did not make progress toward benchmarks were eventually referred for evaluation and a special education diagnosis. The 2004 reauthorization of the Individuals with Disabilities in Education Act explicitly supported this approach, stating that "children may be identified for special education only with documentation that low achievement is not the result of inadequate instruction."[8]

Drew credited the inclusion work that was completed in the first year as instrumental in helping teachers see the possibilities. "I think that there was an organic RTI thing that no one outside of the special education team would have recognized. All the teachers knew were that people were being more supportive." A teacher acknowledged, "Teachers appreciated when there was so much support and they had the opportunity to throw ideas off each other. Over the past three or four years it was accepted and anticipated that you would have a lot of people in your classroom. I think it was a change for the better."

For Drew and the special education team, the first step was identifying assessments to begin the process. By the second and third years, the team had identified and purchased a commercially available assessment system that worked well with the Readers and Writers Workshop model.

Drew hired a highly competent former Title I teacher to lead the RTI effort. She developed the first data sheets and served on the data team. After the initial assessment, they identified the bottom 20 percent of students in each class and began discussing where to focus instruction for individual children over the next six weeks, after which they would be reassessed. She then created a document that outlined who was responsible for what aspects of the interventions, and copies were distributed to Drew and all the teachers. "The sheet made it easy for me to check up with people about what they were supposed to be doing and the timelines," Drew recalls. "It became a great prompt for me to ask teachers about their work with students."

RTI in Action

Using the data sheet, one of the teachers pointed out a specific first grade student to show the impact early interventions had on his reading.

> When he came in at the beginning of first grade, this student wasn't able to access an A-level text (middle of kindergarten level), so in September we identified him as a student who qualified to receive Title I targeted services. We put him in a small group that met five times a week for forty minutes of guided reading and phonics during the class's regular reading period. In January, when we reassessed him, he had made a gain but was still below benchmark, reading at a level D (beginning of first grade level). So we continued to work with him, and then he made a huge developmental jump in the spring, so that by the end of the year he met the benchmark on the leveled books gradient. And according to the Newton Words

Survey Decoding Assessment, he went from being able to de-code one word to exceeding the benchmark and decoding 123 words in June.

Based on the success of the early interventions, this student would not have been included in the small group when he began second grade.

But the teachers could point to another first grader for whom the RTI process seemed to be less successful. "This student," said Stephanie,

was someone we were concerned about and wanted to start a special education evaluation on early in his first grade year. He began not able to read an A-level text, and in spite of the work he did in the small group, in June he was still only able to access a D-level text, and could only decode thirty-three words when the benchmark is ninety. So sometime in the middle of the year he began receiving special education, using a Wilson phonics system, phonics instruction in our small group, and phonics instruction in the classroom. It was just too much for him, and it wasn't all one consistent system. But because of the interventions he received, we feel fairly confident that the IEP for learning disability is valid.

His failure to respond to the Tier 2 interventions meant that he would receive an individual education plan (IEP) to offer him more intensive services. Though there are differences in the ways schools implement RTI, Tier 1 interventions are typically implemented by general education teachers and may involve changing strategies. Tier 2 usually involves individual student help provided by a teacher skilled in helping children who struggle with reading. In the case of the Tucker and many other schools, Tier 3 involves a referral to special education.

Funding

At the Tucker, the RTI model is closely connected with the sources of funding. Because the Tucker is a targeted Title I program. Teachers and staff identify specific students who qualify for services at the beginning of the year; this roster does not change during the year. In the RTI model, students who responded successfully to interventions after eight to ten weeks could be moved out of Tier 2 intervention groups, but for the most part by a highly trained special education teacher and a Title 1 teacher, who work with the same students all year.

Previously at the Tucker, Title I teachers were more often used in the classroom as "glorified aides" without clearly delineated responsibilities. But with the addition of highly qualified and experienced teachers, Title I teachers began working with the special education staff and the teachers to coordinate much of the assessment and became integral to developing accommodations and modifications to the curriculum.

Results

When the first year's MCAS scores were released, the Tucker school saw that their hard work had been rewarded. Their ELA MCAS scores had increased from 42 percent passing to 72 percent passing, with similar increases in math. And they went from being the lowest-scoring school in the district to the highest-scoring school in the district. The percentage of students with IEPs dropped from 30 percent to around 14 percent, the lowest percentage in the district. This universally designed approach clearly yielded good results.

Taken from [NG] and Hehir, 2010 in press.

Universally Designed Positive Behavior Supports

Teachers in the three schools were focused on creating school communities that proactively taught and supported positive behaviors. Even though these schools enrolled students with a diversity of behavioral needs, teachers did not focus their efforts on reacting to instances of students' misbehavior. Teachers and administrators focused on creating a positive school culture by teaching and rewarding positive behaviors. They were clear that with respect to behavior, their task was to work with all students, and as with instruction, no one teacher was solely responsible for any individual or group of students. As Karen said, "Everybody in this building is responsible for all these kids."

The behavioral supports developed at each school were aimed at teaching students appropriate and constructive behaviors rather than reacting to inappropriate and destructive behaviors. Heather explained that both teachers and administrators at BAA "approach[ed] behavior from a proactive stance, as opposed to [a] reactive [stance]." She explained that they worked "to create a certain culture within the building, so it's not just the policies don't do, don't do, don't do, it's a bunch of to-dos also that we try to have permeate the culture at all the different levels, administrative, teacher classroom, interpersonal, et cetera." Similarly, at the O'Hearn, Mary described their "schoolwide expectations" as "very, very positive." Maricel explained that the level of student engagement and lack of student misbehavior at the O'Hearn was deliberate, "not necessarily anything magical. I think it's more that there's that whole structure in place."

Similar to the academic supports, the behavioral supports and practices at these schools adhered to the principles of universal design; that is, they

> *The behavioral supports were aimed at teaching students appropriate and constructive behaviors rather than reacting to inappropriate and destructive behaviors.*

were developed to meet the needs of a diverse array of students. Each school developed general schoolwide practices, and then they further created varying degrees of supports for those students who required more. These three schools did not use the same practices, and no school relied on any one established model. Each school developed and grew its own unique practices, all based solidly on proactive supports designed universally, with all students in mind. This included students with disabilities for whom complying with behavioral norms can be more difficult. As Blair stated, "We differentiate behavior management."

In developing the schoolwide expectations and practices, teachers examined behavior through the lens of building an inclusive community. Heather explained that teachers "all try to have that same vision in terms of the mission, in terms of the shared values." Karen described Mason's "shared core values" and explained that "community building in . . . classrooms, that's probably . . . the most profound layer. . . . It's probably the deepest work that people do." Samantha said that at the O'Hearn, they strived to "keep [the school] a community." Heather at BAA described how she worked to "establish a certain kind of culture in [her] classroom," with a focus on "language and interaction." In her classroom, she explained how she worked with students.

> *I start out with this idea of being like a community, and what does that mean. And we talk about it. And I call kids out positively and negatively on behavior that contribute to [being a community]. And*

then, you know, when someone's not using appropriate language, you say something like, "Use loving words with each other." It's not typical that you hear the word love a lot in a classroom, I think, but I use it a lot because I expect the kids to create a loving nurturing environment for learning. So I'm like, "Those aren't loving words." And then, like, later on, you'll hear them repeating, "Those aren't loving words Melissa." You know, and maybe they're kind of making fun of it. But the idea, at least the expectation, is there.

Teachers explained that they were working to create in students the ability to accept and embrace all types of people into their worlds. As Mary described, in her school, the behaviors she witnessed transcended what was considered the norm to the point that the norm had to be redefined. "Everything is the norm," Mary explained. "Sometimes, somebody's making a lot of noise, and we just go on with it. . . . They just kind of accept things. . . . There's a kid who talks differently. We can't understand what he's saying, doesn't talk, he's in a wheelchair, looks totally different, does these strange things with his hands, and it's like, Yes, that's just what he does." What was considered acceptable was broadened for all students. Noel explained; "I think. . . kids with behavioral issues start to see more what a normal classroom should function like. And I think for . . . kids without behavioral issues, [they get] a broader view of the world and the general public . . . and learn how to deal with different things."

Teachers considered the building of inclusive communities as more than simply classroom management, but rather helping to mold future strong leaders. Samantha described this vision: "Hopefully that's the inside story of this, is that we become inclusive in our outside world and not just in our school. And if that could happen, I mean, especially for people who are decision makers, maybe there'll be a shift here in thinking where the world of disabilities opens up more. I mean, we can only hope."

Examples of the general schoolwide practices used in these schools include training at the Mason in a curriculum aimed at building social competence. Melissa explained that this program provided teachers with information that helped them to "get the kids to talk about problem solving, talk about feelings, anger management, all sorts of emotions." Melissa also described her school using an "incentive program" that "encourage[d] the good behavior, as opposed to always highlighting the negative behavior."

Teachers at the O'Hearn described numerous opportunities to focus on positive behaviors. Maricel explained, "There's a lot of opportunities . . . especially for kids that struggle with behavior, when they do something well. . . . We can praise them in here." At the O'Hearn, the greatest reward was to earn leadership privileges, such as tutoring younger children. Mary said, "It's considered a reward and a privilege. And they know that it happens when they've shown good behavior." Both first grade classes at the O'Hearn were working specifically on students complimenting each other. Bev, a first grade teacher, described using a training program for her whole class that was developed specifically for students with autism. She found that the focus of teaching students the skills of showing respect, such as tapping a student on the shoulder, using each others' names, making eye contact, and taking turns would support students to "increase conversation and their interactive play."

At BAA, teachers focused a great deal on positive behaviors. To begin, teachers examined their curriculum. Blair explained, "I think most people here put the effort into looking at their teaching in order to manage the behavior." Reflecting a major UDL principle, Heather said that her "first approach to behavior" was to ask, "Is my curriculum engaging?" She explained, "I think a lot of behavior issues come up because the curriculum is off, it's not touching the kids, they can't relate." BAA also adhered to the school district's general code of discipline, as well as "community standards" that were developed by the school and "designed to support [their] shared values." The community standards included thirty-three items, each with a paragraph of explanation.[9] The first item was "respect for cultural diversity." The handbook reads, cultural diversity "extends to matters of language, race, gender, sexual orientation, class, religions, disabilities and other cultural traditions." Students were "expected to offer the same kind of respect they would demand from others and may suffer disciplinary action if they fail to do so."[10] Addressing respect for diversity at the beginning of the standards sent a clear message to students that the value of relationships with others in their community was of paramount importance.

Other standards addressed sexual harassment, the use of cell phones, and appropriate attire. Each topic was explained in detail and written for students.

These shared values or community standards were discussed daily over morning announcements at the school. Heather explained that Carmen Torres, one of the co-headmasters of the school, each morning over the loud speaker "usually highlights one of our shared values." At BAA behavior was addressed through a conceptual framework termed "RICO" (an acronym for refine, invent, connect, own) developed by the school that that organized all aspects of the student's school experience, from academics to social behaviors, and focused on developing the "habits of the graduate."

Intensive Supports for Some Students

Teachers in each school expected that some students would not be able to work within the margins of the general schoolwide practices, and they developed more intensive levels of supports. Teresa described Mason's "crisis team" that, while used "rarely," was in place if needed for students experiencing behavioral crises. More likely, however, if the standard behavioral expectations were not working for a particular child, teachers such as Teresa would simply take "different measures," such as calling a meeting with the parent, principal, and the student and coming up with an individual plan to help the student meet the school's expectations. Similarly, while there were schoolwide expectations at the O'Hearn, Bev explained that she had worked with one first grade student who had a difficult time transitioning from play to work. She said that she had taught him to "raise [his] hand and say, I need a minute . . . [and then he could] let the rest of the class line up and walk in and he [could] walk in alone." Bev realized that some days were "just overwhelming" for him. At BAA, the school followed a code of conduct listed in their student handbook, yet individualization was the norm. Noel explained that students even understood the need to individualize behavioral expectations for some of their peers: "I can think of a kid who called out all the time. And when he only called out once or twice in a class, I might go to him at the end [of the class], and the other kids in the group would hear, [and] I'd say, 'You know, you did a good job not calling out today.' And I think kids kind of get that it's sort of okay if that kid calls out a couple times in class, because that's so much less than fifteen, which is on a bad day."

That some students would need more supports was taken in stride, and no teacher appeared surprised. Teachers in these schools not only accepted a variety of behaviors, they expected them, and they were not shocked or surprised but also actively sought to shape students' behavior to a more acceptable form.

Teachers Working Together to Improve Student Behavior

Similar to instructional practices, teachers worked together to support all students' behavior. Together, teachers developed schoolwide behavioral expectations that supported the school's inclusive communities. They collaboratively problem-solved to meet the needs of students who had or who they believed would have a difficult time meeting these expectations.

Teachers in all three schools explained that because their standards were developed together, the expectations they had of students were similar, allowing teachers to be consistent with students throughout the school. As Teresa explained, "Everyone has similar expectations for the kids in terms of how they treat others and how they behave in school. . . . It's not like you go to one class and it's a free-for-all, and then the next class, it's much more structured." Maricel said that at the O'Hearn "the kids know it's not like good parent/bad parent, good cop/bad cop. . . . They cannot . . . run to somebody or get away with something. There are norms that everybody upholds." She said that teachers worked to "always appear to be on the same page as the other adult [that students were] working with. . . . They know if I say no, and then they go to [another teacher], she's going to say no, too." This is not to say that teachers' supporting one another was always simple. Maricel said that sometimes, appearing as a "united front" was difficult: "It's like parenting. . . . You have to agree with the other person, and uphold whatever they say, regardless or whatever you think. So that's, kind of, a challenge. . . . But if you can do that, then it makes it, I think, very effective, even more than just having one person in front of you, because you have two adults who are presenting a united front."

Teachers also relied on each other to develop the capacity to address student needs that required more supports. Each school had structured formal Student Support Teams (SSTs) in which an established group of teachers and administrators met regularly to address the concerns of individual students. Heather explained that when students' "behavior issues are, like, maybe too much . . . we have the whole area called SST." Teachers could go to SST meetings to raise concerns that they had about individual students and receive guidance and support from their colleagues. In addition, at BAA, teachers worked together on case studies of individual students. Heather explained that in a case study, they looked at "particular students with IEPs [individualized education plans]" and "talk[ed] about the students in depth [to come] up with strategies."

Teachers relied on each other informally for support. Bev at the Mason explained that she depended on her colleagues as "resources," and Karen from the O'Hearn "[sought] out other people [for] help," explaining that the one colleague she went to most often was very strong at managing behavior. "It's not that I'm horrible at it," she said, "it's that she's better." Teachers consistently spoke with each other either in person or via email. According to Noel at BAA, "We do email. We do a lot of email. If the kid is really acting up . . . I'll email the advisor and say, 'Listen, what's up?'"

Teachers relied on each other to support all students, and again, no one teacher was solely responsible for any individual or group of students. Had teachers not been working in relation to each other, they would not have been able to address successfully such a wide range of student needs. As measured by the percentage of out-of-school suspensions, these schools had lower percentages of students suspended than both the city and the state. The reader is also reminded that these schools enrolled students with a diverse array of disabilities, including students who were classified as seriously emotionally disturbed and autistic, two disability classifications often tied to inappropriate behaviors and often connected to concerns about the viability of their inclusion in the general education environment.

The Role of Professional Development

The universally designed practices described thus far were closely connected to the extensive opportunities provided by these schools for professional development described in Chapter Two. The depth and breadth of professional development in these three schools was significant and was focused on improving practice at the classroom and school level. Much of this work centered on the principles of universal design, with teachers and administrators seeking multiple ways in which to provide students with improved access to education.

THE ROLE OF ADMINISTRATORS

Administrators in these schools implemented practices that supported universally designed instruction and positive student behaviors. Administrators worked to create opportunities for teachers to work collaboratively on professional development activities. These leaders of these schools—both principals and teacher leaders—fostered relationships between teachers by creating a collaborative culture in the schools, by staffing teachers in a matter where no one worked in isolation, and by dedicating time for teachers to collaborate.

Collaborative Culture

Administrators were clear that they could better meet their mission of educating all students to high academic standards in inclusive environments if they developed cultures that supported collaborative practices. Michelle, a special education supervisor, explained, "[It all] comes back to relationship. With adults, there needs to be the high level of openness. The speech therapist needs to feel comfortable, as she did this morning, say, saying, 'I don't agree with the approach you're taking here. Let's talk about it.' You know? But that kind of positive accountability takes a relationship." By developing relationships with each other, these administrators understood that teachers could share their expertise and become better teachers for all students.

The collaborative cultures developed by administrators focused on teachers' problem-solving with each other. Henderson, principal of the O'Hearn, explained, "Collaboration . . . that's the hardest part because . . . there's not always one way of doing something. There's not only a right way. And people's personalities get in the way. . . . [However], it [isn't] just collaboration for teaming's sake. But it [is] collaboration to figure out how we can be successful."

To be sure, administrators defined success as strong outcomes for students with and without disabilities, and the ability of teachers to be able to address the needs of students with disabilities was a benefit to all. Torres, co-headmaster of BAA, explained that having students with disabilities in the school made her teachers stretch professionally: "I think because it really gets you to be more thoughtful about reaching kids. And you can't make assumptions. And you have to try different things. . . . So you have to be open. You have to be patient. You have to ask questions.

Those questions were asked by teachers and other school staff of each other. Michelle explained, "One of our strengths is that we don't just have [one] conversation, and then we're done. We're always talking about what are . . . the different kinds of ways they present in the classroom? What are the different kinds of strengths and challenges they have? What are the different things they need?"

Staff Placement

These principals did not staff their schools in the traditional manner of one teacher responsible for one class. Teachers in these schools taught together. At the O'Hearn, there were two teachers in each class, one general and one special educator. At the Mason, there was one teacher in each class who was certified in both special and general education, usually assisted by an intern and intermittently by a special education teacher and other specialists. BAA had a combination of dually certified teachers and co-teaching. In each school teachers had a great deal of time to plan together.

What was also clear in each school was that the administrators supported both special and general education teachers to learn from each other. Because, as Michelle explained, there was a need to "push the special educators to think more like regular educators and . . . push the regular educators to think more like special educators." Leigh, the special education supervisor at the Mason, explained that those teachers who could address the needs of students with disabilities were stronger teachers overall. She said, "I've seen teachers who have become better with their students with special needs, become better teachers overall, and actually . . . they feel so much better about themselves."

Those teachers who could address the needs of students with disabilities were stronger teachers overall.

These administrators were also aware that to do the complex work of teaching all students to high standards meant having adequate staff. Henderson explained, "I get angry with university folk and policy makers who think, you know, that—you can teach children, with or without disabilities, and not have the person power to do it. I mean, the needs are tremendous of so many kids. So, if you're going to take more kids with needs . . . you're going to need the supports. So if you have a school that you're skimping on the supports . . . it's going to fail, because you got to have enough person power.

To be sure, in each school there were paraprofessionals and at BAA interpreters, most attached to whole classes rather than to individual students. There were also a large number of student teachers in two of the schools, and at the other, full-year residents from the district's alternative certification program. These administrators worked to provide adequate and appropriate human supports for all students through various entrepreneurial and political actions. Leigh described her school as utilizing well "the delegation of the other people in the classroom . . . the [alternative certification] residents, the paraprofessionals, the . . . tutors from [a local university]."

Having adequately staffed personnel is crucial to the success of these schools. However, without the time to create their practice together, more adults in a classroom might simply be more adults in a class, not necessarily better practices.

Dedicated Time

Perhaps the most important resource that administrators used to support instructional innovations was time. The administrators here dedicated significant amounts for their teachers to be able to develop strong working relationships. Time was set aside for professional development activities. Time was scheduled daily for teachers to plan together. Time was built into the schedule for grade-level team and staff meetings. Linda Nathan, co-headmaster of BAA, explained, "We always have thought of ourselves as having a rich, professional learning community, and in order to have a rich, professional learning community, you need some things in place. Obviously you need time."

As a resource, time is costly. Yet the leaders at these schools emphasized the importance of teachers having time to problem-solve around issues of practice. At all three schools, administrators were clear that they did not want to rely on using the "specialists," such as special education teachers, art teachers, music teachers, and such, to make time for other teachers to meet. Instead, these administrators saw benefit in developing working relationships among all faculty. Henderson explained that those who were at the "front line" but with "[fewer] degree[s]" often were those "people that make it or break it." Michelle said that including specialists in meetings is "an important part of our story."

As described in the Introduction, BAA and the Mason were district pilot schools, which meant that they had autonomy in budget, staffing, curriculum, and school calendar while adhering to all other guidelines of the district. Does a school need to be a pilot school to create the time to effectively teach students with disabilities in inclusive settings? Michelle explained that she thought pilot school status helped but was not necessary.

> *I think what's really important is [an] administration-down-to-teacher-aide vision. . . . Does it need to be a pilot school? No. But there needs to be a clear through-line. It can't just be the project of the few teachers or one cluster or particularly the special ed department. It has to be a whole-school conversation that everyone's involved in. And I think maybe, this is my bias; I think whole-school conversations are sometimes difficult in a traditional school model, although not impossible. . . . I think you need lots of time. You need lots of adult time. . . . And I don't see how you do inclusion without it.*

The most significant point, however, is that these administrators were at the very foundation of creating these collaborative effective schools. Administrators set the tone concerning high expectations and inclusion. They actively sought teachers who shared that vision and provided them with the opportunities to work together and grow professionally.

TO SUM UP

- Universal design principles have greatly enhanced the ability of teachers to allow students with disabilities to access academic curriculum.
- Universally designed RTI approaches at the Tucker have been successful in reducing overplacement of students of color in special education while improving literacy scores.
- Universally designed behavior supports have been an essential component for these schools to educate students with significant behavioral issues.

- Universally designed approaches have benefited all students in these schools.

- Leaders of these schools have provided staff development and time for teachers to work together in order to implement universally designed approaches.

Because these schools are largely achieving the policy goals of NCLB, higher academic achievement for diverse groups of students, and IDEA-appropriate, individualized integrated education for students with disabilities, we believe these schools provide important lessons for how policy makers might approach the difficult work of improving schools for all students.

In the next chapter we discuss the lessons for practitioners that emerge from this research. Given that these schools have demonstrated that the presence of highly diverse populations of students has led to innovation and greater effectiveness, we utilize the lens of universal design to help organize our discussion of implications.

PART THREE

How to Create More Inclusive Schools

CHAPTER SIX

Making Schools More Inclusive

Lessons for Educators and Parents

As should be apparent to the reader thus far, the schools profiled in this book were dynamic problem-solving organizations in which highly skilled educators produced results. Strong leadership from the schools' principals created both a sense of common purpose and internal accountability as well as the conditions for high-quality teaching and learning to take place. The leadership was distributed, particularly to competent veteran teachers. The communities from which these children were drawn were actively involved in the schools. Children were highly engaged and, where appropriate, took responsibility for their learning. Teachers who were attracted to and worked at these schools shared the vision and common purpose upon which the schools were based. They were given extensive opportunities for professional development to improve their practice.

The lack of effective models of inclusive education led us to do the research that forms the basis for this book. These schools profiled provide hope that effective models can be developed. However, it appears that this work is more complex than many might assume. The creation of effective inclusive schools, though difficult, can be accomplished even in low-income urban environments. However, the work that must be sustained takes time and is never really complete. There are always new challenges and areas that need improvement.

The factors leading to success are remarkably similar across the three schools. In attempting to relay the implications of our findings to practicing school leaders and teachers, we noticed just how complex and inter-related the factors that appeared to undergird the success of these schools actually were, defying definitive prescriptions for practitioners. This very inter-relatedness and mutual dependency constitutes our major lesson for practicing educators.

THE INCLUSION CACOPHONY

Numerous academics and practitioners have proposed prescriptions for promoting inclusive education. Among the more popular ideas include appeals to "differentiate" instruction, recommendations to establish team-taught "inclusive or collaborative classrooms," assigning full-time paraprofessionals to students with disabilities, providing teachers with training on individualization, and increasing the use of technology in education. Each of these may have merit and indeed might improve education for children with disabilities if implemented well. But none alone is sufficient, and some may have negative effects. "Differentiated" instruction may lead to overmodified curriculum if schools do not emphasize high expectations.[1] A district's implementation of collaborative team-taught inclusive classrooms without implementation of other effective practices may lead to a new form of segregation in which students and staff are separated within the class or in which "inclusion classes" become isolated within schools. There is a growing belief among some educators in districts that have implemented isolated, co-taught "inclusion classrooms" that children with disabilities "need" the full-time help of a special educator when in a general education class. Paraprofessionals assigned to individual students in a general education setting may serve to remove children from interactions with teachers and other children.[2] The schools highlighted in this book have been successful because of comprehensive schoolwide approaches on a number of levels. First, a clear vision of high expectation and inclusion that involves the whole school, not isolated classrooms, has been established by leadership. Second, universally designed instructional practices that address both academics and behavior have been implemented, along with significant ongoing professional development for teachers. This occurs within coherent school cultures in which teachers and administrators exhibit a high level of personal responsibility and collective accountability.

The inclusion of students with disabilities with complex needs illustrates the inter-relatedness of these factors. One factor that created the opportunities for these students to be educated more effectively in all three schools was that these schools had become problem-solving organizations. The presence of students with more significant disabilities may have supported this change. Most of our interviewees reinforced that such students led to adhocratic problem-solving organizations that benefited all students.

However, simply enrolling those students does not, in and of itself, lead to effective education. Indeed, one school in Boston that had made major efforts to include students with significant disabilities did not meet our selection criteria for this study due to low academic performance. However, enrolling these students may be a necessary condition to promoting schools that are more equitable and effective for all.

In the case of the schools profiled, the inclusion of these students was accompanied by strong values-driven support from school leaders. The expectation that inclusive education of these students was central to the mission of the schools and being successful with these students was non-negotiable. This expectation was accompanied by supportive structures. Teachers were given the time to problem-solve around the needs of these students and often provided in-class support. Expert special educators were made available to assist teachers, and extensive professional development was available. It is clear that these schools would not have been as successful without these supportive structures and cultures. The full participation of students with significant and complex disabilities created a condition that required all the educators in these schools to examine their practices critically and to develop new approaches and structures that made these schools more effective for all students.

SEVEN LESSONS FOR SCHOOL LEADERS

Our challenge in this chapter is both to respect the complexity and inter-relatedness of these schools and to avoid simplistic prescriptive implications for educators while also communicating important lessons to practitioners. Universal design for learning (UDL) provides a useful and comprehensive framework for determining guidelines for practitioners.[3]

In Chapter Five we detailed the ways in which teachers were implementing universal design at the classroom level. Universal design requires more than teachers learning new skills and children having greater access to technology. To implement UDL effectively, schools have to provide opportunities for teachers to problem-solve and to learn new skills. Practices like school discipline and behavioral supports need to be approached universally across the school. Other universal structural supports include expanding the time available for learning, increasing early education options for preschool children, and providing comprehensive wraparound services for children and families in crisis.

This comprehensive concept of universal design uniting curriculum and school design is beginning to be implemented by innovative educators. A week-long institute at Harvard's Graduate School of Education on universal design for learning has sold out every year for the past three years, and publications are coming forward regularly on the subject. The pioneering organization that developed many of the original products and strategies for UDL, CAST (formerly known as the Center for Applied Special Technologies), has expanded from a couple of visionaries in 1987 to almost 50 people in 2011. The concept of UDL has begun to enter into educational policy as well. (See Chapter Seven.) Former Assistant Secretary of Education Madeline Will describes UDL as "one of the most exciting developments in pedagogy in a quarter century."[4]

The schools profiled in this book exemplified much of what has been developed in the field of universal design both at the classroom and the school levels. Within these problem-solving cultures, practices evolved that benefited many other children. The following recommendations for school leaders arise from our study of these schools.

1. Establish a Strong Inclusive Vision

All four of these school leaders are visionaries. As strong symbolic leaders, they were unwavering in their support for the concept that "all mean all." There were times when this stance caused problems with staff or within the school system, yet they did not waiver in this belief. The impact of their values-based leadership has had a wide-ranging impact on their schools.

First, they resisted the temptation to remove children who were most challenging. In addition to providing these children with the opportunity to have highly effective educations that might otherwise have been denied to them, keeping these children in the schools was central to establishing the schools' cultures and practices.

Further, the forceful visions of these leaders when developing these inclusive schools likely influenced their strong levels of internal accountability. Teachers who did not share these leaders' vision would be unlikely to remain in these schools; the principals were forceful about the visions, and the teachers were committed to the schools' inclusive missions. Inclusiveness and high expectations were necessary conditions upon which universally designed approaches were built.

2. Practice the Principle of Distributed Leadership

These leaders set the tone but allowed teachers to create classroom and school solutions. These principals were not micromanagers; rather they distributed leadership to the teachers. However, these leaders did not simply pass the buck. They invested a good deal of resources in staff development and allowed teachers to experiment with new approaches. This freedom to experiment allowed teachers to innovate and design new approaches to better educate all children. Further, the leaders spent a good deal of time in classrooms and working with teachers on instructional initiatives. Janet, principal at the Mason, had spent much of her first year observing classrooms. "I had been at the high school level for so many years I needed to understand elementary classrooms better. I think taking that year was important because it gave me a better idea what the teachers needed and gave me credibility with them."

3. Establish Structures That Enable Teachers to Work Together

These schools had developed collaborative problem-solving cultures. The leaders of these schools created opportunities for teachers to work together, both within the classroom and in groups addressing instructional issues. Each leader did this differently. (See Chapter Two.) Without time structured into the day for teachers to work together, it is doubtful these schools would have been so successful.

4. Seek Entrepreneurial Opportunities

Resources were a continual struggle for these leaders as they tried to meet the needs of highly diverse student bodies within the constraints of a large urban district. All reported that they could use more help. However, they creatively used the resources they had been given by the district, and all brought significant resources into their schools beyond those provided by the district. Each leader approached his or her budget in two ways. First, all approached the district budget given to them by putting their resources in "one basket."[5] For instance, they united their categorical resources from special education, bilingual education, and Title I around whole-school improvement. Second, each aggressively sought outside resources to augment his or her school's resources. They refused or reduced outside resources when funders were not willing to fund activities central to their missions.[6] They did not go after funding for funding's sake but rather sought outside resources that would enable them to support the direction of their schools.

5. Establish Strong Relationships with Parents and the Community

All of these leaders deeply valued parent and community involvement. The O'Hearn's inclusive education model would not have happened without the advocacy of parents of children with disabilities. The early efforts at the Mason to include students with disabilities were presented by the leadership to both parents of students with disabilities and parents of nondisabled students. The support of both groups was considered important to the ultimate success of the effort by the Mason's leadership. The birth of Boston Arts Academy (BAA) was greatly assisted by the arts community in Boston who strongly advocated for an arts high school. The support of both groups was considered important to the ultimate success of the effort by leadership. Though leaders valued parent involvement, there were times when the leadership of the schools conflicted with individual parents who advocated for approaches that were not consistent with the direction of the schools. The O'Hearn had gone to due process hearings with parents allowed by the Individuals with Disabilities Education Act (IDEA) over disagreements around inclusive approaches. Again, the picture that emerges is of leaders who are confident in the direction of their schools.

6. Situate Reforms in the Instructional Core

These leaders focused their activities around teaching and learning. At all three schools, the education of children with dyslexia was focused on how to achieve high levels of literacy rather than on the disability, and these practices in turn supported the reading achievement of all students. These leaders focused their efforts on improving the delivery of the curriculum. Bill Henderson, principal of the O'Hearn, expressed his view of a failed inclusive school's shortcomings: "The [school] did not have a strong instructional core. You can't do inclusion without a strong instructional program for all kids."

"You can't do inclusion without a strong instructional program for all kids."

7. Support School-Level Universal Design for Learning at the School and Classroom Levels

Though UDL is often described as approaches employed at the classroom level, school leaders created the conditions under which UDL flourished. The previous six recommendations reflect the behavior of all four principals profiled. Taken together, they provide the foundation upon which effective universal design practices were built. Though these schools all began with a desire to be inclusive, only one, BAA, consciously thought about the concept of UDL as they initially developed their school. All three schools, however, came to implement approaches that exemplified UDL. The leadership at BAA incorporated UDL in the design of the school when the school opened. Within the entering class at BAA were several students who were deaf, and co-headmasters Linda Nathan and Carmen Torre hired a teacher of the deaf. The teacher advocated to these school leaders that the school become "universally accessible to deaf students." This concept resonated with Linda. "We [she and Carmen] both came from a bilingual education background. We thought, yeah, that's exactly what English Language Learners need; schools universally designed to provide language access."

The other two schools seem to have developed universal approaches naturally, spurred on by the establishment of problem-solving structures that sought to educate children with the greatest challenges. This aspect of all three schools seems central to their development of universally designed approaches. In a sense, the desire to be inclusive was largely philosophically driven, but the philosophy needed practices to accompany the beliefs. These schools were committed to inclusion long before other urban schools in Boston had embraced the concept; thus there was little precedent to rely upon. UDL evolved into the practice necessary to implement the philosophy.

The leaders of these schools set the tone and expectation that their staffs must determine how to be effective with all students. Linda sums up this expectation well. "Why this was all so important to us is the subtext. . . . What does it mean to create success for all students, taking into account, not regardless of, race, gender, socioeconomic background, language background, disability, artistic background, family, cultural background, you name it?" Carmen, Bill, and Janet expressed similar beliefs. Janet, talking about her belief in the importance of high expectations, said, "[Teachers hold] the same expectations for every single child. There may be a different road to get there for different children, but their expectation is that we're all going to get there."

These beliefs about diversity and the responsibility of schools to be successful with all students were internalized by teachers. The inclusive belief system established by the leaders and embraced by the teachers was structurally supported by the opportunities to problem-solve around individual students. A teacher at the Mason reinforced that this structure influenced practice "where people are just constantly investigating how, what is the best practice, and how they can get to a child."

Over time this opportunity for problem solving around individual children appears to have influenced schoolwide practices by promoting universally designed approaches. These schools have also provided vehicles whereby staff can examine schoolwide issues. This is most evident in the areas of literacy and positive behavior and support. The shared beliefs that are evident in each of these schools reflect their tight coherence (see Chapter Four) and have led to universal approaches particularly in the area of literacy. All of these schools have universal expectations that all children interact frequently with challenging text and at the same time individual children have opportunities to get intensive help in skill development. (See description of the BAA literacy program in Chapter Three.) Children are given multiple means of access to reading materials such as screen readers and video. Literacy is reinforced in highly engaging ways through both the selection of text of high interest to students as well as through the arts.

Behavior is another area where these schools have developed effective universal approaches. Universal expectations are communicated clearly to students and families and reinforced by teachers and administrators.

Though each of these schools has high standards for student deportment, there is recognition that behavior may have to be approached differentially for students because of the nature of their disabilities. As another BAA teacher stated, "We differentiate behavior management." At the O'Hearn, where there are a number of students who exhibit very atypical behavior as a result of their disabilities, children handled this differentiation well. Though the school has a clear and consistently applied norm of behavior, some children can't control certain behaviors that might be out of the norm. Bill's successor,

Trish Lampron, discussed an incident with a student who showed significant behavior issues. The boy was upset that one of his classmates, a child with autism, had refused to run the bases during a kickball game. The boy said, "That kid is weird. I just don't understand why he didn't run." Trish responded, "You know last year he didn't even kick the ball. So kicking the ball was a big improvement for him. You know we all are different. You know next time, how about if you be the pinch runner. You know the Red Sox do that sometimes and you can too." The boy nodded and said, "Yeah, I can do that. I'm a good runner."

The need to be aware the effect that total environment has on children's behavior and to universally design consistent approaches extends beyond the classroom at O'Hearn. Bill underscores this principle. "The more vulnerable the kid, the more important that stuff becomes. See, if you're a brilliant kid, you can have a jerk for a bus driver, and you're going to figure out how to do well in math. But if you're a vulnerable kid and you have a bus driver who is mean or unpleasant, you're going to start off the day wrong."

Leaders in these schools provided necessary conditions under which UDL could flourish at the classroom level. Janet, principal of the Mason, explained that her teachers had "the same expectations for every single child. There may be a different road to get there for different children, but their expectation is that we're all going to get there."

Teachers had "the same expectations for every single child. There may be a different road to get there for different children, but their expectation is that we're all going to get there."

At the O'Hearn, Bill provided for co-taught classes so that students with significant disabilities could be included. Some teachers at the Henderson had difficulty naming the students with disabilities in their classrooms. It is doubtful that this teacher would have the same reaction if she were teaching this class by herself.

Another design feature of these schools was the opportunities for teachers to work across grade levels. Teresa explained that for a student who was working on reading comprehension but had difficulty decoding words, she might provide him with "a book on tape that his guided reading group [was] doing," and to accommodate the students in her class who were reading at higher levels than her other fourth graders, she had them "go and meet with [a fifth grade teacher] for guided reading twice a week." Teachers worked across grades and disciplines to support student learning.

The development of effective, inclusively designed schools appears to require active, involved leaders who created the conditions that allowed for innovation. These leaders were clear about their beliefs about children, respected their teachers and parents, and worked effectively to provide for the school's needs.

SIX LESSONS FOR TEACHERS

The implication for teachers of this research is complex; the success of these schools is the result of interdependent factors that contribute to the success the teachers enjoy in the classrooms. These teachers do not practice their trade in isolation but rather work in collaborative environments in which significant support is available. We recommend the following guidelines for teachers.

1. Seek Out Schools with Strong Inclusive Problem-Solving Cultures

Our first recommendation is for teachers to seek out situations in which collaborative inclusive problem-solving cultures are the norm. Some people have the ability to choose schools in which to teach; choosing a school like those profiled can greatly enhance one's effectiveness and job satisfaction. The teachers profiled in this book were enthusiastic about their work, and many had actively sought out these schools due to their missions and their reputations for supporting teachers. Though teachers work very hard in these schools and often work long hours, we were impressed by their high morale and diligence. When openings arise in these schools, there are many applicants.

Though the ideal may be to teach in these schools, most teachers will not be able to secure such assignments. These schools are far from the norm in Boston, and we assume this is the case in other settings. But teachers can take away lessons from the schools, leaders, and teachers profiled. We would not want this work to reinforce what Richard Elmore refers to as the default culture that so often pervades urban education in which teachers and administrators externalize responsibility for improving their practice. In other words, we would not want readers to assume that unless they work in schools like these there is little they can do. Teachers can work with their colleagues within schools to begin to build inclusive problem-solving cultures through grade-level teams, instructional departments, or through professional development activities.

2. Implement Universal Design for Learning in Your Classroom

Individual teachers can do much to incorporate the principles of UDL in their own teaching. Providing multiple means of presentation of lessons will greatly enhance the ability of diverse learners to access the curriculum. Allowing students multiple ways of demonstrating what they know and are able to do will enhance student achievement while allowing the teacher to do a more accurate assessment of student learning. Allowing students multiple means of engagement can keep students motivated. Efforts in implementing UDL at the classroom level are greatly enhanced by the use of new technologies, many of which are free or at relatively low cost. For instance, using books on tape will allow students with dyslexia access to high-level literature, and digitally organizing the classroom through class websites enables students who might use screen readers to access content while at the same time saving paper.

However, implementing UDL at the classroom level is relatively complex, and teachers should seek out training in this area. Increasingly, school districts are sponsoring such efforts, and universities are offering courses. Most teachers participate in professional development during their careers, and we recommend UDL training as a powerful vehicle. For a good introduction to UDL at the classroom level, we recommend Rose and Meyers's *The Universally Designed Classroom*.[7] For an online orientation to UDL, we recommend the CAST website www.cast.org, which provides tutorials and materials to use.

> *Implementing UDL at the classroom level is relatively complex, and teachers should seek out training in this area.*

3. Seek Active Collaboration to Better Educate Students with Disabilities

Though many teachers may work in schools that do not resemble the collaborative problem-solving schools described in this book, the requirements of special education law promote both integration and collaboration. Teachers in these schools who had students with disabilities in their classrooms received assistance from special educators in assuring successful educational placements. Though some teachers were struggling in determining the best approaches for some students, no teachers said they lacked support in educating students with disabilities. The teachers were sophisticated in their understanding of the complexity of the instructional issues they faced. Recognizing that there were no "cookbook" solutions to the challenges they faced in the classroom, teachers in these schools were continually innovating in collaboration with one another to produce more effective approaches. (See Chapter Three.)

The working conditions these teachers enjoyed are in sharp contrast to those of most of their colleagues working in more traditional schools. As teacher educators who have taught hundred of teachers over the past decade, we find that the level of frustration reported by many teachers in our courses is considerable. A common lament of the general education teachers in other schools is that they know little about the children integrated into their classrooms, nor do they receive much assistance. One veteran teacher said in speaking of a child in her class, "I knew he had an IEP [individualized education plan] but I did not know what I was supposed to do to meet his needs." Another stated, "When I finally got his IEP, it told me nothing that was useful in my classroom." Frustration also can be heard from special educators. "They put a kid with autism on my case load and I know nothing about autism. I was trained in LD [learning disabilities]."

Teachers who have students with disabilities in their classrooms can seek expert assistance from special educators who are knowledgeable about the nature of a child's disability, how that disability affects the ability of the child to access the curriculum, and how to provide the child access to the highest possible standards. Therefore, we recommend that teachers advocate for the assistance both they and their students need to be successful.

4. Know the Law

Teachers, both special education and general education, should use the law to promote more effective collaborative practices and to advocate for the education of students with disabilities in the general education class with access to the general education curriculum. Many students in our classes have expressed the belief that special education law is too complicated to understand. This is understandable, as there are many regulations surrounding special education. However, teachers should not lose sight of the forest for the trees. There are relatively straightforward and powerful principles that undergird special education law that support good inclusive practices. The teachers in this study were aware of these principles.

The vehicle that drives IDEA in schools is the IEP process, a collaborative process whereby teachers, service providers, and parents or caregivers come together to make important decisions about a student's education. General education teachers and parents have been required participants since 1997. However, in many places these meetings take on a rather pro forma tone, and very little problem solving takes place. As the teachers in these schools profiled did, teachers should work together with parents and administrators, and when appropriate, students, to make sure these meetings are valuable and that all participants leave with a good understanding of the accommodations and or modifications that the child will need and the support she or he should expect to assure success.

The plain language of the IDEA also makes it clear that Congress envisioned that children with disabilities would be educated predominately in the general education environment. IDEA states:

> *Each public agency must ensure that . . . (i) To the maximum extent appropriate, children with disabilities, including children in public or private institutions or other care facilities, are educated with children who are nondisabled; and (ii) Special classes, separate schooling, or other removal of children with disabilities from the regular educational environment occurs only if the nature or severity of the disability is such that education in regular classes with the use of supplementary aids and services cannot be achieved satisfactorily.*

In addition to the preference for integration, the law in its definition of special education goes further to promote access to the general education curriculum as well as addressing the unique needs that arise out of the child's disabilities. IDEA states:

> *Specially designed instruction means adapting, as appropriate to the needs of an eligible child . . . the content, methodology, or delivery of instruction—(i) To address the unique needs of the child that result from the child's disability; and (ii) To ensure access of the child to the general curriculum, so that he or she can meet the educational standards within the jurisdiction of the public agency that apply to all children.*

Reading these two parts of the law together, it becomes clear that Congress intends that children and their teachers have the support they need to be successful. Armed with this understanding of the law, it is perfectly appropriate for a teacher to bring up concerns she may have concerning the types of support she can expect in order to make inclusive practices successful. For instance, a teacher who knows nothing about the unique needs of a child with autism and how he is going to be met should bring this up at a meeting. Another teacher who may believe that a child could access higher levels of curriculum through the use of technology would be well within the law to advocate for this in a meeting.

5. Work with Parents and Caregivers

The staffs at all three of these schools viewed parents and caregivers as essential partners. Parents, to the educators in these schools, were integral members of the school communities. For teachers serving children with disabilities in their classrooms, parents can help assure that children and teachers get what they need. Parents have a good deal of power through the due process protections of IDEA. The law states specifically that "a parent . . . may file a due process complaint on any of the matters . . . relating to the identification, evaluation or educational placement of a child with a disability, or the provision of FAPE [Free Appropriate Public Education] to the child" (IDEA Section 1415).

Though educators and parents should try to resolve disputes in less adversarial means than due process hearings, the fact that parents ultimately have these rights predisposes school officials to try to mediate disputes over placements and services.[8] Therefore, it is likely that when parents and teachers are in agreement on placement and service issues, districts and schools are more apt to provide what children and teachers need.

FIVE LESSONS FOR DISTRICT LEADERSHIP

The schools profiled had mixed support from central office leadership. On the one hand, each leader reported strong support from the superintendent in their entrepreneurial endeavors and in their efforts to support instructional improvement. On the other, they reported inconsistent support from the special education department, some of whose leaders they viewed as at best not supportive of inclusive education and at times antagonistic. Further, there was little evidence that the superintendent or board promoted inclusive education systemwide. It is our hope that central office leadership in cities provides more effective support for inclusive practices employed by their schools. With that goal in mind, we offer the following lessons.

1. Support Inclusive Education

There is a tendency in many large school districts for superintendents and in some cases principals to "delegate" special education.[9] This is a mistake on many levels. First, special education is a major part of school district budgets, with many districts spending 20–25 percent of their budgets on special education. Second, special education can become a costly source of litigation, either through individual due process hearings or class action litigation. More important than these concerns, however, is the fundamental lesson demonstrated by the schools profiled in this book that students with disabilities provided a major impetus for instructional improvement for all students. By establishing problem-solving organizations in which teachers grappled with the most effective approaches to educate complex students, these schools created strong instructional approaches that benefited all children. This is exactly what superintendents should be seeking in all of their schools. Rather than being viewed as a "burden" or a mandated "obligation," students with disabilities were an asset to the schools profiled. Further, the significant fiscal and human resources devoted to special education were utilized to improve the instructional core for all students.

2. Create Specialized Inclusive Schools in Large Urban Districts

As veteran special educators we supported the principle of serving students in home schools for administrative reasons. Serving children in home schools vastly cut down the costs of transportation and resulted in a more even distribution of students throughout the system. This practice also increased the potential for integration into general education classrooms as no one school or grade had inordinate numbers of students to integrate.

However, this research for this book has made us think differently on this issue, though we still support this principle as an ideal. The logic is compelling, and the alternative of segregated, clustered programs organized by disability type reproduces a past that resulted in significant educational inequities. However, we have come to believe that a rigid application of this principle might harm some students, particularly those with low-incidence disabilities, those conditions that occur in less than 1 percent of the population, such as blindness, deafness, significant intellectual impairment, and so on. These schools do not serve "natural" populations of students with disabilities but have attracted specific populations of children because of the choice system that operates in Boston as well as the desires of leadership to be inclusive.

The schools profiled have become highly specialized. The O'Hearn has developed deep expertise in educating children with developmental disabilities, and BAA has deep expertise in deafness. We believe that large urban districts should encourage the development of such specialized inclusive schools.

The principle of "home school placement" assumes that eventually all schools will develop the capacity to serve the children that would naturally attend the school. The school would have the specialists on site and the general education teachers would become skilled in providing accommodations for students with disabilities. In practice, the implementation of home school placement has proved daunting, and other models have developed that may be more desirable for some children.

Though we continue to support this principle from both an equity and a managerial perspective, we have come to believe that the achievement of this ideal is based on several assumptions that have proven formidable in practice and may represent a level of naïveté concerning school change.

In order to implement home school policies, schools must develop the capacity to serve a diverse population of students with disabilities in a relatively uniform way; that is, each school must have the capacity to serve a diverse population of students with disabilities. Schools must be able to serve both students with high-incidence or common disabilities as well as those who have more significant or rarely occurring conditions.

Approximately 90 percent of students with disabilities fall into five categories of disability: learning disability, mild intellectual disabilities, speech and language disorders, mild to moderate behavioral disability, and other health impairments such as attention deficit/hyperactivity disorder. Together, these conditions represent close to 10 percent of children overall.[10] Given the frequency with which these disabilities occur, and that in general the needs of these children are similar to those of nondisabled students, it is reasonable to expect that most schools should develop the capacity to serve these students. Most school districts increasingly do expect this of their schools.

For students with less common and often complicated needs, the expectation that every school can develop the capacity to serve these students needs to be reconsidered. The ability of each school to meet the needs of students with complicated needs is variable. If No Child Left Behind (NCLB) has taught us anything it is that many schools struggle even with delivering the standard curriculum. The expectation that a struggling school can then develop the capacity to serve a child with complex needs is clearly questionable.

This is not to say that schools are unable to develop the capacity to serve students with low-incidence disabilities in the school the child would attend if nondisabled. Many schools have. Indeed, many schools in rural areas have been doing this for years because practical alternatives do not exist. In urban areas there are also effective inclusive schools that have developed the capacity to serve students with very complex needs in the mainstream. However, these schools tend to be exceptionally strong schools overall with strong leadership and highly skilled teachers. Though they may be the ideal, the expectation that highly effective schools can be replicated on the broad scale has yet to be shown.[11]

Because expecting all schools to develop the capacity to serve students with complex needs may be unrealistic, the second assumption that needs to be questioned is whether clustering students with a particular disability is always undesirable. In addition to the problem of whether the goal of high-quality education for students with disabilities is achievable in all home schools, there is the question of whether this arrangement is desirable for every student with complex or low-incidence needs both educationally and socially.

The proposition that all children be served in their home school mathematically means that most children with low-incidence disabilities will likely be the only children in their age group with their type of disability. Though this may represent an integrative ideal, the need for students with disabilities to have associations and friendships with others with similar disabilities has long been recognized by writers with disabilities. Judy Heumann, one of the foremost leader in the disabilities rights movement and a strong advocate for inclusion, speaks fondly of her experience attending a summer camp for children with physical disabilities.[12] Adrienne Asch, a blind woman who was fully included in her home school in New Jersey in the 1950s, has written about the importance meeting other blind people had for her development.[13]

Neither Heumann's nor Asch's insights are not in and of themselves arguments against home school placement. Both of these advocates have strongly supported this principle. However, their writing does argue for the importance of children meeting other children with similar disabilities as an important part of identity formation and political solidarity. If the child is the only child in the school with his or her disability, it is important that opportunities are created. This can happen naturally if the child attends a school with others who have similar disabilities.

Educationally, the needs of these students are diverse and complex. One of the debates that has swirled around special education for decades is whether special education is specialized.[14] We are deeply impressed with how specialized these teachers have become. They have implemented techniques to provide previously nonverbal students with the ability to speak through computer-assisted devices. They have developed behavioral approaches that enable children with autism to engage in instruction in integrated settings. Skilled educators assist deaf children whose primary language is American Sign Language to learn to write at high levels in standard English. These are but a few of the specialized interventions and supports that are so evident in this research. These represent major advances that can greatly enhance educational access for these children.

Some might argue that the regular education teaching force should be trained to implement these techniques. This makes sense for disabilities such as dyslexia that teachers see frequently. Every teacher needs to understand how to address the needs of these students in their classrooms through accommodations and universally applicable teaching methods. However, this logic falls apart with students with infrequently occurring disabilities whose needs are complex. It makes no sense to train all teachers in educating deaf children when a teacher may not have a deaf child in her class for years at a time.

Given these real problems with the implementation of the home school principle, we believe we must actively support the development of more schools that specialize in the education of students with low-incidence needs, particularly in densely populated areas where populations are sufficient to support such schools. Both special and general educators in these schools have had to continually innovate to meet the needs of these students and have deep understanding of how to educate these children in inclusive environments.

The important dimension that separates BAA and the O'Hearn from home schools is the concentration of a significant number of students with the similar disabilities in a mainstream school. Further, the leaders of these schools were given the resources generated by the students to develop capacity within the general education program. A single child does not typically generate enough resources to do this. The dimension that distinguishes these schools from typical segregated cluster programs still prevalent in many cities, including Boston, is the fact that these schools have been designed to meet the needs of students with complex needs within inclusive environments. These schools are fundamentally different from traditional urban schools in design, classroom practice, and culture.

3. Selectively Support Entrepreneurial Principals

All of the school leaders profiled were exceptionally entrepreneurial, using the resources they had creatively and bringing in additional resources to augment their schools' programs. Entrepreneurship is encouraged by many policy makers and school district leaders. The promotion of charter schools, school-based management, and for-profit reform initiatives are all examples of the level of support within education for entrepreneurial activity. However, there is little evidence that these activities have produced widespread improvement.[15] Indeed, the now longstanding charter school movement has failed to provide equitable access for students with disabilities and English language learners.[16]

As the charter school experiment demonstrates, simply unleashing entrepreneurship isn't sufficient to promote more effective and equitable education. Indeed, the failure of most charter schools to serve diverse populations of students with disabilities results in the traditional public schools having to serve most students with significant disabilities. Therefore, we recommend that district leaders selectively support entrepreneurship among school leaders. The concept of allowing every principal to put all their resources in "one basket," as these school leaders have done, should be predicated on the requirement that school leaders serve all children more effectively while the needs of individual students with disabilities are also met. Simply encouraging flexible use of resources may result in failure to meet the needs of the students for whom categorical programs were developed.

4. Support Efforts to Extend Time

This study supports the growing body of literature that demonstrates the importance of extending time in school for students who have disabilities. All of the schools profiled have extended their time options for students. Teachers believe that virtually all students can achieve at high levels, but that for many the school day and school year need to be extended. For instance, the impressive literacy gains experienced by many students at Boston Arts Academy would not have happened without significant time devoted to improve these skills among students.

> *Teachers believe that virtually all students can achieve at high levels, but that for many the school day and school year need to be extended.*

5. Hold Harmless Resources

As schools develop more universally designed approaches, some students may not require special education services, or the services may change and not fit into traditional resource allocation structures. One reason for this is more appropriate referrals to special education. For example, we found at the Mason a concerted effort to prevent inappropriate referrals to special education of African American children. Similarly, as schools develop more universally designed approaches, more students will achieve success, and those with less significant disabilities may not require special education services. (Readers are reminded that a student must meet a two-pronged requirement to receive services under IDEA: they must have a disability *and* require specialized or related services.) In addition, none of these three schools had any full-time self-contained special education classes, the model in many districts that garners the most funding. And, the schools rarely used one-to-one paraprofessionals, a resource many schools rely on to educate students with disabilities in the general education class.

It is important for districts not to disincentivize schools from engaging in these innovative and successful efforts. These principals were concerned that if the special education resources declined, they would lose the very resources they had used to be successful. Leaders of other schools worried about changing their practices because of a concern for losing the very resources they need. District leaders should therefore hold these schools harmless as they relate to their special education resources. That is, if the number of students needing special education goes down due to implementing UDL, as was the case at the Tucker (profiled in Chapter Five), the school will not lose teachers.

TWO LESSONS FOR PARENTS

Parents have played a powerful role in promoting and supporting the reforms in these schools. The development of the O'Hearn as an inclusive school was largely the result of the activism of parents of students with disabilities. Both parents of students with disabilities as well as parents of nondisabled students supported moving the Mason from a segregated model of special education to an integrated one. The administrators demonstrate in both word and deed the importance of close collaboration with parents and the power of parent advocacy.

What should other parents do to support schools like those in this study? We believe there are several actions parents can take to support these schools.

1. Minimize the Negative Impact of Disability and Maximize Opportunities for Students to Participate

Most parents of children with disabilities face difficult decisions about how best to address the needs of their children. We hope that most would see in the descriptions of these schools a vision of effective education for children with disabilities, one of high expectation and achievement and belonging. Parents ask, "How much integration is desirable, how many hours of related services should I seek? Should my child attend his neighborhood school or one that has more expertise in his disability?" There are no simple answers to these questions, as each family and each child is different.

> *How much integration is desirable, how many hours of related services should I seek? Should my child attend his neighborhood school or one that has more expertise in his disability?*

This framework developed by Thomas Hehir concerning the role of education in combating ableism described in Chapter One was derived from the narratives of adults with disabilities and from those of parents of children with disabilities. These narratives are rich and varied and span several decades. Noteworthy among them is the work of Adrienne Asch, who teaches at Wellesley College and is blind. Asch analyzed various narratives of adults with disabilities about their experience as children and identified themes that emerged concerning the way in which their parents and educators responded to their disability, some being viewed as more positive than others.[17] One common response was to overact to disability by excessive concern and sheltering. Asch theorizes that this response is underrepresented in narratives because individuals who experience this type of upbringing do not have the sense of personal empowerment to write narratives. Another reaction conveyed to children was that nothing was "wrong." This was communicated to these children through parental silence or denial. One narrative relates how a young woman with significant vision loss was not given any alternative but the use of her vision even though she experienced significant academic problems. Another common theme was the ill-conceived attempts to fix disability. Marylyn Rousso's narrative is an example of this:

My mother was quite concerned with the awkwardness of my walk. Not only did it periodically cause me to fall but it made me stand out, appear conspicuously different—which she feared would subject me to endless teasing and rejection. To some extent it did. She made numerous attempts over the years of my childhood to have me go to physical therapy and to practice walking "normally" at home. I vehemently refused her efforts. She could not understand why I would not walk straight.[18]

Asch, recalling her own upbringing and education, described a more positive response to disability. That is, she credits her parents with minimizing the impact of disability while assuring that that she had a full life:

In thinking about the writing of disabled adults and reflecting on my own life, I give my parents high marks. They did not deny that I was blind, and did not ask me to pretend that everything about my life was fine. They rarely sheltered. They worked to help me behave and look the way others did without giving me a sense that to be blind— "different"—was shameful. They fought for me, to ensure that I lived as full and rich a life as I could. For them, and consequently for me, my blindness was a fact, not a tragedy. It affected them but did not dominate their lives. Nor did it dominate mine.[19]

We believe that Asch's narrative provides useful guidance for defining the purpose of special education.

Minimizing the negative impact of disability and maximizing the opportunities for children with disabilities to participate in schooling and the community is a framework that parents can use when addressing the education of their children who have disabilities. It assumes that most children with disabilities will be integrated into general education and be educated within their natural communities, with special education serving as a vehicle for access and service that addresses the specific needs that arise out of their disabilities.

Minimizing the negative impact of disability does not involve attempts to cure disability but rather involves giving the child the skills and opportunities needed to live as full a life as possible with his or her disability. For a blind child, this could mean learning Braille, orientation and mobility skills, and having appropriate accommodations available that would enable her to access education. Special education would thus provide her with the necessary means of access that would minimize the impact of her disability. The student and her family would not be required to disrupt their lives in order to receive the specialized services she needed. She could live at home and attend her local school.

Certainly, for blind children it has been demonstrated that services can be brought to children in typical community settings and that most students can thrive in such environments. The schools in this study have made such highly specialized services available while providing opportunities for inclusion and access to the curriculum.

Schools have long adopted roles that go beyond academic learning. Sports teams, choruses, clubs, and field trips are all fixtures of American education that provide significant benefit to children. Children who participate in these activities develop friendships, learn important skills, and cultivate leisure interests that enrich their lives. Again, Adrienne's narrative testifies to the importance of full participation to her childhood experience: "For me participating meant joining chorus, the drama club, writing and debating groups. It meant not being excluded from after-school activities and class trips by teachers, club leaders or the transportation system."[20] The schools profiled here have developed multiple opportunities for students to participate in all aspects of school life, maximizing their opportunities to participate.

We believe parents should seek schools in which children are welcomed and included in all aspects of school life. Parents and schools should explicitly seek to minimize the negative aspects of disability while celebrating the positive aspects of having a disability. The negative impacts of children's disabilities are minimized through both specialized and universal approaches while recognizing that children with disabilities bring unique and wonderful assets with them that benefit the whole school community. Shouldn't we seek this for all children?

2. Support Universally Designed Inclusive Education

Though this may sound like an obvious idea, in reality it may require parents to examine some of their assumptions about what may be best for their individual children. And, in some instances they may have to make what initially appear to be compromises around individual needs for the opportunity to be part of an inclusive community. Parents of children with disabilities may have to question the individualized approach espoused in traditional special education approaches. For instance, the parents at the schools profiled allowed the special education teachers dedicated to their children to work with nondisabled children as well. The vast majority of parents of students with significant disabilities at the O'Hearn have forsaken one-on-one aides in favor of more flexible supports within the classrooms. Some parents have decided not to have their children pulled out for related services in order to assure they will not miss important academic instruction.

The fundamental dilemma parents face is balancing the individual needs that arise out of their children's disabilities with their desires for their children to have access to the general education curriculum, to be part of a community that includes nondisabled peers, to develop friendships, and to have appropriate role models. Is it possible to meet individual needs while at the same time being part of an inclusive classroom? What most parents of children with disabilities must therefore face is making decisions about interventions and access.[21]

In traditional special education programs in which children are grouped by disability type and are often segregated from their nondisabled peers, students optimally get a good deal of specialized individual attention focused on the unique needs that arise out of their disabilities. However, in these models children have much fewer opportunities to be integrated with nondisabled peers, often have restricted access to the general education curriculum, and lack typical role models.

Further, most research indicates that integration is associated with better outcomes.[22] At the same time, however, other research indicates that some students with disabilities are not getting specialized services. Children who are blind who are not proficient in Braille are less employable (National Federation for the Blind), and children who are deaf who have not had appropriate development of language have significant educational deficits.[23]

The parents and teachers in these schools actively struggled with this dilemma and, in the true nature of a dilemma, the problem was never put to rest. However, the success of these schools, we believe, was based on the fact that, as parts of problem-solving organizations, these teachers and parents were conscious of meeting the needs of individual students while at the same time promoting inclusive practices. For instance, children who were blind at the O'Hearn had a Braille teacher available to them as well as an orientation and mobility instructor. At BAA, there was a teacher of the deaf as well as several American Sign Language interpreters.

There were times when parents and teachers could not resolve this dilemma satisfactorily. We became aware of a situation at the O'Hearn in which a parent demanded three hours a day of pull-out services for her son. The school resisted, and the parent went to a due process hearing. However, these are the exceptions, not the rule. Parents of students with disabilities actively sought out all three of these schools, and parents with and without children with disabilities were comfortable with the decisions they had made.

This balancing of individual needs with being part of an inclusive community reflects what Martha Minow refers to as the "dilemma of difference."[24] In our efforts to extend education to all students with disabilities we may inadvertently reinforce historic discrimination by emphasizing difference. Traditional segregated programs reflect this. However, Minow warns that ignoring difference can be equally problematic in that the needs of individuals can be ignored. This framework acknowledges that "differences" that arise out of childhood disability matter, and therefore it avoids the pitfalls of what Minow refers to as "impartiality" or what some disability activists would consider denial. "Through deliberate attention to our own partiality, we acknowledge the dangers of pretended impartiality. By taking difference into account, we can overcome our pretended indifference to difference and our tendency to sort the world into same and different."[25] Minow goes on to advocate for universally designed approaches as a way to address this dilemma.

Parents who are seeking inclusive education for their children should actively engage in discussions with educators about addressing this dilemma. They may have to be willing to compromise what they perceive to be their child's individual needs in favor of the child's participation in an inclusive classroom. However, it is never productive to force a viewpoint on a parent struggling with the decisions involving his or her own child. It is perfectly legitimate for a parent to decide that addressing the individual needs of their children outweighs the benefits of participating in an inclusive environment.

As Bill Henderson stated, "This is not the right placement for every child. Every year it seems we have a student who goes to a more restrictive environment and that's okay if that's what he needs."

TO SUM UP

- School district leadership can support the development of effective inclusive schools by supporting entrepreneurially visionary principals.

- Principals can support the development of effective inclusionary schools by establishing a clear mission, implementing collaborative problem-solving cultures, and providing teachers with staff development designed to improve their skills in educating diverse students in the mainstream.

- Teachers can support inclusive education by implementing principles of UDL in their classrooms and by developing collaborative relationships with like-minded colleagues.

- Parents can support the development of inclusive options for their children by working with educators to minimize the negative impact of disability while seeking the full participation of their children in all aspects of the school.

Can the type of reforms demonstrated by the schools profiled in this book become more widespread? We believe that many more effective and inclusive schools can be developed. However, the promulgation of such schools has policy implications writ large. Policy was important to all participants; their profiles yielded examples of how policy has both promoted and inhibited their success. Therefore Chapter Seven addresses policies that might better support the expansion of schools such as these.

PART FOUR

The Big Picture of Special Education

CHAPTER SEVEN

How Education Policy Affects Our Schools

The schools profiled in this book, like all schools, exist in a complex policy milieu in which local, state, and federal policies seek to influence the people working in them. The interviews we conducted with school and district leaders contained many examples of how policies both supported or inhibited their efforts to develop effective inclusive schools. There were remarkable similarities among interviewees, and some divergence of opinion among the leaders in their assessment of the degree to which local, state, and federal policies supported their efforts. However, all agreed that these policies played a major role in their schools.

From the perspective of building-level administrators, the source of any policy is often unclear.

From the perspective of building-level administrators, the source of any policy is often unclear. This is understandable given the complex, interrelated system of governance in education.[1] For instance, sometimes the interviewees would refer to "the state" when they were actually referencing a federal program. Or they would not know how a collaborating local agency funded a program that supported their schools. While all interviewees correctly identified Title I of No Child Left Behind (NCLB) as the source of regulations pertaining to school-level accountability that required schools to make adequate yearly progress (AYP), they identified many of the discretionary programs funded under the federal act as "state programs." Indeed, this makes sense, as many of these programs were administered by the state using federal funds.

The policies most cited by these administrators as having influence on their schools have some relationship to the two large federal education programs that affect students with disabilities and students reaching high academic standards: IDEA (the Individuals with Disabilities Education Act) and NCLB (also known as the Elementary and Secondary Education Act, or ESEA). This is understandable in that this study involved special education within the era of NCLB. Special education has been the most

States have a good deal of discretion in how they implement federal programs.

federally controlled and supported area of education since the passage of the first special education law, P.L. 94-142, in 1975. NCLB has aggressively brought federal policy to the school level in a way never before experienced in the United States.

Policies for the state of Massachusetts and the Boston Public Schools also influenced these schools in several ways. First, states have a good deal of discretion in how they implement federal programs; they can regulate beyond what is required by federal law, or they can define certain aspects of the law. Second, they have a great deal of discretion in focusing discretionary grant programs. Third, they support state-level initiatives that may have little or no relationship to federal programs. Beyond education, states implement other programs, such as Medicaid, that may affect schools and students. On a day-to-day level, the local education agency has enormous influence on these schools, both in implementing federal and state programs and in promoting local policies and initiatives.

The policy backdrop for schools thus involves local, state, and federal policies and programs, all of which seek to influence the operation of schools or support the children and families who attend them. Courts also can become sources of policy, particularly in areas involving civil rights. In general, these levels of government are seeking to accomplish various goals through a variety of policy mechanisms.[2] The most prominent mechanisms involve:

1. Regulations
2. Capacity-building grant programs
3. Direct assistance to children and families, and
4. The "bully pulpit," the pronouncements of powerful people like presidents, governors, and superintendents

Of these, the most frequently cited policy mechanisms in this study are regulation and capacity development grants. Regulations seek to prohibit or promote certain behaviors on the part of school leaders and teachers. Capacity-building grants figure prominently and were used entrepreneurially by these leaders to improve teaching and learning in their schools. Some of these resources came from private sources, but most appeared to be connected to federal programs administered by the state or the school system. Children and families received important support from some programs, particularly

Medicaid. Leadership from outside the policy makers' use of the bully pulpit was also noted as important to promoting change.

In this chapter, we detail how federal, state, and local policies supported and at times inhibited these leaders in improving their schools. Though we begin with the federal level and move to the local, we attempt to underscore the relatedness of all three.

> We did not take interviews in this area at face value due to the confusion the interviewees had regarding the sources of policies and programs. Our discussion in this section is augmented by our own knowledge of federal, state, and local education policy as well as additional research. We did to try to locate the source of programs and policies mentioned in the interviews.

FEDERAL EDUCATION POLICY

Many of the regulations that influence schools derive their authority from civil rights legislation. The 1964 Civil Rights Act bans discrimination based on race. Title IX seeks equal treatment for students across gender lines. Section 504 of the Rehabilitation Act of 1973 seeks full access for students with disabilities. These civil rights statutes have been part of the education milieu for decades but are reinterpreted over time by the courts and the U.S. Department of Education's Office of Civil Rights. For instance, a major Supreme Court decision concerning desegregation (*Parents v. Seattle,* 2007) has greatly restricted the options of school districts that are attempting to desegregate their schools. Essentially these laws either prohibit certain behaviors (discrimination) or require others (expanding athletic opportunities for girls). Though many advocates, ourselves included, would contend that there remains much to be done in the civil rights area, these statutes have become a fixture in American education policy and have significantly improved access for previously excluded groups.[3]

As we detailed in our description of the leaders of these schools in Chapter Two, the civil rights movement had a major impact on their development as professionals and influenced the values they brought to their work. We contend that the schools they developed would be very different without the foundation laid by the civil rights movement. As Martha Minow, dean of the Harvard Law School, wrote, "Largely missing from the public discussions was the enormous influence of *Brown* in schools beyond race. The Supreme Court's embrace of the ideal of equal opportunity and its critique of the separate-but-equal approach to education transformed the treatment of immigrants, students learning English, girls, students with disabilities, and poor students in America's schools."[4] Boston's specific history with racial desegregation also influenced the parental choice system in which these schools have flourished. However the only specific mention of court involvement involved the O'Hearn. The genesis of this school's inclusionary approach was greatly enhanced by parents involved in a lawsuit with the district over its failure to implement federal and state special education law (*Allen v. McDonough*).

As previously mentioned, the two major federal education programs that influence these schools are IDEA and NCLB. Title I of NCLB (originally the Elementary and Secondary Education Act of 1964) and Part B of IDEA (originally the Education of All Handicapped Children Act of 1975) provide financial assistance to schools to promote federal goals laid out in Section 504 of the Rehabilitation Act of 1973. In exchange for receiving funds, school districts and states are required by regulation to engage in certain activities and are prohibited from others.

The Elementary and Secondary Education Act

In the case of Title I of the Elementary and Secondary Education Act, the historic goal has been to promote educational improvement for low-income students. Originally the act was also used to promote racial desegregation of the schools, particularly in the South. The provision of funds to schools in exchange for desegregation was viewed as a more effective mechanism than court-ordered desegregation by the Kennedy administration, and indeed the act spurred much progress in this area.[5] Over time, Title I evolved into a largely pull-out program providing tutoring and compensatory services outside the classroom to low-income students. As the nation became more concerned with the inadequacies of the educational system after *A Nation at Risk* was published in 1981,[6] Title I was increasingly under attack for its failure to produce improved educational performance among low-income students. The Clinton administration promoted and Congress passed major revisions to Title I, with the requirements that states establish performance-based accountability systems in 1994. (The act was retitled the Improving America's School Act [IASA].) Though the act required significantly expanded accountability around educational performance, it relaxed many regulations particularly around the use of funds. Schools were given much more flexibility around how Title I funds were used, particularly in schools where many low-income students were enrolled. The law promoted schoolwide approaches to improving results for low-income students.

Though the IASA represented a significant departure from the previous Title I program, there appeared to be no meaningful way to enforce the new requirements. As late as 2002, only sixteen states had fully complied with the law.[7] The current Title I program, renamed the No Child Left Behind Act in 2002, was promoted by then President George W. Bush and enthusiastically embraced by important Democrats in Congress. According to two influential policy advisors, the regulatory philosophy at the time sought to significantly improve the accountability structure of the law: "Making accountability consequential requires policy makers to link sanctions or rewards to results."[8] The resulting system of school-based accountability requiring adequate yearly progress is probably familiar to the reader. Essentially schools must make enough progress yearly to enable all children to be proficient by the 2013–2014 school year. Schools that fail to meet this standard are subject to various sanctions that can include the closure of the school and dismissal of teachers and administrators. An important provision of NCLB relevant to this study is the requirement that the performance of students with disabilities be disaggregated as well as that of other subgroups, such as by race, socio-economic status (SES), and English Language Learner (ELL) status. At the writing of this book NCLB is very controversial and may be significantly revised by Congress. However, when this study was conducted the provisions of NCLB were in effect and appeared to be a major part of the policy milieu.

The leaders in these schools differed significantly in their assessment of the importance of standards-based reform represented by NCLB. Views about standards-based reform were conflated in these interviews with the Massachusetts Comprehensive Assessment System (MCAS) standards system that pre-dated NCLB. Janet Palmer Owens, at the Mason, described standards-based reform as "the best thing that has happened in my career." She decried the historic low expectations educators held for African American students and expressed her view that a strong external force was necessary to jolt educators into changing their practices. Bill Henderson felt similarly: "Challenging [students] is a huge issue. We baby kids with disabilities—so standards, I would say that standards reforms in Washington and MCAS, No Child Left Behind, even in our school which had higher expectation[s], that even took us to another level."

Carmen Torres and Linda Nathan at Boston Arts Academy (BAA) were vocal opponents of MCAS and NCLB. When the name of the state secretary of education came up, Linda stated, "He'll know that I'm the anti-MCAS lady." In response to a direct question about whether she supported MCAS, Carmen responded, "Oh, no. I mean, I think it's one way, but it can't be the only way [to get a high school diploma], and I think that that's the problem. I grew up in New York and we had to take . . . the Regents. But it wasn't the only way." However, the staff at BAA occasionally used the threat of not passing MCAS as a vehicle to motivate individual students. Despite the views of the leadership and many of the teachers at BAA toward MCAS, the vast majority of the students passed the test. Linda stated, "We just did our second certificate of attendance this year with a kid that was cognitively delayed. But everyone else passes." It appears however that the leadership did not need the threat of MCAS to spur innovation at BAA. After a lengthy discussion of how students who could not read had caused to the school to significantly revamp its literacy approach (see Chapter Three), Linda was asked if the student passed MCAS. She responded, "He's pre-MCAS."

Though there was disagreement among the leaders concerning standards-based reform generally, they all expressed concerns with the specific model of school-based accountability under AYP. Further, at both the Mason and the O'Hearn, even though by all measures these schools were high performing, they both experienced the threat of being labeled as "failure to meet AYP" for students with disabilities on two occasions. In both instances, this designation appeared to be inappropriate and was reflective of what statisticians refer to as a "small numbers problem." Given that these were small schools, a few children can skew the data significantly. However, the existing system is not sensitive to this problem, and the threat of the designation caused significant concern to the principals and parents and negatively affected the morale of the teachers. In the case of the Mason, as we related in Chapter Three, one year of poor data in the fourth grade put pressure on Janet not to admit complex students with disabilities. Further, this experience caused Janet to relax her insistence that every child take the standard MCAS; she began to use alternate assessment for some children with intellectual disabilities, potentially creating a lower standard for the children involved—a compromise that she felt very uncomfortable with.

The Individuals with Disabilities Education Act

IDEA has had more consistent goals over time and has not been subject to the types of radical shifts that Title I has endured. Responding to the widespread exclusion of students with disabilities, IDEA sought to give students access to education through its requirements that school districts engage in "Child Find" and that all children with disabilities be provided "Free Appropriate Public Education" (FAPE). IDEA has always sought to have children be educated as much as appropriate with their nondisabled peers through its Least Restrictive Environment (LRE) provisions. Finally IDEA has given parents significant rights concerning the placement of their children through the due process protections incorporated in the law. Though the law has been relatively stable, there have been numerous amendments over time, mostly with the goal of strengthening its original intent. Courts have also influenced policy in this area, particularly in their support for the LRE provisions for the law.[9] Further, the 1997 amendments to IDEA promoted "access to the curriculum" and an increased emphasis on inclusion. The revised law also allowed more flexibility in the use of funds.

The leaders of these schools as well as the teachers were generally very supportive of inclusion, so we can assume that the LRE provisions of IDEA were in concert with the direction these schools were going. The due process protections in IDEA seem not to have had much influence on BAA or the Mason. However, the O'Hearn enrolled a number of children over the years whose parents had filed for due process hearings. Some were assigned to the O'Hearn as a result of mediated agreements with parents who had been dissatisfied with the inclusive opportunities elsewhere in the system. In this way, due process may be indirectly benefitting the O'Hearn, as the Boston public schools would be in a significantly weaker position in due process hearings without this option to offer parents. Other parent at the O'Hearn had rejected their children's individualized education plans (IEPs), seeking different types of services than those available at the school. In general the school was able to accommodate them, and it appeared that the school may have improved as a result of this advocacy, particularly for children with autism. However, there were times where parent advocacy and school leadership were in conflict and a successful resolution was impossible. Bill related one incident when a parent wanted a good deal of pull-out while keeping her son at the O'Hearn: "You can't have three hours of ABA [applied behavioral analysis, a one-on-one behavioral therapy provided outside the classroom] and still have inclusion. It's incompatible. I counsel such parents to seek another type of program."

The requirement of "access to the curriculum" incorporated into the 1997 amendments to IDEA seemed to have had an impact an all three schools. The term was mentioned in many of the interviews, and the concept was incorporated in the universally designed practices evident in our observations. Bill emphasized the importance of these changes to the law in how students with disabilities were educated: "The IEP was all about the minutia of different subsets of skills. And those kids didn't take the standardized test. . . . So you could do your worksheets and work on the 'cuh' sound and the 'ah' sound and the 'ih' sound and say they're doing great and meeting all their IEP objectives. I'm not saying we didn't do more than that. We did . . . [but] IDEA '97 ramped it up for the kids with disabilities. And MCAS ramped it up for everybody."

Federal Research and Capacity-Building Grants

Both NCLB and IDEA have discretionary funding programs that seek to build the capacity of schools to better educate the targeted groups. NCLB has a number of programs with relatively significant funding that has been used by these schools to innovate. A good deal of the success of these schools was likely the result of extensive capacity building. Michael Fullan describes the importance of capacity development to school improvement and its link to policy. "It is not that NCLB is entirely wrong, but more that it was fatally flawed by failing to concentrate on capacity development. To make my point, capacity building is more important than accountability because the former is a route to the latter. Clearly you need both."[10] The data in this study strongly supports Fullan's assertion.

Bill echoes Fullan:

> *I really think most schools are doing a better job, although I am fearful now with the reduction in resources from the federal and state government. I don't even know if we can sustain what we've been able to do. And I think that is—you know, it'd be kind of like saying, "We're going to increase our military presence for antiterrorist activity," and gave fewer resources to the airports and the people in Iraq to do that. I mean, who's kidding whom? It takes people power. And it takes informed and trained people. And class sizes are going up. Needs are increasing. The time isn't—you have to fail for three or four years before you get those additional levels of supports.*

The sources of support for extensive capacity development in these schools were complex and uncertain at the building level. It took exceedingly entrepreneurial political leaders enormous amounts of effort to amass the resources to do capacity development. Mason and BAA had even hired staff to raise money for development.

These leaders did not often know whether the resources they had used for innovation were from federal state or local sources. However, it was clear that federal discretionary programs played a significant role in capacity development. BAA used Perkins Act federal vocational education money to expand its arts options. Linda considered this funding crucial to the evolution of the school: "After all, the arts are vocational." BAA and the other schools had benefited from technologies, such as text-to-speech technology, originally developed under the IDEA Part D discretionary programs. Staff at all three schools mentioned "mini-grants" from the state to support inclusive education. We assume that these were funded under what is called "local capacity development" under IDEA. The O'Hearn benefited by technical assistance provided by CAST (formerly known as the Center for Applied Special Technologies), a federally funded technical assistance provider under IDEA. Bill spoke of support received from the Massachusetts Federation for Children with Special Needs; an IDEA-funded parent training center. Several other capacity-building programs initiated by the state and district also were partially federally funded, most notably after-school and summer programs.

Another federal policy mechanism that was mentioned by both Bill and Janet was the "bully pulpit." Janet and the staff at the Mason were justifiably proud of their designation as a Blue Ribbon School. This designation by the U.S. Department of Education helped support and sustain their efforts. Janet also mentioned how important the support of Governor Deval Patrick was to her school. Bill talked about how the support of the U.S. Secretary of Education and his staff was critical in the early years of the O'Hearn. In 1994 the Secretary of Education, Richard Riley, the Assistant Secretary, Judy Heumann, and Tom Hehir visited the O'Hearn. Bill later said, "I can't tell you how important it was for me to say that the Secretary and Judy and Tom support us. Inclusion was new at the time and we were pushing the envelope. So what's a mid-level bureaucrat going to say when you have the Secretary of Education behind you? You need powerful allies."

The other federal program that has been important to the schools in the study was Medicaid. Most of the students in the study were eligible for the program that entitled them to comprehensive services through the Early Periodic Screening and Testing Program (EPSDT). The leaders in all three schools recognized the importance of meeting the health care needs of the students they served. Of particular importance was mental health. All three schools had brought clinical services into the schools and considered them central to their success. At the time of this research, the state of Massachusetts was being sued by advocates for failure to meet the needs of children with psychiatric disabilities under Medicaid. A resulting consent agreement required the state to work cooperatively with schools in responding to the needs of these children by coordinating educational and mental health systems. It was not clear whether this suit influenced the availability of these services.

The schools may have benefited indirectly from the school district's pursuit of Medicaid funds to help subsidize the cost of special education. Though the schools did not know the amounts these efforts garnered for the system, schools were given comparative data on the numbers of eligible children and the degree to which schools had been successful enrolling students. Bill reported that he was motivated to reach 90 percent. "I actively pursued parents."

In summary, the overall federal milieu in which these schools operated strongly required greater attention to accountability around standards through NCLB. IDEA was also emphasizing higher standards and inclusion for students with disabilities. The two large federal programs were both allowing schools more flexibility in the use of federal funds. Both laws were providing funds for the extensive staff development all three schools engaged in. These laws rested on a foundation of civil rights legislation that greatly influenced the values of the leaders of all three schools and the school cultures that emerged.

STATE EDUCATION POLICY

States play a major role in implementing federal programs and are required by Congress to oversee the implementation of both IDEA and NCLB. Though we primarily focused on Massachusetts, the influence of states in general on local school districts and schools seems to be increasing with programs like Race to the Top. Therefore, the experience of these schools with the state can provide important lessons for other states and for school districts and schools that interact with the state.

States play a major role in implementing federal programs and are required by Congress to oversee the implementation of both IDEA and NCLB.

In Massachusetts, the goals of both major federal programs are strongly supported in state policies and practices. Indeed Massachusetts had already passed comprehensive standards-based accountability legislation long before the passage of NCLB. In 1993, Massachusetts passed the Education Reform Act that established the Massachusetts Comprehensive Assessment System. The act required students to pass an exit exam in English language arts and mathematics. The test is based on the Massachusetts Curriculum Frameworks and requires testing of students with disabilities as well as students with limited English proficiency.

The teachers and administrators profiled had been working in a standards-based environment for nearly a decade prior to the implementation of NCLB.

The state had gone beyond the requirements of NCLB by requiring that students pass a high school exam as a condition of graduation. When NCLB was introduced, the test was used to determine whether schools had made adequate yearly progress. As such, the federal program became intertwined with the existing state program.

In the area of special education, the state of Massachusetts also preceded the federal government by requiring the participation of students with disabilities in the state accountability system. The state has allowed for rather robust accommodations on the state assessments, including the use of screen readers on some assessments. However, the state discretion in determining accommodations allowed on state assessments for the purposes of NCLB has created problems for the schools. Of particular note is whether screen readers can be an allowable accommodation on the language and literacy tests beyond the primary grades when decoding is being assessed. This accommodation is controversial with some educators and policy makers who consider accessing text through screen readers "not reading." Bill and many in the disability community have had to fight back efforts to drop this accommodation from the list of acceptable accommodations. Further, Bill, a screen reader user himself, has persuasive data from his school showing that students with dyslexia can comprehend text at much higher levels using screen readers than via traditional sight methods. This continual struggle exacerbates Bill: "I just wish the feds had defined what is acceptable." He is optimistic that disability advocates in Washington can secure this accommodation.

Another area in which the state and NCLB become intertwined is in determining subgroup size for the purposes of state accountability under NCLB—the size of groups of students like students with disabilities or English language learners whose performance must be reported to determine whether schools are making adequate progress. Massachusetts sets this number at 40. This is in contrast to California, where the subgroup size is 100. By keeping this subgroup small, Massachusetts has assured that almost all its schools are held accountable for the performance of students with disabilities.

A related state issue has involved the issue of alternative assessments under NCLB. Essentially, schools can exempt certain students with significant intellectual disabilities from grade-level assessments, and if children pass an alternative individualized assessment they are counted as proficient under NCLB.

The vast majority of students in alternate assessments are considered proficient, thus helping a school meet AYP.[11] As the Mason case illustrates, there is much confusion in the schools about how these provisions apply. This is true in other schools as well. This policy not only threatens a highly regarded integrated option that prepares students for employment but possibly serves as a disincentive for the development of other options desperately needed by adolescents with significant disabilities.

Another example of how the state may inadvertently be providing disincentives at the school level to enrolling students with intellectual disabilities was found at the O'Hearn as well. Though the children at the O'Hearn were considered proficient for NCLB purposes, Massachusetts reported these children in the "warning" category because they were taking the alternate assessment and unlikely to pass MCAS. Thus the O'Hearn appeared to be doing poorly with a large group of students because it chose to provide inclusive education to a large number of children with intellectual disabilities. Clearly, the way Massachusetts handles the 1 percent may be working against the interests of students with intellectual disabilities.

Though these problems exist within the accountability structure in the state, there has been some support for inclusive practices for students with disabilities, and the state has used discretionary resources to support inclusive programming and integrating assistive technology. The "minigrant" programs supporting innovations in inclusive practice is evidence of this.

Finally, Massachusetts has supported significant options for parent choice through support for cross-district enrollment, within district choice, a suburban racial desegregation program, and charter school development. Schools in cities in Massachusetts are thus competing for students and run the risk of being closed if enrollments are insufficient. Indeed, at the time of this writing, Boston is contemplating closing nine schools. The primary reason given for this action is under-enrollment and the need to bring expenditures in line with projected revenues. Though each of the schools in this study is heavily chosen by parents, and therefore benefit from school choice, that was not always the case. The early reform efforts at the Mason were influenced by the threat of closure due to under-enrollment, and the Henderson was under-enrolled when Bill was appointed principal.

Being situated in Massachusetts has meant that these schools were ahead of the federal policy curve. Educators and students were accustomed to a standards-based accountability system that included students with disabilities. Inclusive education was supported at the state level. Schools in other states that did not have this environment may not have evolved in the way these schools have, that is, becoming high-achieving inclusive urban schools.

LOCAL POLICIES

Some local policies at the district level had a significant and mostly positive impact on these schools. The option for starting charter-like pilot schools in the district was viewed as essential to the success of BAA and Mason. Like charters, pilots were given significantly more autonomy from district policies and some union rules. They had greater discretion in hiring teachers, in curriculum, and in budgeting. BAA started as a pilot and remained so. The option to start a school for the arts was an opportunity seized by Carmen and Linda as the district was actively encouraging the establishment of these "in-district charters." The Mason, a hundred-year-old school, converted to a pilot under Janet's leadership to, among other things, increase the length of the school day. This required a two-thirds vote among the faculty. Though Bill considered converting the O'Hearn to a pilot, he did not see the benefits outweighing the potential consternation that such a move would create among his staff.

Pilots were part of a broader array of choices available to Boston parents. The support for parent choice in Boston first grew out of its efforts to find alternatives to desegregate its schools. Over time, Boston's student assignment evolved from one that was based on neighborhood and race to one that allowed for significant parent choice. Parents can choose from an array of geographically based public schools and twenty-one citywide Boston-run pilots, as well as numerous independent charter schools. Many parents also participate in a long-standing suburban desegregation program, METCO. Parent choice in Boston is thus even more extensive than in the state as a whole. Thus the schools profiled, which are highly desired by parents, were advantaged. This advantage not only provided protection from closing but also may mean the student population is more apt to have actively involved parents. Even though significant choice is available to parents, many choose not to actively participate in the program and are assigned by the district. Bill described the potential effect of this on the population at the O'Hearn: "Once you're known as a good school, parents seek you out. However, some parents don't participate in the school choice process. So you

> *"Once you're known as a good school, parents seek you out."*

get parents who are more apt to be involved in their kids' education. This means you are more likely to be successful with the children."

However, parent choice for parents of children with disabilities was not nearly as extensive. Evidence of this can be found in the relatively low participation rates in charters of students with disabilities, particularly those with significant disabilities.[12]

In addition to limited access to charters, Boston students often are assigned to schools based on their disability. When we were conducting our research, Boston had an elaborate coding system for assigning students with disabilities to schools based on the level of need. And, leaders in these schools viewed this system as incompatible with providing individualized inclusive opportunities for students across disability types that these school leaders were creating. Carmen detailed how this system conflicted with their vision to include all their students.

> *You know, most of the time, there are no special needs services in any of the arts schools. You have to come in being sort of a high achiever academically or else you don't have access to the other stuff. And we said we definitely don't want that to be us. And . . . we really were intentional in our mission statement to say we educate a diverse community of learners. . . . It's front and center from the beginning when people come to know about us. . . . [In] the beginning, they would assign kids that had certain categories [and say that the others] can't go [to BAA] because you don't have [programs] X, Y, and Z. But we don't do it that way.*

This locally designed system of categorizing children was mentioned by each leader as an impediment to inclusion that at times served to limit, not expand opportunities for individual children with disabilities. Further, dealing with this system created significant work for administrators who appeared nonproductive. Linda spent years trying to address this.

The Importance of Support from the School Superintendent

Another local special education policy issue that was supportive of the leadership of these schools was the strong insistence by Superintendent Tom Payzant that all pilots must enroll students with more significant disabilities. This is in contrast to the lack of enrollment of these children in most charter schools throughout the country.[13] In discussing this issue, Payzant was reflective: "I wish I had done it sooner. It was the right thing to do."

Another local policy that seemed to have been favorable to these schools related to the strong support provided by Payzant for experimental entrepreneurial school leaders. Janet, Bill, and Linda all spoke of how supported they felt by the superintendent. They all clearly had a relationship with Payzant and spoke warmly of him. The same was true of the superintendent. In speaking of these leaders and his high regard for them, he elaborated on his administrative style: "I spent a lot of time in the schools. You have to and I really got to know them. Like Janet, every time I went to the Mason I wanted to clone Janet a hundred times. . . . My job was to support them."

Payzant focused significant attention to improving teaching and learning at the classroom level during his ten-year tenure in Boston and devoted significant resources to staff development. These schools benefited from these efforts. Bill and Janet spoke of how effective training in Readers and Writers Workshop was for their teachers. The district provided literacy coaches who would model and observe lessons within the classrooms. The school leaders lauded this approach. This effort was not funded from The Reading First Program funded under NCLB but rather by the Annenberg Foundation with matches from other sources. Boston had been denied funding from the federal program in the beginning because it refused to focus its efforts (in Boston's view) inordinately on phonics. Recalling the time, Tom Payzant said, "You know it was the only time I had a major disagreement with Dave Driscoll [then state commissioner of education]. We did not want to take such a narrow approach."

Boston eventually got Reading First money, which helped the system continue to develop capacity to improve its literacy program. Like the principals in this study, Tom Payzant was entrepreneurial, bringing significant resources into the district. However, he did not go after resources for resources' sake; they had to fit into his goals for the system. In retrospect, this decision to pass up Reading First may have been vindicated by the increase in literacy scores enjoyed by Boston in subsequent years. Boston's gain since 2003 on fourth and eigth grade literacy totaled 9 points and surpasses the 4-point gain nationally and 6-point gain experienced by large cities (NAEP, Trail Urban District Assessment). The Superintendent's concerns were prescient given the scandal that enveloped Reading First at the federal level over how money was rewarded.[14]

Boston also made significant investment in training teachers in a districtwide math program. These entrepreneurial leaders seized on these opportunities for professional development for their staff and customized them for their buildings. For instance, Bill talked about the need to adapt the program for students with intellectual disabilities: "To say a kid with an intellectual disability in the fifth grade should be doing a highly abstract constructive math program at grade level was absurd. However, we felt it was important we do the program. Prior to implementing it the city had no real curriculum and it provided a necessary push that benefited the kids."

The local context thus is one in which stable leadership in the superintendency largely supported the efforts of these innovative schools. The establishment of pilots created the opportunity for BAA to emerge and gave the Mason important flexibility. However, the existing special education system was a barrier to the type of universally designed individualized approaches being implemented in these schools. Though the policy environment was largely favorable, these leaders were policy entrepreneurs who used policy to advance their goals. Of particular importance were the opportunities provided by the district to develop the capacity of the teachers in the schools to deliver higher-quality instruction.

TO SUM UP

- Federal civil rights policies were very influential in these schools by providing an imperative to promote racial, gender, and disability equity. These statutes not only provided an outside force for change but also influenced the values of leaders and staff within these schools.

- Policy consistency for more than a decade concerning standards, accountability, and inclusion at the state level assisted these schools in promoting higher levels of learning for all students.

- A superintendent of schools who supported entrepreneurial principals and allowed for flexibility greatly enhanced the work of these schools. The fact that Superintendent Payzant remained in the position for more than ten years provided unusual and welcome stability for these schools in a large urban district.

- Federal, state, and local capacity-building grants were critical sources of staff development resources without which these schools would not have been successful.

As one who has been at the "policy level" at the district, state, and federal levels, I (Hehir) was forced to be introspective about the role of policy in promoting and at times inhibiting the development of effective inclusive schools. In Chapter Eight I share my thinking on how we might better promote and support the promulgation of more schools such as those profiled here.

CHAPTER EIGHT

Where Special Education Needs to Go

In attempting to glean the policy lessons from this research, I (Tom Hehir) struggled between my desire as a researcher to adhere closely to our data and my desire as one who has spent a good deal of his career in the policy arena at the classroom, district, state, and federal levels to communicate the impact that my encounter with these schools has had on me. I have chosen the latter.

Before I go specifically into policy recommendations, I share some principles that have guided my thinking on education policy. These principles derive from years of experience, the accumulated exposure to the literature in this area, and the experience of conducting this study.

POLICY PRINCIPLES: COMPLIANCE AND QUALITY

1. No One Policy or Set of Policies Creates Good Schools

No one policy or set of policies caused the schools profiled in this book to be high performing. For these schools, policy, particularly regulatory policy, is in the background, not the foreground. In short, these schools are not being led by policy, but rather policies, at their best, are used to promote already established values and goals. Policy at its worst becomes an obstacle these schools must problem-solve around. The effectiveness of these schools is largely driven by competent, focused, values-based leaders and skilled, committed teachers working within collaborative problem-solving organizations.

2. Policy Is Important

Policy was likely a necessary condition for promoting these effective, diverse, inclusive schools. School leaders were driven to promote justice and diversity. They all spoke of the importance of the civil rights movement on their own development as leaders. Similar themes emerged from many of the teachers. As one who worked in Boston during the initial phases of court-ordered desegregation, where I witnessed race riots in high school corridors, I cannot help but marvel, when walking through the halls of BAA, at the young people from all types of backgrounds walking through the halls of Boston Arts Academy (BAA), relating across boundaries with boisterous enthusiasm. In my view, such a school would not have been possible in Boston without the force of policies that promote racial justice.

In a previous chapter we mentioned the O'Hearn student with significant intellectual and physical disabilities who performed as a German soldier in *The Sound of Music* with his wheelchair transformed into a tank. I think back to the naked children lying on floors in institutions I visited in the early 1970s. I doubt that O'Hearn would have evolved into the inclusive school it is today without the force of the Individuals with Disabilities Education Act (IDEA) and the disability civil rights movement.

When I see a young African American fifth grade girl who lives in a housing project nearby to the Mason writing a composition worthy of a high school freshman, I cannot help but contrast that with the low expectations many low-income African American children suffer from in too many schools. I am persuaded by Janet Palmer Owens that the standards-based reform movement represented by Massachusetts Comprehensive Assessment System (MCAS) and No Child Left Behind (NCLB) have provided the necessary jolt that helped move the Mason to higher levels of performance.

These powerful policy directions have thus helped create the necessary conditions that have enabled these schools to flourish. Further, those policies that have sought to provide assistance in capacity development have greatly benefited these schools. However, other schools in Boston have existed in the same policy arena without similar outcomes. This reality supports Principle 1. Further, the lack of similar outcomes may also reflect the ways in which policy makers approach schools with relatively uniform approaches. This leads to my next two principles.

3. Policies That Seek to Reform Low-Performing Schools May Hurt High-Performing Schools

The adequate yearly progress (AYP) system under NCLB was designed with low-performing schools in mind. However, in two of the schools profiled, this system had a negative impact. As the O'Hearn and Mason worked to meet AYP status, their MCAS scores were becoming a concern because they had included students with disabilities, particularly those with significant disabilities. Similarly, IDEA was designed to hold schools accountable for the education of students with disabilities. A focus on schools who do not promote this goal has led to a focus on compliance and resulting volumes of paperwork. Yet in these schools where the intent of IDEA, Free Appropriate

Public Education (FAPE) in the Least Restrictive Environment (LRE) provisions, is clearly being met, the centralized special education assignment system coupled with this paperwork may be detracting from achieving this result by consuming resources for unnecessary activity.

4. Policies Designed for High-Performing Schools May Have Negative Impact on Low-Performing Schools

Though we did not study low performing schools for this study, I have spent a good deal of my professional life working in and with school districts where low performing schools were far too prevalent. The policy milieu in which low-performing schools operate contain policies designed for both low- and high-performing schools. For instance, the relaxing of the rules concerning the use of federal funds under IDEA and NCLB are clearly beneficial to schools for which schoolwide approaches to curriculum and instruction benefit students with disabilities, low-income students, and English language learners as well as those not targeted under the federal programs. However, if those funds are used indiscriminately in low-performing schools, the intended beneficiaries of the federal programs may suffer. The same is true for capacity-building grant programs. For instance, one could interpret the O'Hearn's support for the increasingly popular practice of co-teaching as an answer to the problems presented by disability inclusion. However, I have observed many such classes in which no children with significant disabilities are enrolled and where many students from general education who are struggling are assigned.

I observed a co-taught high school English class in a highly regarded suburban high school in which students on individualized education plans, none of whom had significant disabilities, were grouped with other students with low literacy levels. The twenty students took turns reading paragraphs out loud while the two teachers occasionally assisted students with words they were struggling with. There was no expectation that students do any homework nor was there any evidence of individualization or universal design for learning (UDL). In another school where I was observing co-teaching, I asked the special education teacher if there were children with intellectual disabilities enrolled, to which she replied that they were "inappropriate for co-teaching" and that they were in a "life skills" class. In these schools a practice designed to promote inclusion appeared to be just another version of segregation, and an expensive one at that.

In effect, some districts placing students in collaborative team-teaching classes is resulting in a new form of tracking, losing sight of a focus on what services individual students need to succeed in truly inclusive environments. This is the opposite of the inclusive co-taught classes at the O'Hearn in which teachers worked together to provide individualized, challenging instruction to highly diverse students. At the O'Hearn, co-teaching is not a "program" but rather a means to the end: highly effective challenging education for all children.

Given the differential effects of policies on high- and low-performing schools, the quest for the perfect policy is likely an elusive one. Policy makers need to be able to implement policies differentially at the school level, taking into account the uniqueness of each school and its capacity to innovate.

5. Practices Are More Important Than Programs

There is a tendency among district, state, and federal leaders to promote programs rather than practices in the hope of reforming schools. Often derived from practices of high-performing schools, innovations such as school-based management balanced literacy reading approaches, responsive classroom behavior management, co-teaching, positive behavior intervention and supports, response to intervention, universal design for learning, and even full inclusion are all examples of effective practices promoted by districts and states. All have merit, but when lifted as static programs and placed into schools, they are insufficient in and of themselves to turn around failing schools and can have a negative impact in the hands of incompetent administrators. Yet, too often I encounter central district administrators or even state level leaders who are quick to latch on to a program as a districtwide solution without regard for the practices and processes needed to implement change in individual schools.

The successful schools profiled were not created through programs but through practices. It's not that programs were not useful to these schools, as the Readers and Writers Workshop example shows. However, these practices were implemented in schools in which teachers had developed highly effective practices of collaborative problem solving, and in fact the practices were different in each school. For instance, at BAA, universal design of their literacy approaches was not a program but rather the result of years of teacher problem-solving efforts concerning the best way to improve competencies in literacy. The practices of individually assessing the needs of all students, providing an array of options for improving students' skills, and providing access to challenging text through screen readers were not created by a program, but rather the

The successful schools profiled were not created through programs but through practices.

practices that evolved over years. The O'Hearn also practices principles of UDL in reading that looked different than those at BAA. At all three of these schools, universal design evolved and is a deeply embedded way of thinking that had strong impact on teacher learning.

6. The Further Removed from the School Level Policy Makers Are, the Decreased Likelihood That Policy Can Take into Account Important Differences in Schools

The history of state and federal policy does not always reflect this. Though many have debated the proper role of various levels of government in education, Richard Elmore contends that there is no doctrinal or constitutional prohibition against the various levels being involved in education as agents of the people. He contends that what is most important for policy makers to consider are the strategic questions. Writing in 1986, Elmore asserted, "If federal policymakers have erred, their errors have been strategic. . . ."[1] I believe the same can be said today about all three layers of governance over schools: federal, state, and local.

One thing that struck me most when I was in Washington was the degree of sanctimony that accompanied the discussions of many policy makers far removed from classrooms. It seemed the level of sanctimony increased the further you were removed from the difficult work of teaching or leading schools. What often accompanied this level of sanctimony was a desire to fix the problems of schools through regulation. I am sure I was guilty of this myself. However, policy is a blunt instrument that is often applied equally to the guilty and the good. And, as one moves away from schools, one's ability to customize policy to the particular circumstances of schools is greatly diminished. NCLB is an example of this type of remote, decontextualized type of policy making.

Though many schools, particularly those in urban districts, may need greater oversight (and some far less), the blunt instrument of AYP has treated all schools alike. This well-intentioned policy may be producing more harm than good. For the schools profiled in this book, the harm was minimal and the strong leadership provided by the principals of the O'Hearn and the Mason sheltered the schools from what could have been inappropriate demoralizing negative assessment. However, there is evidence that some schools may be restricting the enrollment of students with disabilities in various school choice programs, such as charter schools and in-district programs, in an effort to "not look bad" under NCLB.[2] In a recent meeting with a cross-section of fifty parents of children with disabilities in Houston, I asked them if they felt they had the same choices within the extensive choice system in the city. The parents responded to the question with an instant and resounding "No!" One said, "I can't find a principal who will take my autistic son." Another was fearful that her dyslexic third grader with a disability would "get kicked out" of the magnet school she attended because she was struggling to learn to read. So the well-intentioned federal policies of accountability and parent choice enshrined in NCLB may actually be hurting these children and their families. This is clearly a strategic error.

SPECIFIC POLICY RECOMMENDATIONS

Though most of the following policy recommendations focus on the two large federal programs affecting public education, these programs are administered by states that have a good deal of discretion in their implementation. The recommendations are written with this intertwined role in mind. Therefore, even without federal action, a state might have discretion to implement some of these recommendations.

The Elementary and Secondary Education Act

At the time of this writing, the Elementary and Secondary Education Act (ESEA) is up for reauthorization and is still named No Child Left Behind. It is likely this name will be changed, so I refer to the act here as ESEA unless I am referring to a specific provision of NCLB. Also, the federal role in public education has been significantly enhanced through the Race to the Top program funded under the American Recovery and Reinvestment Act, commonly known as the stimulus bill. This program offered states $4 billion in additional aid in return for the states instituting several reforms. Among these are linking teacher evaluations to student performance, encouraging the development of charter schools, and the adoption of common core standards among the states. Though only twelve states received grants in the second round, forty-six applied, and most had to alter policies to be eligible. Race to the Top was compatible with elements of ESEA and represents President Barack Obama's administration's priorities in education policy; it is likely to be part of the proposed changes to ESEA. The following discussion concerning ESEA incorporates elements of Race to the Top:

1. Accountability for the Performance of Students with Disabilities Must Be Clarified in ESEA

The inclusion of students with disabilities in performance accountability systems at the building level may be a necessary condition to promote access to more effective instruction. Bill and Janet clearly thought so, and the theme of standards and accountability emerged in many teacher interviews. These policies did not "cause" these schools to value high achievement for all students; at best they enhanced the effort. Though these schools may not have needed the push of federal policy to be accountable for their students with disabilities, many schools undoubtedly do.

The current building-level accountability system allows for far too much state-level discretion in the determination of (1) the ways in which students are assessed, (2) subgroup size upon which schools are judged, and (3) the ways in which schools are held accountable for performance. This discretion allows many schools to shirk accountability for the performance of students with disabilities and may in time provide incentives for schools either to not enroll certain students or to modify and lower expectations for students with disabilities.

The types of accommodations allowable should be robust and seek to be valid measures of what students know and are able to do. Further, accommodations used in testing should be accommodations used in instruction. For instance, if the test is measuring whether children can comprehend text, the accommodations used in instruction, such as the use of screen readers, should be used in testing. This allows for the test to maintain its construct validity, accurately measuring what it is purporting to measure. However, if the test is measuring decoding skills, such an accommodation would be inappropriate as the construct measured is decoding. The ultimate goal of testing should be to have accurate measures of what children know and are able to do, while encouraging educators to have children access instruction in a manner most efficient for them.

> *Accommodations used in testing should be accommodations used in instruction.*

The O'Hearn has experienced confusion and uncertainty regarding the use of screen readers in assessing literacy comprehension. The teachers at BAA and the O'Hearn have been very successful in their efforts to provide students with dyslexia access to high levels of literacy through the use of screen readers. Fortunately, as previously mentioned, advocates have been successful in turning back those who would change the policy regarding MCAS testing. However, many states do not allow this accommodation. This is disturbing. A major impact of dyslexia is fluency problems that affect the ability of students to comprehend text. Screen readers or taped books can greatly enhance the ability of students with dyslexia to comprehend text.[3] The fact that this accommodation is not allowed in testing in some states and school districts probably influences whether teachers employ these practices in instruction. The result may be that many children are being instructed in lower-level texts and are reading less. This practice contradicts the goals of the ESEA and IDEA, both of which seek to promote high expectations and achievement for students with disabilities.

The failure of the federal government to lead on this issue is not only likely affecting instructional practice but also makes it difficult to compare testing data among and within states. The lack of uniformity means that some states may be underestimating the abilities of students with disabilities. Further, given that sanctions and rewards of states, schools, and even teachers may be tied at least partially to the performance of students with disabilities, it is important that accurate measures are used. Finally, and most important, test results in some states are tied to whether a child moves from grade to grade or gets a diploma. Failure to assure appropriate accommodations can thus have a lifelong and potentially discriminatory impact.

States are given wide discretion in determining the size of the groups relevant to school-level accountability provisions of ESEA, the size of a given population at the building level must reach before the building must report the test results for a group and be held accountable for making AYP for that group. States vary from twenty to one hundred in their determination of subgroup size for students with disabilities. So, in California, where the subgroup size has been set at one hundred, the vast majority of schools are not reporting on the performance of students with disabilities.[4] A federal rule that was designed to shed light on the performance of children with disabilities appears to have been subverted by some states. This state-level flexibility in determining subgroup size again limits state-to-state comparisons and may divert schools from focusing on the needs of students with disabilities. Yet, focusing on the needs of these very students leads to much of the innovations the schools profiled implemented.

Finally, the ways in which the performance of students is counted in the sanction and reward systems promulgated by the states and federal government may need revision. Approximately 3 percent of children (or 30 percent of children with disabilities in a district that identifies 10 percent of children as in need of special education) may not be in the standard accountability system. These nonstandard treatments are based on the recognition that some children with disabilities have intellectual disabilities and holding them to grade-level standards is inappropriate. Originally the federal government only allowed 1 percent of children to be assessed through alternate assessments (the "1 percent rule"). If children passed these individualized assessments, they would be counted as proficient under NCLB. After complaints by many school districts that the 1 percent rule was too narrow, the Department of Education established an additional rule that 2 percent of children could take modified grade-level tests. If students passed these tests, they were considered proficient for the purposes of NCLB. Many disability advocates, myself included, think this rule is too liberal and is taking too many students with disabilities out of the standard accountability systems.

Texas provides an interesting case that demonstrates how the newer rule has played out in practice. Texas developed a modified state accountability test called the TAKS-M. This test purports to measure grade-level standards but has only three choices in multiple-choice questions and limits the number of open-ended response items. The state school-level accountability program does not count students who take the TAKS-M or students taking the alternate assessment in its systems of rewards and sanctions. In the city of Houston as well as the state as a whole, large numbers of students with disabilities, more than 50 percent, in the city are taking the TAKS-M or alternate assessments, thus removing their performance from the accountability system.[5] It appears the Texas system has created a disincentive to include students with disabilities in school level accountability. It should also be noted that there are consequences for students being placed on TAKS-M. If they do not pass the standard TAKS by graduation, they may be ineligible to attend state universities and to qualify for certain scholarship programs.

The high use of the TAKS-M in Texas has had an interactive effect with NCLB, as the Texas test is used for accountability purposes under the federal law. Thus Texas has far exceeded the level of 2 percent allowed under NCLB and has been cited by the federal government for noncompliance with NCLB. Texas is in the process of remediating this situation.

In conclusion, the positive movement by the federal government to bring students within state accountability systems has been hampered by state-level discretion. Not all states have behaved the same way as Texas and California but all would benefit from more uniform rules. The goal at both the federal and state levels should be to use their state accountability system to leverage better instruction for students with disabilities. To do this, policy makers should

1. Allow robust accommodations that enable students to demonstrate what they know and are able to do within the standard assessment

2. Standardize subgroup size so most buildings will be held accountable, and

3. Provide incentives to include students with disabilities in reward and sanction programs

2. The School-Level AYP System Should Be Significantly Revised

Though states have significant flexibility around certain aspects of NCLB, they must implement rather uniform federal regulations regarding school-level accountability. The current system requires states to identify schools that have failed to make adequate yearly progress as a whole and among the various subgroups and to move aggressively over a five-year period to employ increasing levels of sanction to failing schools, to the point at which schools must undergo "restructuring." Districts must implement one of five strategies, including replacing all or most staff, reopening the school as a charter, or contracting with a private entity to run the school. The state-level subverting of the intent of federal law previously described may have been a reaction to this federal rigidity.

This lockstep linear system assumes schools improve in a rather linear fashion. This is not the case. Schools that are improving often experience a plateau in performance after they have innovated successfully and don't show further gains until they initiate a new innovation (School Reform from the Inside Out). Innovations are experimented with, evaluated, and revised over several years as better practices are institutionalized. A new challenge is then identified that receives attention. For instance, at BAA, after the school had significantly improved its literacy approaches, the school focused its attention on reducing dropouts. These schools focus and innovate, and real substantive change does not happen quickly.

Another reason for revising the school-level AYP structure is that it may, in a given year, identify a school or a subgroup as failing to meet AYP. This is particularly true in states with low subgroup sizes. This happened at both the O'Hearn and the Mason for one year and served no constructive purpose. A revised school-level accountability system should involve growth-model data that evaluates the performance of a school over time, one that might assume plateaus between innovations. Such a system might reduce pressure on individual schools and states to "game" the system and might foster a greater degree of reciprocity between districts, states, and schools. The ultimate goal of the school-level accountability system should be to foster improvement in schools that serve all students, a system that both holds schools responsible for the education of all children and develops the capacity of schools to be more effective.

3. Support Discretionary Programs That Assist Schools in Developing Their Capacity

Discretionary programs played a major role in the improvement efforts of the schools profiled in this book. These entrepreneurial leaders have used these programs and others to expand the capacity of the teachers and to implement more effective practices. Though most educators know the major features of Title I of NCLB, few, including those profiled, are aware of the discretionary programs it funds. This could portend a political problem if these useful programs are eliminated because of their relative lack of visibility. The federal government should be increasing, not decreasing these programs. Capacity development and the expense involved in innovation are important to school success. However, though it is important to increase these resources, it's important to customize its use to the needs of local school systems and schools. As the Reading First example shows, a school district such as Boston was denied funding due to excessive federal control even though it had a cogent approach that ultimately proved successful in improving literacy performance within the city. Capacity development cannot be micromanaged from Washington.

Capacity development cannot be micromanaged from Washington.

Capacity development takes place within the context of schools, and schools vary tremendously both in need and ability. Therefore, federal discretionary programs need to be administered by those who are more apt to be able to discern these differences—those closer to the schools. For instance, though after-school programs have been shown to be effective in some schools, giving money for after-school programs to a school that is poorly run and has a weak academic program would be a waste. Such a school would likely benefit from a change in leadership, coupled with capacity-building resources that are focused on improving the delivery of the core curriculum first.

4. Adopt the Principles of Universal Design for Learning into ESEA

Universally designed instructional practices support all students. In these three schools, teachers developed instruction based on the principles of universal design for learning, and students in these schools, those with and without disabilities, were reaching high academic standards. Universal design for learning is a process, based on research of how the brain learns, of developing instruction that provides access to a diverse array of learners. There is currently a national movement to promote the use of UDL in classrooms. The National Universal Design for Learning (UDL) Task Force is made up of more than thirty-five national disability and education groups representing higher education and general and special education interests working together. The state of Maryland recently passed a bill to develop a statewide Task Force to Explore the Incorporation of the Principles of Universal Design for Learning into the Education Systems in Maryland. UDL has the power to transform not only the instructional practices but the perceptions of what and how students can learn.

5. Efforts to Connect Teacher Evaluation with Student Performance Must Be Inclusive of All Children and Recognize That Student Success Is Often the Result of Collaborative Effort

The Race to the Top priority given to linking teacher evaluation to student performance should proceed in a way that promotes the type of successful teaching for all children evident in the schools profiled. These systems need to first assure that teachers are accountable for all children and that incentives are not created not to enroll these children. As the Texas system demonstrates, perverse incentives can remove children from the accountability loop and may promote a lowering of expectations for these students.

A further concern is that many of these evaluation systems assume that the success of students is the result of the impact of individual teachers. In the schools profiled, success is the result of collaborative effort. Bill responded to a question concerning how individual awards would affect his school: "Individual awards would be disastrous in my building. How can you determine if the success of children is due to one teacher or another? What about special education teachers working with students in general education classes? Let me use a sports analogy. The Patriots are not successful due to Tom Brady alone. Let me use another example. At BAA, how do you know

"Our success is the result of collaborative effort."

that the math results aren't influenced by the music program? This is why I never nominated a teacher in my school for a Golden Apple award. Our success is the result of collaborative effort."

Though Bill reacted negatively to the concept of individual awards, he did not reject the notion of additional pay for better performance: "I'm with Kim Marshall on this.[6] You could reward teams of teachers for extraordinary performance. Or you could reward even an individual who became expert in a particular area such as technology with the expectation that she would then work more hours to help the others teachers learn how to do it."

6. School Choice Programs Need to Be Fully Inclusive

We have engaged in a major experiment in this country over the past twenty years in school choice: charter schools. Though the evidence concerning the efficacy of these schools is decidedly mixed, the enrollment of children with disabilities has been problematic, with few charters serving children with significant disabilities. Traditional public schools are serving far greater numbers of students with disabilities than are charter schools, particularly students whose disabilities require significant special education services.

Research conducted in a number of major cities bears this out. In San Diego, where close to 10 percent of all students now attend charter schools, and the enrollment of students with disabilities in the district approaches 12 percent, the average enrollment of students with disabilities in nonconversion ("from scratch") charter schools during the 2005–2006 school year was 5.8 percent.[7] For students requiring extensive special education services, the imbalance is even more dismal. For example, during the 2005–2006 school year there were only three children classified as having mental retardation in all San Diego nonconversion charter schools. Traditional schools across the district, meanwhile, educated nearly one thousand students classified as having mental retardation. That same year, nonconversion charter schools in San Diego educated just two students with autism.

The picture is quite similar in Los Angeles. The enrollment of students in charter schools throughout the city is large (approximately 8 percent); the enrollment of students with disabilities across the district averages more than 11 percent, while the enrollment of students with disabilities in independent charter schools averages under 7 percent.[8] As in San Diego, the distribution of disability types within independent Los Angeles charter schools is skewed; for students with disabilities requiring extensive special education services, the likelihood they will be enrolled in independent charter schools is one-fourth that of traditional public schools.

Similar data emerges for charters serving urban areas in Massachusetts (for example, Boston, Worcester, Springfield, Lowell, Lawrence, and others). For the 2006–2007 school year, the percentage of enrolled students with disabilities in traditional urban schools was 19.9 percent ($n =136,587$), while the percentage of enrolled students with disabilities enrolled in urban charter schools was significantly lower, 10.8 percent ($n = 12,562$). Like San Diego and Los Angeles, significantly fewer students who had mental retardation, emotional disturbance, specific learning disabilities, autism, or developmental delays were enrolled in all urban charter schools in Massachusetts in 2006–2007. Several cities' charter schools enrolled zero students who were deaf, who were blind, who had physical or orthopedic impairments, who had multiple disabilities, who had autism, or who had traumatic brain injury.[9]

Though the aggregate data from these three metropolitan areas are discouraging, there are some hopeful trends among some charter schools. In one of the Massachusetts studies, Wilkens found that charters were much more apt to serve students in inclusive settings.[10] Further, charter schools nationwide may be less inclined to label children. Given concerns about the overplacement of minority students in some special education placements, this trend should be further examined. Moreover, there are individual charters that enroll large numbers of students with disabilities who have demonstrated impressive results. Among these are Community Day Charter School in Massachusetts, Democracy Prep Charter School in Harlem, New York City, CHIME Charter Elementary and Middle schools in Los Angeles, and Kipp Tech Valley in Albany, New York. Like the leaders in the schools profiled, Seth Andrews from Democracy Prep in Harlem credits having students with disabilities in his school with making it a better place for all children. Even though he has many more students applying for each seat in his school, Seth actively recruits students with disabilities from New York City's special education District 75. And, in 2010, Democracy Prep was rated the number one middle school in New York City.[11]

It is time for policy makers to directly address the issue of imbalanced enrollment of students with disabilities in charter schools. Though some may have argued in the past that charter schools needed time to get established, and to have flexibility to experiment, not including students with disabilities does not prepare them for this eventuality. In addition, charter schools are now a well-established segment of American education. It is time to make sure that charters and other programs of parental choice, such as the pilot schools profiled in this book, become options for all students, including students with disabilities. Without such insistence, we run the risk of both over-estimating the performance of choice schools while vastly restricting the options of parents of children with disabilities. With few choices, these children will be concentrated in a few schools. This has both civil rights and fiscal implications.

Individuals with Disabilities Education Act

1. Provide Free Representation to Low-Income Parents

Compelling data suggests that IDEA has influenced widespread research-based improvement in educational practice for students with disabilities. Despite these positive effects for students and teachers, it is clear that youth from low-income backgrounds are not showing the same academic post-secondary education and employment gains as students from middle-income and upper-income households. The vast majority of students with disabilities in Boston do not enjoy the type of educational opportunities that are provided the students in the three schools profiled in this book. One likely reason for this may be the failure of the school district to implement practices associated with better outcomes for students with disabilities. Another factor that may explain this disparity between the implementation in districts serving affluent families and those serving low-income students may be the relative lack of access for low-income parents to the due process hearings of IDEA as a means of change in schools.

The due process mechanisms are powerful and, as inclusion cases such as *Holland* and *Oberti* have demonstrated,[12] can have an enormous influence on educational practice. Some might argue that funding to enable poor parents to effectively use due process might, in some places, simply result in more children being placed in private schools. However, the use of due process by more advantaged parents is much more complex than that. Many parents use the threat of hearings to secure greater integration for their children with disabilities, and

The due process mechanisms are powerful and . . . can have an enormous influence on educational practice.

many of those cases never proceed to hearing because districts settle given the LRE imperative in IDEA law.[13] It is undoubtedly that threat that accounts for some of the movement of middle- and upper-income students to more inclusive settings between the two NLTS studies.

Though this proposal might sound utopian in the current political climate, there is a practical way it could be accomplished even in part: fund existing Protection and Advocacy Centers (P&As) to selectively provide representation to parents within the centers' current legislative mandate. These centers, currently funded under the Developmental Disability Act, serve individuals with significant disabilities and their families, and their legislative mandate is to prevent institutionalization and to promote integration. Funding these centers to provide representation would thus increase pressure on districts to provide more effective integration for students with significant disabilities.

The California Protection and Advocacy Center has implemented a model of how this might be implemented. Currently the center funds a skilled educator who works mostly with low-income parents seeking more inclusion for their children within the Los Angeles Unified School District. This educator has worked with scores of parents over the years and has helped promote more inclusive practice within the district.

2. Promote More Strategic Litigation and State-Level Intervention Focused Systemically on Changing Practice

There are two potential sources of intervention in districts serving predominantly poor children that have the potential to promote more systemic reform in the courts and the states. These mechanisms need to be utilized in a way that promotes the development of more schools like the three schools featured here. Though it is my opinion that class action litigation and state oversight has on the whole had a positive impact for students with disabilities, the primary impact has been in assuring implementation of IDEA's procedural elements. Though this is important in that children with disabilities need to be identified and receive services, the overall impact of these litigations on district instructional practice can be questioned.[14] For instance, a number of districts that have been under consent decrees for years, including Boston, Los Angeles, New York, and Washington, D.C., continue to segregate large numbers of students with disabilities at rates that are far above national averages and forces attention on compliance rather than on the capacity of schools to educate students with disabilities to high academic standards in inclusive environments.[15] Though the *Allen* litigation in Boston gave parents some leverage in advocating for the establishment of the O'Hearn, this is the only inclusive school in the system with a direct tie to this litigation.

The focus on procedural compliance by states and courts is understandable, in that IDEA is a law of individual entitlement with prescribed procedural elements. These procedural elements lend themselves to oversight and enforcement (for example, whether the student had his or her evaluation conducted on time or not, whether the student received a service or not). However, it is far more difficult to evaluate whether a child has received a free appropriate public education in the least restrictive environment. Though these are legal requirements, both contain an element of regulatory vagueness that is difficult to assess.

Though both FAPE and LRE are relatively vague, they are central to IDEA and should be viewed as the main entitlements of the law, designed to confer benefits on children. As the research has shown, and these schools demonstrate, integration is associated with better outcomes for students with disabilities, and FAPE ultimately should ensure that the effects of students' disabilities are minimized through the provision of special education services and access to general education with individualized disability accommodations.

Though these are vague concepts, class action litigations have been successful in finding districts and states in noncompliance with these elements, either through court action (for example, *Corey H.*) or through negotiated settlements (for example, *Chandra Smith*). Further, the 2004 reauthorization of IDEA has required states to develop data-based performance plans that may lend themselves to more robust and effective interventions.

To increase the likelihood of districts implementing practices that will improve outcomes, class action litigation or state interventions must focus more closely on educational practices and move away from their current emphasis on procedural compliance through "top-down" bureaucratic intervention. They need to promote changes in educational practice at the school level where children are educated. This is admittedly difficult to do, because each school, like those profiled in this book, is an organization that is semi-autonomous.[16] However, the fact that schools are individual organizations may explain some of the failure of traditional bureaucratic interventions; they are apt to treat all schools as if they are the same. A more effective intervention strategy by either a court or the state would thus highlight schools that have failed to implement effective practices and require improvements. A major element of this effort must focus on capacity development.

3. Support Capacity Development by Expanding Discretionary Programs

Many of the innovative practices employed by the schools profiled were developed under discretionary research and technical assistance programs funded under Part D of IDEA. These include the development of technology that enables screen readers to go from text to speech, behavioral approaches that benefit children with autism, practices in universal design for learning, access to digitized materials through the National Instructional Materials System (NIMAS), as well as effective interventions for students with dyslexia. It is doubtful that these schools would be as effective without these federally supported innovations.

TO SUM UP

- Policy—particularly that involving civil rights—helped give birth to the schools profiled in this book.
- Capacity development programs provided the fuel for innovation. But, ill-conceived policies became an obstacle these schools had to strategize around.
- However, the people in these schools mattered more than policies.
- It appears that policy at its best can reinforce the competent and well intended while shedding a light on those who are failing children.

It is hoped that policy makers can embrace the lessons contained in this book and create a framework of accountability that is inclusive of all children. These schools have demonstrated that when teachers, parents, school leaders, and policy makers work together we can have schools that live up to our ideals of excellence and equity for all children.

Transitioning to a Full Adult Life

Ultimately the goal of inclusive education is preparing students for full adult lives, one with careers, friends, and interests within integrated communities. The schools in this study are doing their part to achieve that goal. The students at Boston Arts Academy (BAA) go on to college at a more than 90 percent rate, and many pursue successful careers in the arts. Many students leaving the Henderson and the Mason go on to selective public and private high schools, and most are well prepared for middle and high schools.

However, many parents of children with more significant intellectual disabilities in the two elementary schools express frustration over the lack of similar high school options for their children in Boston. Though Boston has begun to develop more inclusive options, more needs to be done. Boston is not alone in struggling with developing effective high school and transition programs; many parents throughout the country express disappointment with the lack of effective transition programs. This need not be the case.

Brian also has Down Syndrome and attends Newton North, a large suburban high school that enrolls close to 1900 students. He, along with other students with significant disabilities from Newton North, has spoken to my class at Harvard concerning inclusion and transition from high school to employment and community inclusion. Over the years I have had over twenty students from the school speak and have been so impressed with how effective the school has been in providing individualized inclusive opportunities to a broad array of students with significant disabilities. Students receive both opportunities to be included in general education classrooms as well as intensive

Newton North: A Suburban High School's Success with Inclusion and Transition for Students with Significant Disabilities

A recent article in a suburban paper highlighted the success of one student, Brian Heffernan, who is transitioning from Newton North High School, a large suburban high school that enrolls close to 1,900 students. Brian has Down syndrome. Heffernan has been taking classes in courses like criminology, mass media, and career and life planning at MassBay for the past two years through the school's partnership with the Newton Public Schools. The Inclusive Concurrent Enrollment grant program allows public high school students with severe intellectual disabilities who are between 18 and 22 and have not yet passed the MCAS test the opportunity to take inclusive college courses aligned with a career goal.

"I'm really proud of the career and life planning class," Heffernan said. "It made me think a lot about my career."

During the school year, Heffernan takes public transportation from his house in Newton to the Wellesley Hills MassBay campus, takes general college classes with his peers, and works out after school in the school gym. Last summer, Heffernan was looking for activities to join on campus and noticed that the college didn't have a glee club like his favorite TV show, "Glee," so he researched and sought out the required number of signatures to form his own glee club. Heffernan said his classes at MassBay have helped him decide that one day he wants to have a career in the film or television industry. He's already written a 52-page TV script, "The Heffernan Show," loosely based on "The Cosby Show."[1]

Brian has been successful in advocating that the Massachusetts legislature pass a bill to improve transition services for young people with disabilities. Brian's testimony in front of the legislature may have been critical in passing the bill.

individual and small group support. Each student has as typical a high school experience as possible, tailored to their own needs and interests for four years. At 18 most students with significant disabilities enter the school's transition program, which diverges significantly from their high school experience. Unlike many high schools, where students' significant disabilities continue in virtually the same program (usually segregated) for eight years, the students at

North are provided a variety of transition options that are geared to preparing students for employment and community integration.

In addition to the experience at MassBay, students explore various career options. Another student speaking to my class related that he had tried a placement at a veterinary hospital and discovered he hated working with animals. He found his match at another placement working in a nursing home. "You know I love working with old people." He eventually landed a job doing this work. Further, the program worked to transition him into an apartment with another man with intellectual disabilities where they receive some support from the state office of developmental disabilities. One of the teachers told me that she recently got a call from this young man inviting her to a home-cooked dinner, describing the night as a highlight of her career as a special educator. Another student who had been integrated into the school's vocational education program discovered a talent for baking. She has started a Web-based company to sell cookies that rival Mrs. Field's.

These young people that speak to my class demonstrate the results of years of thoughtful inclusive education, as many have been included since preschool. They are self-assured with a good sense of themselves and speak freely about their disabilities. One student with autism stood in front of my class looking down, rocking back and forth. "I am autistic and that means that you can be looking at me and be smiling and I don't know if you are happy. You have to tell how you feel because I can't read faces. Autism also means I am much better at math than most kids."

It is the authors' hope that the examples of successful inclusive schools described in this book will help other schools implement more effective and equitable practices for all children. We seek a future in which all children with disabilities receive effective inclusive education that enables them to live fulfilling lives. We seek a society in which those who have learned together create a world that truly values diversity, a world where justice and equality is the norm.

Questions for Discussion

CHAPTER 1

- Do these schools seem exceptional to you? In what ways?

- Are you aware of any schools in your district whose missions are deeply connected to the concept of inclusion? Has that commitment made a difference?

- Can you give examples in schools you know where teachers, parents, and administrators have clearly demonstrated their commitment to inclusion?

- Can you think of incidents involving students with disabilities in a school that provided an opportunity for leaders to reinforce the importance of inclusion to the school's mission?

- What should schools do when some staff do not embrace inclusion? How should parents be involved in establishing schools with inclusive missions?

CHAPTER 2

- Is it possible to find principals like these in your community?

- What essential characteristics do these leaders have that have been central to their successes?

- Can you identify a structural change in a school that enhanced inclusive education?

- Can you identify a "human resources" approach in a school that promoted inclusive education?

- Can you identify a symbolic activity that reinforced the importance of inclusive education in a school?

- How has politics been used to promote inclusive education in a school you know?

- How can parents support the development of effective inclusive schools?

- Are you aware of a school with a collaborative culture such as those profiled in the book? How did it come about? Has it made a difference in student outcomes?

CHAPTER 3

- Can schools effectively implement inclusion without questioning existing practices concerning curriculum, instruction, and behavior management?

- Can you think of successful examples where teachers and parents have collaborated and come up with effective innovative approaches to reach students who were previously unsuccessful?

- Can you think of examples where teachers' and parents' successful problem solving concerning students with disabilities have resulted in better practices for other students as well?

- Do special educators always need to be in general education classrooms in order for inclusive education to be successful?

- How could time be built into the schedule of your school to provide for collaborative problem solving?

- Are teachers with specialized expertise needed in order to provide successful inclusive practice?

CHAPTER 4

- How can schools recruit and hire staff who have a strong sense of personal responsibility for student learning?

- How should school leaders foster personal responsibility among teachers for assuring high-quality education for all learners?

- How can your school foster collective responsibility among teachers and administrators for student outcomes?

- How have external accountability systems influenced coherence within your school?

- How can external accountability systems be used to foster coherence in your school?
- How can parents help foster greater coherence in inclusive schools?

CHAPTER 5

- Can you identify an example where universal design for learning (UDL) has improved your life?
- Can you give examples of how universal design principles have enhanced teaching and learning?
- Are students with disabilities in your school encouraged to learn and express what they know in a manner that is most **efficient** for them?
- Is technology necessary to implement UDL?
- Has your district implemented RTI (response to intervention)? How successful has that been? What might make it more successful?
- How can school leaders and parents promote universally designed behavior management approaches that will enable children with behavioral issues to thrive in inclusive environments?
- Can you identify staff development activities that have been particularly effective in your career? What made them effective?

CHAPTER 6

- Can you identify schools in your area that have successfully implemented inclusive education? How have these schools become successful?
- How can school districts support more schools in becoming inclusive?
- How can parents partner with educators to promote more successful inclusion?
- What should educators or parents do when there is a significant disagreement around the education of students with disabilities?
- Can you give examples of how principals, teachers, and parents have worked together to promote inclusive practices?
- What resources outside your school district may be available to promote inclusive education in your district?

CHAPTERS 7–8

- Can you think of examples where federal policies have helped or hindered the implementation of inclusive education?

- Can you identify ways in which the state has helped or hindered inclusive education?

- How effective has district leadership been in promoting inclusive education in your district? What might be done to enhance district leadership on this issue?

- How is federal special education money and Title I money being used in your district or school? How might they be used more effectively?

- How are discretionary grant programs designed to build capacity being used in your district or state? How might they be more effectively used?

- How can school-level staff and parents influence decisions "made from above" to promote more effective inclusive education?

Appendix B

Information on the Research Study

In our research study we sought to identify successful schools that were inclusive of students with a range of disabilities and had strong academic outcomes for both students with and those without disabilities. We selected schools based on the following criteria:

1. Schools had to have higher large-scale test scores for students with disabilities as well as those without disabilities than what would be predicted by socioeconomic class, race, and disability. These test scores had to have been consistently high for at least three years. We sought schools that, in the case of high schools, had low dropout rates, and for all levels, schools with low suspension and expulsion rates.

2. The schools had to be inclusive of students with disabilities. Our functional definition of *inclusive* required that schools educated children with disabilities predominately in general education classrooms, with no children placed in separate special education classrooms for the majority of the day. We also sought evidence that the schools were intentionally inclusive through school mission statements and school websites.

3. We sought schools that enrolled a broad range of students with disabilities. A school was considered enrolling a broad range of students if it enrolled students with both high-incidence disabilities like dyslexia and low-incidence disabilities, such as deafness, intellectual or developmental disability, or autism, that occur in less than 1 percent of the population.

Applying these criteria to a broad array of Boston schools yielded five schools. One was dropped as a potential site because the principal was new and the school was focused on becoming a pilot school; another, a large comprehensive high school, was dropped because it was divided into three small schools as a part of an overall high school reform initiative in the district. The final sample included two elementary schools, the Patrick O'Hearn[1] (O'Hearn) and the Samuel Mason (Mason), and one high school, the Boston Arts Academy (BAA), all located in the city of Boston.

SCHOOL ACADEMIC DATA

Each school had better than district average passing rates on the Massachusetts Comprehensive Assessment System (MCAS), the state's large-scale assessment. As shown in Tables B.1 and B.2, the percentage of students who passed the MCAS in English language arts (ELA) and mathematics in the fourth and the tenth grades were higher in these schools than they were in the district as a whole, and in some cases, the passing rates were higher than state averages.[2] Schools in Massachusetts are prohibited from reporting on subgroups with fewer than ten students, and there were fewer than ten students with disabilities taking the fourth grade ELA MCAS at both the O'Hearn and the Mason in 2005 and fewer than ten students with disabilities taking the fourth grade math MCAS at the Mason in 2005. The data closest to

Table B.1 2005 MCAS English Language Arts Scores

Fourth Grade		All Students	Students with Disabilities
	Massachusetts	90	69
	Boston	73	42
	Patrick O'Hearn	80	NA*
	Samuel Mason	92	NA*
Tenth Grade			
	Massachusetts	89	69
	Boston	73	39
	Boston Arts Academy	92	83

*According to state regulations, scores not available for fewer than ten students with disabilities.
Source: Massachusetts Department of Elementary and Secondary Education, 2005

Table B.2 2005 MCAS Mathematics Scores

Fourth Grade		All Students	Students with Disabilities
	Massachusetts	84	62
	Boston	68	41
	Patrick O'Hearn	78	71
	Samuel Mason	86	NA*
Tenth Grade			
	Massachusetts	85	61
	Boston	67	33
	Boston Arts Academy	80	83

*According to state regulations, scores not available for fewer than ten students with disabilities.
Source: Massachusetts Department of Elementary and Secondary Education, 2005

2005 for which there are scores for these subtests are shown in Tables B.3 and B.4. Table B.3 compares the percentage of students who passed the ELA MCAS for students with disabilities at the O'Hearn in 2004 and the Mason in 2006 with both district and state rates. In both cases, the percentage of students with disabilities who passed the English language arts MCAS in the fourth grade were higher than the percentage of students with disabilities passing the ELA MCAS in the district, and for the Mason, the percentage of students with disabilities passing was higher than that of the state. Table B.4 compares passing rates for students with disabilities on the math MCAS at the Mason in 2006 with both district and state scores. Once again, the rates for students at the Mason were higher those of the district and the state.

Table B.3 2004 and 2006 MCAS ELA Scores for Students with Disabilities

Fourth Grade		Students with Disabilities
	Massachusetts (2004)	72
	Boston (2004)	46
	Patrick O'Hearn (2004)	50
Fourth Grade		
	Massachusetts (2006)	64
	Boston (2006)	41
	Samuel Mason (2006)	100

Source: Massachusetts Department of Elementary and Secondary Education, 2004 and 2006

Table B.4   2006 MCAS Math Scores for Students with Disabilities at the Mason

Fourth Grade	Students with Disabilities
Massachusetts	61
Boston	47
Samuel Mason	90

Source: Massachusetts Department of Elementary and Secondary Education, 2006

In these schools, populations of students with disabilities ranged from the national average (12 percent at the high school) to higher than the national average (20 percent and 34 percent at the elementary schools).[3] They enrolled students with high- to low-incidence disabilities, meaning that students in these schools were classified with, for example, more common disabilities such as learning disabilities and serious emotional disturbances, but also less common disabilities such as deafness, developmental disabilities, and autism. More specifically, each school enrolled students with specific learning disabilities and emotional disabilities, considered high-incidence disabilities, as well as students with the low-incidence disability mental retardation. The O'Hearn and Mason also enrolled students with autism, and BAA enrolled students who were deaf or hard of hearing.

DEMOGRAPHICS

We examined data from these schools for racial disproportionality in special education—that is, we looked to see whether these schools over-represented or under-represented students in disability categories by race. Currently, and historically, students of color, particularly African American students, are over-represented in special education categories.[4] As evidenced in Table B.5, we found no significant disproportionate representation in these schools.[5] In addition, while not statistically significant, all three schools enrolled a higher percentage of White students than of students of color who received special education services, a trend quite the opposite from the disproportion found in national data. This may be due to the fact that Boston is a district that allows for a good deal of

Table B.5 School Demographics (percentages)

	African American	Asian	Hispanic	White	Native American	Native Hawaiian, Pacific Islander	Multi-Race, Non-Hispanic
Boston	42.8	8.5	33.4	13.6	0.5	0.1	1.1
Patrick O'Hearn	47.1	8.5	4.9	27.8	5.4	0	6.3
Samuel Mason	63.7	0	25.6	7.9	0.5	0	2.3
Boston Arts Academy	43.1	3.5	29.1	20.6	0.3	0	3.5

Source: Massachusetts Department of Elementary and Secondary Education, 2005

parent choice and thus may reflect the impact of "social capital" among White parents. (See Chapter Five.) At both the Mason and the O'Hearn, a lower percentage of African American students received special education services than did African American students in the general school population, and at both the Mason and BAA, a lower percentage of Hispanic students received special education services than did Hispanic students in the general school population. That is, there does not appear to be a problem of over-placement of minority students in special education at these schools. The sensitivity of the leaders of the schools to these issues and the way in which they have designed their schools may have had an influence on this. (See Chapter Two.)

The suspension rates of BAA (2.5 percent), Mason (0.5 percent), and the O'Hearn (0.4) were considerably lower than those of both the district (7.6 percent) and the state (6.0 percent).[6] The dropout rates for Boston Arts Academy (4.6 percent) were lower than the district average (7.7 percent), yet slightly higher than the state average (3.8 percent).[7]

In these schools, the education of students with disabilities occurred predominantly in their age-appropriate general education classes. Special education classes existed only for the provision of some of the related services, such as speech and language services or occupational therapy, and in the high school, in the learning center where students enrolled for no more than one period per day.

DATA COLLECTION AND ANALYSIS

Data was collected during the 2006–2007 and 2007–2008 school years, primarily through interviews, observations, and document reviews. Interviews were conducted with nineteen teachers, four principals,[8] three school-based special education leaders, twenty-four parents, and the superintendent of Boston public schools. Interviews were conducted with a semi-structured protocol. Interviews ranged from one to five hours, with each session lasting approximately one hour. Follow-up conversations with school leaders were conducted to verify various data. We chose to focus our efforts on targeted grades for greater depth in data collection. In the two elementary schools, we looked carefully at the first and fourth grades, and in the high school, the ninth grade. Certification of teachers included special education, elementary education, secondary English, math, art, and music. The majority of teachers interviewed were either dually certified in one general education area and special education or were working toward this dual certification. Each of these schools was independently encouraging teachers to become dually certified, so we believe the teaching populations we interviewed were roughly similar to the faculties as a whole. Combining teachers and administrators, we interviewed with twenty-two women and four men; thirteen were White, four African American, three Latino, and one Asian. All teachers and school-level special education leaders were promised anonymity, and for them, we use pseudonyms. Principals allowed us to report their actual names as well as their schools' names.

Data collection also included twenty-nine direct observations in first, fourth, and ninth grade classrooms, in leadership meetings, and in special education meetings such as special education evaluations and annual reviews. Observations provided data that supported or contradicted interview data, providing us with findings that were more robust. We also observed three of the four principals speak publicly about their schools to audiences of educators. When possible, two members of the research team, which included the authors, two doctoral students, two undergraduate students, and one special education teacher, conducted classroom observations. We also examined quantitative data on achievement scores, disability classification, placement, and graduation, which allowed us to support or refute findings as they emerged. Finally, we collected school documents, such as mission statements and codes of conduct, in print and on the Web. In the case of the Mason, we used data from two case studies of the school conducted by Harvard faculty.[9]

Our data analysis began with coding all interviews and observations, searching for themes raised by specific questions in the interview protocols and ideas and concepts that emerged from the interviews, observations, quantitative data, and documents. Once initial coding was complete, we developed case studies of each school, identifying individual schools' values and practices. We then employed the analytic strategy of explanation building,[10] in which we examined data across schools and participant groups within the schools to identify similarities and differences. Our data were analyzed by codes and memos with the support of NVIVO, a computer program used for qualitative data analysis. The research team developed all codes, and more than one team member coded each transcript. We presented our findings to the interviewed principals and school-level special education leaders and university colleagues before completing this final analysis. The responsibility for the findings in this book, however, lies solely with the authors.

Finally, while not a quantifiable variable, these schools each had a reputation for effectively serving students with disabilities among parents of students with disabilities and among local educators. We ascertained this through discussions with educators and parents as well as through media reports. We hoped to understand why these schools were held in high regard, and further, we believed that by understanding the underlying reasons for their reputations, we might be able to find the less obvious values and practices for which we were searching.

THEORETICAL FRAMEWORKS AND ANALYSIS

To analyze these pathways and bring structure to our data analysis, we utilized the organizational theoretical framework developed by Bolman and Deal, the four frames of leadership.[11] Bolman and Deal contend that effective and sustainable change occurs only when leaders address several fronts or frames concurrently: the symbolic frame, the structural frame, the political frame, and the human resource frame. The symbolic frame addresses the values and culture of the organization. The structural frame attends to the organization of the institution, its resources, and policies. The political frame addresses how the organization deals with power, and the human resource frame deals with how individuals within the organization are treated, supported, and developed. Our analysis found strong evidence that the leadership in these schools attended to all four frames and developed school-level teacher leaders who also attended to the four frames. Though utilizing widely varying strategies, each frame received considerable attention by leaders and teachers in the schools, reinforcing the utility of Bowman and Deal's framework.

Thomas Skrtic

We were greatly influenced by Skrtic's work in conducting this study as well as in our teaching. In the interest of full disclosure, both Thomas Hehir and Lauren Katzman included his work in edited books each has published, with Hehir having originally solicited Skrtic's article for the *Harvard Educational Review*.[12] We used this theoretical framework to help analyze our data, and indeed we found much support for his theory within the practices of these schools. (See Chapter Three.)

However, though we admire Skrtic's work, we have found using his articles in courses to be challenging due to the density of his writing and the prior knowledge required of the reader to understand the text. Therefore, we have to "deconstruct" Skrtic to make it accessible to most of our students. We make the same assumption of readers of this book, so will attempt to summarize the main argument Skrtic developed in his 1991 seminal piece.[13]

First, using an extensive review of organizational theory and research, Skrtic concludes that schools are essentially professional bureaucracies. That is, from a structural frame of reference, school systems and schools are bureaucratically organized entities in which professionals, mostly teachers, implement standard programs. Schools are not true machine bureaucracies because these structures are only effective where work is relatively simple and certain. However, the work of educating children is relatively complex and uncertain. As a result, traditional schools are organized into professional bureaucracies, where work is divided among specialists, grade-level teachers, and support staff, who are trained to do their job for a group of assigned students. The third grade teacher, for example, is a specialist in educating eight-year-olds in the third grade curriculum. The special education teacher is an expert in educating children with a particular type of disability who may have difficulty fitting into the standard program. These professionals are overseen by a bureaucracy that seeks to standardize the preparation of these professionals and to supervise the fidelity with which they deliver their assigned roles.

However, as it relates to the education of students with disabilities and other students who do not prosper in the standard program, problems arises because professionals have a finite repertoire within their standard programs. There is a room for some adjustment, but not enough for students who fall outside the margins, as many students with disabilities do. Without this room for adjustment, there are perceived limited choices. According to Skrtic, "Teachers, whether in regular or special class environments, cannot escape the necessary choice between higher means [that is, maximizing mean performance by concentrating resources on the most able learners] and narrower variances [that is, minimizing group variance by concentrating resources on the least able learners] as long as resources are scarce and students differ."[14]

This fundamental dilemma plays out within professional bureaucracies through the establishment of the "decoupled unit" or the special class or resource room. The establishment of these special programs is consistent with the fundamental structure of the professional bureaucracy and thus, according to Skrtic, buffers the organization from change. However, this response fails to meet the needs of many children with disabilities in that they tend not to be truly individualized and do not promote integration. Students who do not fit must be removed rather than adjusting the program to meet the students' needs.

The framers of the Individuals with Disabilities Education Act (IDEA) envisioned the need to create custom individualized program for students with disabilities through requirements for individualized education programs, or IEPs. Further they recognized the desirability of integration through the incorporation of the Least Restrictive Environment (LRE) provisions. Added to this was the force to spur implementation through the due process options given to parents, allowing them to look to the law to uphold these standards. However, Skrtic would contend that this bureaucratic approach, using rules and pressure, was inadequate to promote true equity for students with disabilities and failed because it was naive in its inability to

> *If we do not address fundamental questions about schools as organizations, they will continue to perpetuate inequity.*

recognize the organizational reality of traditional schools. Indeed the ubiquity and growth of resource rooms and special classes in response to the passage of the original IDEA, P.L. 94142, lends considerable credence to Skrtic's theoretical framework.

Skrtic posits that the creation of special programs reflects organizational failure. If we do not address fundamental questions about schools as organizations, they will continue to perpetuate inequity.

> *Given the inevitability of human diversity, a professional bureaucracy can do nothing but create students who do not fit the system. In a professional bureaucracy all forms of tracking—curriculum tracking and in-class ability grouping in general education, as well as self-contained and resource classrooms in special, compensatory, remedial, and gifted education—are organizational pathologies created by specialization and professionalization and compounded by rationalization and formalization.[15]*

Skrtic proposes that schools evolve into problem-solving organizations in which the fundamental structure of the classroom is replaced with more flexible structures that are more adhocratic in nature or focused on problem-solving—organizations in which educators customize programs for individual students. For Skrtic, in a problem-solving organization, disability becomes an opportunity to innovate and improve. "Regardless of its causes and its extent, student diversity is not a liability in a problem-solving organization; it is an asset, an enduring uncertainty, and thus the driving force behind innovation, growth of knowledge, and progress."[16]

Richard Elmore

In addition to the early work of Skrtic, we have been influenced by more contemporary work in school reform and improvement, particularly that of Richard Elmore. Over two-plus decades, Elmore has sought to examine how policy plays out at the classroom and school level. His years of research and thinking on this fundamental problem of educational policy are summarized in his book, *School Reform from the Inside Out: Policy, Practice and Performance.* His thesis is best expressed, "The problems of the system are the problems of the smallest unit."[17] The guiding principle behind his career of research and writing is that for school reform to work, it must happen from the "inside out." Elmore's work on school-level interpretations of accountability helped us analyze how the schools studied all met the standards of the MCAS, yet none had put the MCAS at the forefront of their work. (See Chapter Four.)

In "When Accountability Knocks, Will Anyone Answer," Elmore et al. spoke to educators in twenty diverse schools (traditional public, charter, and parochial) in two metropolitan areas (one on the west coast and the other on the east) to ascertain how accountability influenced their daily work.[18] They used as their conceptual framework a theory drawn from the work of R. B. Wagner. Elmore posited how a school would react to external accountability requirements by examining a set of relationships among three factors: "individual conceptions of responsibility; shared expectations among school participants and stakeholders; and internal and external accountability mechanisms."[19] As Elmore explained, "An individual school's conception of accountability, in our view, grows from the relationship among these three factors."[20]

Responsibility in this framework is individual and refers to the educators' sense of personal responsibility for their work. Largely stemming from personal values and experience and influenced by their experience with others, educators may have strong beliefs about their work, about the capacity of their students and their responsibility toward parents and toward one another. Assuming that teachers largely work in isolation, Elmore posits, "We assume that organizational and external influences may play a part in teachers' perception of role, but that individual values are certainly influential."[21]

Expectations in this framework are collective in nature and are characterized by "shared norms and values of school participants developed in order to get the work of the school done."[22] Examples of collective expectations include the responsibility of teachers at one grade level to prepare students for successive grade levels, student discipline, and the school values that students are expected to reflect. Expectations constitute beliefs about the behavior of others, though individuals may include themselves. These expectations may be held by all parties or by groups within the school, such as teachers who teach the same grade or subject. However, the fact that expectations are shared does not mean they reflect a consensus. Teachers in these schools have deeply held values of personal responsibility coupled with a strong sense of responsibility to one another.

Elmore et al. define accountability mechanisms as the ways, both formal and informal, by which educators give account for their actions to someone in a position of authority inside or outside the school.[23] An example of internal accountability may be a principal requiring teachers to provide copies of lesson plans or to display examples of student work on a bulletin board. External accountability increasingly involves assessment of student progress through district- or state-administered standardized tests. Other examples include external oversight of curriculum and dropout rates as well as state monitoring of regulatory compliance. Accountability mechanisms vary in terms of consequences: some have relatively low stakes, such as principal disapproval; others have high stakes, such those taking place today when teachers and principals are losing their jobs due to the failure of their schools to make adequate yearly progress under NCLB.

Putting It All Together

Putting this all together, Elmore et al. describe their working theory. "In our working theory, responsibility, expectations, and accountability operate in a close mutual reciprocal relationship with each other, and this relationship takes a variety of forms in different schools. This relationship is captured in Figure 1 [presented here as Figure B.1]. Individual conceptions of responsibility may influence collective expectations or, alternatively, collective expectations influence individual conceptions of responsibility.

Responsibility, expectations, and accountability operate in a close mutual reciprocal relationship with each other.

Similarly, individual conceptions of collective expectations may influence formal or informal accountability mechanisms, or vice versa."[24] According to this theory, they posit that the power of internal accountability mechanisms is

Figure B.1   Interactions and Alignment

Source: Elmore, "School Reform from the Inside Out." p. 141

greatly enhanced when they are aligned with individual responsibility and collective expectations. They further assert that the efficacy of external accountability mechanisms are mediated by internal alignment. The schools' response to an external mechanism would, they assume, depend on the degree of alignment between the purposes of the external mechanism and the internal norms of the school.

Elmore et al. present a series of case studies that place schools within this Venn diagram shown in Figure B.1. One school, for instance, had teachers with a strong sense of individual responsibility, with very little with respect to collective expectations and with weak internal accountability mechanisms. Such a school is atomized and would likely respond to external accountability in a number of ways largely determined by individualized reactions, not by collective action. In such a school, external policy mechanisms such as NCLB would unlikely produce their intended effect.

Using Elmore's Concepts to Analyze Our Data

We found these concepts of individual responsibility, shared expectations, and internal accountability useful in analyzing our data. Also, the ways in which schools dealt with external accountability mechanisms is illuminating. Not only was this framework useful, but our study provides additional evidence that supports this theoretical framework.

All three schools studied were tightly coherent on all three dimensions of Elmore's model. Teachers and administrators had a deep sense of responsibility for providing high-quality education for all students. Teachers had remarkably similar values as they related to their students, their rights, and their capabilities. The "default culture" described by Elmore of externalizing the problems of educating a diverse population of largely low-income students to their backgrounds and communities was not evident in any of our interviews or our observations.

The same was true of disability. As many of the quotes in the book indicate, disability, like family background or poverty, was never cited as a reason that children could not learn; quite the opposite was true.

The pilot school described in Elmore's study (see the Turtle Haven case study in Chapter Four) did not experience a good deal of influence from external accountability mechanisms due to its newness and because pilot schools at the time were freed of much central office involvement. This was not the case for any of the schools in our study, even though two are pilots. This, we believe, was due to the increasing presence of NCLB in the lives of these schools. When Elmore et al. conducted their research, NCLB had yet to be fully implemented. Each of these schools had experienced the impact of NCLB to varying degrees. And, as Elmore would predict, the coherence of these schools around responsibility, expectations, and internal accountability had positioned them well to deal with this external presence. The fact that these schools valued and produced high academic performance has also aligned the goals of NCLB with that of the schools, which has minimized its potential disruptive effect.

Other external accountability influences that appear to have an impact on these schools have to do with special education. As we described in Chapter Two, these leaders have had to at times deal with less-than-supportive central office special education leaders. However, given the schools' strong results and popularity with parents and general education leadership, this potentially negative influence has been checked. However, another potentially more powerful external mechanism, special education law with its individual due process rights, emerged in our study, particularly at the O'Hearn.

TO SUM UP

The frameworks developed by Skrtic and Elmore used to analyze our data proved useful. They helped us see the commonalities of practices that were likely behind the success of these schools. Though these schools have all developed independently, they are remarkably similar when viewed from the perspective of organizational theory developed by Skrtic and Elmore.

- The schools have developed adhocratic cultures and structures that have enabled them to better educate highly diverse populations.

- The presence of students with disabilities who diverge significantly from their age-level peers in academic performance, communication mode, or behavior has made it necessary for these schools to fundamentally question assumptions inherent in traditional professional bureaucracies of schools.

- Students with significant disabilities have provided opportunities to develop new approaches to benefit all children.

- These are schools with high-level coherence with closely aligned responsibility, expectations, and internal accountability. This has positioned them well to deal with external accountability mechanisms such as those employed by NCLB and IDEA.

NOTES

PREFACE: ON ABLEISM

1. Johnson, Akilah. Anthony Curioso: A Disabled Student with Limitless Abilities. *Boston Globe,* April 4, 2011. Video available at: http://www.boston.com/news /local/breaking_news/2011/04/inside_scoop_an.html
2. Hehir, Thomas. *New Directions in Special Education: Eliminating Ableism in Policy and Practice.* Cambridge, MA: Harvard Education Press, 2005.
3. Overboe, James. "Difference" in Itself: Validating Disabled People's Lived Experience. *Body Society,* December 1999, 5(4), 17–29; Weeber, J. E. What Could I Know of Racism? *Journal of Counseling and Development,* 1999, 77(1), 20–23.
4. Rauscher, L., and McClintock, M. Abelism Curriculum Design. In M. Adams, L. A. Bell, and P. Griffin (eds.), *Teaching for Diversity and Social Justice* (p. 198). New York: Routledge, 1997.
5. Smith, Greg. Backtalk: The Brother in the Wheelchair. *Essence,* July 20, 2001, p. 162.
6. Hehir, Thomas. Eliminating Ableism in Education. *Harvard Educational Review,* Spring 2002, 72(1), p 3.
7. Ferguson, P. M., and Asch, A. Lessons from Life: Personal and Parental Perspectives on School, Childhood and Disability. In D. Biklen, D. Ferguson, and A. Ford (eds.), *Schooling and Disability: Eighty-Eighth Yearbook of the National Society for the Study of Education: Part II* (pp. 108–141). Chicago: University of Chicago Press, 1989; Rousso, H. Fostering Healthy Self-Esteem: Part One. *Exceptional Parent,* 1984, 14(8), 9–14; Hehir, *New Directions in Special Education.*
8. Hehir, Thomas. Charters: Students with Disabilities Need Not Apply? *Education Week,* January 27, 2010, 29(19), 18–21.
9. Grindal, Todd, Eidelman, Hadas, Marcell, Elizabeth, and Hehir, Thomas. *A Review of Special Education in the Houston Independent School District.* Cambridge, MA: Thomas Hehir & Associates, 2011.

10. Wagner, M., Newman, L., Cameto, R., and Levine, P. (2005). *Changes over Time in the Early Postschool Outcomes of Youth with Disabilities. A Report of findings from the National Longitudinal Transition Study (NLTS) and the National Longitudinal Transition Study-2 (NLTS-2).* Menlo Park, CA: SRI International.

11. Ferguson and Asch, Lessons from Life, p. 118.

INTRODUCTION

1. Patton, M. Q. *Qualitative Research and Evaluation Methods,* 3rd ed. Thousand Oaks, CA: Sage, 2002.

2. The NLTS-2 conceptual framework and research questions are designed to allow analyses of the relationships between NLTS-2 data and data generated by Office of Special Education Programs' (OSEP) Special Education Elementary Longitudinal Study (SEELS). This six-year study, following a group of students in special education (six to twelve years old as of September 1, 1999), assessed the experiences and achievements of students as they transitioned from elementary to middle and middle to high school. The overlap of NLTS-2 and SEELS students in high school permit linkage of the early school factors measured in SEELS with postschool experiences measured in NLTS2. Available at: http://www.seels.net/grindex.html

3. Wagner, M. The Early Post-High-School Years for Youth with Disabilities. In M. Wagner, L. Newman, R. Cameto, N. Garza, and P. Levine, *After High School: A First Look at the Postschool Experiences of Youth with Disabilities. A Report from the National Longitudinal Transition Study-2 (NLTS-2)* (pp. 1–6). Menlo Park, CA: SRI International, 2005. Available at: http://www.nlts2.org/reports/2005_04/index.html

4. Ibid.

5. National Longitudinal Transition Study-2 (NLTS-2), U.S. Department of Education, Office of Special Education Programs (OSEP 2001–2011) and Institute of Education Sciences (IES 2000–2011), is a follow-up of the original National Longitudinal Transition Study. The original NLTS was designed and conducted by SRI International for OSEP from 1985 through 1993. Available at: http://www.nlts2.org/

6. Wagner et al., *After High School.*

7. Originally named the Patrick O'Hearn Elementary, its name was changed to the William T. Henderson Elementary Inclusion School in 2009, after Bill Henderson's retirement.

8. Bolman, L., and Deal, T. *Reframing Organizations: Artistry, Choice and Leadership*. San Francisco: Jossey-Bass, 1997, pp. 3–17, 280–317.
9. Rose, D., and Meyer, A. *Teaching Every Student in the Digital Age: Universal Design for Learning*. Alexandria, VA: Association for Supervision and Curriculum Development, 2002; Hehir, Thomas. *New Directions in Special Education: Eliminating Ableism in Policy and Practice*. Cambridge, MA: Harvard Education Press, 2005.

CHAPTER 1: THE SCHOOLS

1. The ELA MCAS data for students with disabilities was not available for the 2004–2005 school year. Schools in Massachusetts are prohibited from reporting on subgroups with fewer than ten students, and there were fewer than ten students with disabilities taking the fourth grade ELA MCAS at the O'Hearn during that time. We used the data closest to the previous year for which there are scores (2003–2004). These data show that the percentage of students with disabilities who passed the English language arts MCAS in the fourth grade was higher than the percentage of students with disabilities passing the ELA MCAS in the district. (See Table B.1.)
2. Hassel, Emily. *Professional Development: Learning from the Best*. Oak Brook, IL: North Central Regional Educational Laboratory (NCREL), 1999, pp. 81–82. Available at: http://www.ncrel.org
3. Passing indicates that students met the MCAS standards of Proficient, Advanced, or Needs Improvement. The only other category is Warning/Failing.
4. See note 2.
5. The ProArts Consortium includes Berklee College of Music, Boston Architectural Center, Boston Conservatory, Emerson College, Massachusetts College of Art, and School of the Museum of Fine Arts.

CHAPTER 2: THE LEADERS

1. Shapiro, Joseph P. *No Pity: People with Disabilities Forging a New Civil Rights Movement*. New York: Random House, 1993.
2. Henderson, Bill. Champions of Inclusion: Making the Extraordinary Ordinary. *International Journal of Whole Schooling*, 2007, 3(1), 7–12. (ERIC: EJ847470)
3. Nathan, Linda. *The Hardest Questions Aren't on the Test: Lessons from an Innovative Urban School*. Boston: Beacon Press, 2009.

4. Bolman, L., and Deal, T. *Reframing Organizations: Artistry, Choice and Leadership*. San Francisco: Jossey-Bass, 1997, pp. 3–17, 280–293, 294–317.

5. O'Day, J. Complexity, Accountability, and School Improvement. *Harvard Educational Review,* Fall 2002, 72(3), 293–329.

6. Elmore, Richard F. *School Reform from the Inside Out: Policy, Practice, and Performance.* Cambridge, MA: Harvard Education Press, 2004.

7. Sataline, Suzanne. A Matter of Principal. *Boston Globe,* January 30, 2005. http://www.boston.com/news/education/k_12/articles/2005/01/30/a_matter_of_principal/

8. Singleton, Glenn Eric, and Linton, Curtis. *Courageous Conversations About Race: A Field Guide for Achieving Equity in Schools.* Thousand Oaks, CA: Corwin Press, 2006.

9. Kozol Jonathan, The Shame of the Nation: The Restoration of Apartheid in Schooling in America, Random House, 2005.

CHAPTER 3: COLLABORATIVE PROBLEM-SOLVING ORGANIZATIONS

1. Bolman, L., and Deal, T. (1997). *Reframing Organizations: Artistry, Choice and Leadership.* San Francisco: Jossey-Bass.

2. Skrtic, T. M. The Special Education Paradox: Equity as the Way to Excellence. In T. Hehir and T. Latus (eds.), *Special Education at the Century's End: Evolution of Theory and Practice Since 1970.* Cambridge, MA: Harvard Education Press, 1992, pp. 203–372. (Originally published in *Harvard Educational Review,* 1991, 61(2), 148–206)

3. Ibid.

4. Ibid., p. 207.

5. Tyack, David, and Cuban, Larry. *Tinkering Toward Utopia: A Century of Public School Reform.* Cambridge, MA: Harvard University Press, 1995.

6. Skrtic, Special Education Paradox, p. 238.

7. Grindal, Todd, Eidelman, Hadas, Marcell, Elizabeth, and Hehir, Thomas. *A Review of Special Education in the Houston Independent School District.* Cambridge, MA: Thomas Hehir & Associates, 2011.

8. Skrtic, Special Education Paradox, p. 231.

9. Ibid., p. 238.

10. Tyack and Cuban, *Tinkering Toward Utopia.*

11. Shaywitz, S. *Overcoming Dyslexia: A New and Complete Science-Based Program for Reading Problems at Any Level.* New York: Knopf, 2003; Rose D., and Meyer, A.

The Universally Designed Classroom: Accessible Curriculum and Digital Technologies. Cambridge, MA: Harvard Education Press, 2005.

12. The following description of the summary reading requirements is taken from the school's website:

> *Rising Sophomores*
> *The theme for rising Sophomores is JOURNEYS*
> *GROUP DISCUSSION BOOK: Read one book from the Literature for Discussion list.*
> *SECOND BOOK: Read a second book of your choice from the list below or a book by an author in this booklet.*
> *OPEN HONORS: Read an additional two books from any of the lists in this booklet for Open Honors credit.*
> *PRODUCTS DUE SEPT 14, 2010*
>
> - *Write one essay (2–3 pages, typed, double-spaced) addressing the theme of JOURNEYS in all of the books. Answer these questions:*
> - *What journeys (to new places or through challenges) do the characters in these two/four books undertake? How can you connect your own personal journeys to those of the characters in these two/four books?*
> - *Choose one character from one of the books and create an identity box for that character.*

13. Faggella-Luby, M. N., and Deshler, Donald D. Reading Comprehension in Adolescents with LD: What We Know; What We Need to Learn. *Learning Disabilities Research and Practice*, May 2008, 23(2), 70–78.

14. Otterman, Sharon. Diversity Debate Convulses Elite High School. *New York Times*, August 4, 2010. Available at: http://www.nytimes.com/2010/08/05/nyregion/05hunter.html

15. Ibid.

CHAPTER 4: RELATIONSHIPS, SCHOOL CULTURE, AND ACCOUNTABILITY

1. Elmore, Richard F. *School Reform from the Inside Out: Policy, Practice, and Performance.* Cambridge, MA: Harvard Education Press, 2004.

2. Ibid., p. 3.

3. Abelmann, Charles, Elmore, Richard, Even, Johanne, and Kenyon, Susan. When Accountability Knocks, Will Anyone Answer? Philadelphia: CPRE Publications, 1999. (ERIC: ED428463)

4. Wagner, R. B. *Accountability in Education: A Philosophical Inquiry*. New York: Routledge, 1989, p. ___

5. Abelmann, Elmore, et al., When Accountability Knocks, p. 139.

6. Ibid.

7. Ibid.

8. Ibid., p. 182.

9. Ibid., p. 193.

10. Ibid., p. 139.

11. Ibid.

12. Boudett, Kathryn Parker, City, Elizabeth A., and Murnane, Richard J. *Data Wise: A Step-by-Step Guide to Using Assessment Results to Improve Teaching and Learning*. Cambridge, MA: Harvard Education Press, 2005.

13. Finn, Chester E., Rotherham, Andrew J., and Hokasan, Jr., Charles R. Rethinking Special Education for a New Century. Washington, D.C.: Thomas B. Fordham Institute. May 1, 2001. Available at: http://www.edexcellence.net/publications-issues/special-ed.html

CHAPTER 5: UNIVERSALLY DESIGNED SCHOOLS

1. Lyon, G. Reid et al. Rethinking Learning Disabilities. *Rethinking Special Education for a New Century*. Washington, D.C.: Thomas B. Fordham Foundation and the Progressive Policy Institute, 2001, pp. 259–287; Shaywitz, S. *Overcoming Dyslexia: A New and Complete Science-Based Program for Reading Problems at Any Level*. New York: Knopf, 2003.

2. Snow, C. E., Burns, S., and Griffin, P. (Eds.). *Preventing Reading Difficulties in Young Children*. Washington, DC: National Academy Press, 1998.

3. Sugai, G., and Horner, R. H. The Evolution of Discipline Practices: School-Wide Positive Behavior Supports. In J. Luirelli and C. Diament (eds.), *Behavior Psychology in the Schools* (pp. 23–50). Binghamton, NY: Haworth, 2002.

4. Rose, D., and Meyer, A. *Teaching Every Student in the Digital Age: Universal Design for Learning*. Alexandria, VA: Association for Supervision and Curriculum Development, 2002; Hehir, Thomas. *New Directions in Special Education: Eliminating Ableism in Policy and Practice*. Cambridge, MA: Harvard Education Press, 2005.

5. Rose and Meyer, *Teaching Every Student in the Digital Age,* p. 11.

6. Ibid., p. v.

7. Ibid., p. 75.

8. Fletcher, Jack M., and Vaughn, Sharon. Response to Intervention: Preventing and Remediating Difficulties. *Child Development Practices,* April 2009, 3(1), p. 35

9. *Boston Arts Academy Handbook.* Boston: Boston Arts Academy, 2007, pp. 71–74.

10. Ibid., 71.

CHAPTER 6: MAKING SCHOOLS MORE INCLUSIVE

1. Hehir, Thomas. *New Directions in Special Education: Eliminating Ableism in Policy and Practice.* Cambridge, MA: Harvard Education Press, 2005.

2. Giangreco, M., Edelman, S., Luiselli, T., and MacFarland, S. Helping or Hovering? Effects of Instructional Assistant Proximity on Students with Disabilities. *Exceptional Children,* 1997, 64(1), 7–18.

3. Rose D., and Meyer, A. *The Universally Designed Classroom: Accessible Curriculum and Digital Technologies.* Cambridge, MA: Harvard Education Press, 2005; Hehir, *New Directions in Special Education.*

4. Will, Madeline. Educating Children with Learning Problems: A Shared Responsibility. *Exceptional Children,* 1986, 52, 411–415.

5. *Samuel W. Mason Elementary School,* 1999. This case was prepared by Linda Greyser from an interview of Mary Russo conducted by James Honan and Tony Wagner. It was written for the Harvard Institute for School Leadership: Effective Strategies for School Reform.

6. See case written by Wilkens and Hehir concerning Janet's efforts at the Mason to rein in outside funding. Wilkens, Christian, and Hehir, Thomas. *The Samuel W. Mason Elementary School, Part II.* Harvard Graduate School of Education: Programs in Professional Education. Cambridge, MA: President and Fellows of Harvard College, 2007.

7. Rose and Meyer, *Universally Designed Classroom.*

8. Hehir, Thomas. *The Impact of Due Process on the Programmatic Decisions of Special Education Directors.* Dissertation, Harvard University, Cambridge, MA, 1990.

9. Smith, J. O., and Colon, R. J. (1998). Legal Responsibilities Toward Students with Disabilities: What Every Administrator Should Know. *National Association of Secondary School Administrators Bulletin,* January 1998, 41–53.

10. See Report to Congress on the Implementation of IDEA. OESP Annual Reports to Congress. Available at: http://www2.ed.gov/about/reports/annual/osep/index.html

11. Elmore, Richard F. *School Reform from the Inside Out: Policy, Practice, and Performance.* Cambridge, MA: Harvard Education Press, 2004.

12. Shapiro, Joseph P. *No Pity: People with Disabilities Forging a New Civil Rights Movement.* New York: Random House, 1993.

13. Ferguson, P. M., and Asch, A. Lessons from Life: Personal and Parental Perspectives on School, Childhood and Disability. In D. Biklen, D. Ferguson, and A. Ford (eds.), *Schooling and Disability: Eighty-Eighth Yearbook of the National Society for the Study of Education: Part II* (pp. 108–141). Chicago: University of Chicago Press, 1989.

14. Hehir, *New Directions in Special Education.*

15. Ravitz, Diane. *The Death and Life of the Great American School System.* New York: Basic Books, 2010.

16. Hehir, T., and Mosqueda, E. *San Diego Unified School District Special Education Issues Document.* Cambridge, MA: Thomas Hehir & Associates, 2007; Hehir, Thomas. Charters: Students with Disabilities Need Not Apply? *Education Week,* January 27, 2010, 29(19), 18–21.

17. Ferguson and Asch, Lessons from Life.

18. Ibid., p. 9.

19. Ibid., p. 118.

20. Ibid., p. 129.

21. Hehir, Thomas. *New Directions in Special Education: Eliminating Abelism in Policy and Practice.* Cambridge, MA: Harvard Education Press, 2005.

22. SEELS: Available at: http://www.seels.net/grindex.htm; NLTS: National Longitudinal Transition Study-2 (NLTS-2), U.S. Department of Education, Office of Special Education Programs (OSEP 2001–2011) and Institute of Education Sciences (IES 2000–2011), is a follow-up of the original National Longitudinal Transition Study. The original NLTS was designed and conducted by SRI International for OSEP from 1985 through 1993. Available at: http://www.nlts2.org/

23. Patton, M. Q. *Qualitative Research and Evaluation Methods,* 3rd ed. Thousand Oaks, CA: Sage, 2002.

24. Minow, M. *In Brown's Wake: Legacies of America's Educational Landmark.* New York: Oxford University Press, 2010.

25. Ibid., p. 389.

CHAPTER 7: HOW EDUCATION POLICY AFFECTS OUR SCHOOLS

1. Elmore, R. Education and Federalism: Doctrinal, Functional, and Strategic Views. In D. Kirp and D. Jensen (eds.), *School Days, Rule Days* (pp. 166–185). Stanford, CA: Stanford Series on Education and Public Policy, 1986.

2. Ibid.

3. Minow, M. *In Brown's Wake: Legacies of America's Educational Landmark.* New York: Oxford University Press, 2010.

4. Ibid, p. 1.

5. Graham, Patricia Albjerg. *Schooling America: How the Public Schools Meet the Nation's Changing Needs.* New York: Oxford University Press, 2005.

6. *A Nation at Risk: The Imperative For Educational Reform.* 1983 report of President Ronald Reagan's National Commission on Excellence in Education. http://www2.ed.gov/pubs/NatAtRisk/risk.html

7. Hess, Frederick, and Petrilli, Michael J. *No Child Left Behind Primer.* New York: Peter Lang, 2006.

8. Ibid., p. 33.

9. Hehir, Tom, and Gamm, Sue. Special Education: From Legalism to Collaboration. In Jay Heubert (ed.), *Law and School Reform* (pp. 205–243). New Haven, CT: Yale University Press, 1999.

10. Fullan, Michael. *The New Meaning of Educational Change,* 4th ed. New York: Teachers College Press, 2007, p. 241.

11. Hess and Petrilli, *No Child Left Behind Primer,* pp. 119–134.

12. Wilkens, Christian P., *Students with Disabilities in Urban Massachusetts Charter Schools: Access, Inclusion, and Policy.* Dissertation. Cambridge, MA: Harvard Graduate School of Education, 2009.

13. Hehir, Thomas. Charters: Students with Disabilities Need Not Apply? *Education Week*, January 27, 2010, 29(19), 18–21.

14. National Assessment of Educational Progress (NAEP). http://nces.ed.gov/nationsreportcard/

CHAPTER 8: WHERE SPECIAL EDUCATION NEEDS TO GO

1. Elmore, Richard F. *School Reform from the Inside Out: Policy, Practice, and Performance.* Cambridge, MA: Harvard Education Press, 2004.

2. Wilkens, Christian P. *Students with Disabilities in Urban Massachusetts Charter Schools: Access, Inclusion, and Policy*. Dissertation, Harvard University, Cambridge, MA, 2009; Hehir, T., and Mosqueda, E. *San Diego Unified School District Special Education Issues Document*. Cambridge, MA: Thomas Hehir & Associates, 2007; Marcell, Elizabeth. *Choice, Charter Schools, and Students with Disabilities: Special Education Enrollment in Post-Katrina New Orleans Charter Schools*. Dissertation, Harvard University, Cambridge, MA, 2010.

3. Shaywitz, S. *Overcoming Dyslexia: A New and Complete Science-Based Program for Reading Problems at Any Level*. New York: Knopf, 2003.

4. Cortiella, Candace. *Rewards and Roadblocks: How Special Education Students Are Faring Under No Child Left Behind*, 2009. New York: National Center for Learning Disabilities. Available at: http://www.ncld.org/on-capitol-hill/policy-related -publications/rewards-a-roadblocks

5. Grindal, Todd, Eidelman, Hadas, Marcell, Elizabeth, and Hehir, Thomas. *A Review of Special Education in the Houston Independent School District*. Cambridge, MA: Thomas Hehir & Associates, 2011.

6. Marshall, Kim. Merit Pay or Team Accountability. *Education Week*, September 1, 2010, pp. 20–24.

7. Hehir and Mosqueda, *San Diego Unified School District Special Education Issues Document*.

8. *Independent Charter Schools Accessibility Report*. Los Angeles Unified School District, Office of the Independent Monitor, February 22, 2010.

9. Wilkens, Christian, and Hehir, Thomas. *The Samuel W. Mason Elementary School, Part II*. Harvard Graduate School of Education, Programs in Professional Education. Cambridge, MA: President and Fellows of Harvard College, 2007.

10. Ibid.

11. *Democracy Prep Charter School Progress Report, 2010*. New York City Department of Education.

12. *Sacramento City Unified School District v. Rachel Holland*, 14 F.3d 1398 (9th Cir. 1994); *Oberti v. Board of Education of the Borough of Clementon School District*, 995 F.2d 1204 (3d Cir. 1993).

13. Hehir, Thomas. *The Impact of Due Process on the Programmatic Decisions of Special Education Directors*. Dissertation, Harvard University, Cambridge, MA, 1990.

14. Hehir, T., Karger, J., and Katzman, L. Reforming Urban Education. *Teachers College Record*, December 21, 2005. (ID Number: 12267). http://www.tcrecord .org/AuthorDisplay.asp?aid=19048

15. Hehir, T., Gruner, A., Karger, J., and Katzman, L. *Hancock v. Driscoll: Special education assessment.* Unpublished report, June 2003; Hehir et al., Reforming Urban Education; Hehir and Mosqueda, *San Diego Unified School District Special Education Issues Document.*

16. Weik, K. E. Administering Education in Loosely Coupled Schools. *Phi Delta Kappan,* 1982, 63(10), 673–676.

AFTERWORD

1. Newton Resident Advocating for Changes in Special Ed Law. *Newton* (Massachusetts) *TAB,* July 14, 2011. Available at: http://www.wickedlocal.com/newton/archive/x1223068302/Newton-resident-advocating-for-changes-in-special-ed-law#ixzz1SqisdLm5

APPENDIX B: INFORMATION ON THE RESEARCH STUDY

1. The O'Hearn's name was changed in 2009 to the William T. Henderson Elementary Inclusion School after Bill Henderson's retirement.

2. Passing indicates that students met the MCAS standards of Proficient, Advanced, or Needs Improvement. The only other category is Warning/Failing.

3. Massachusetts Department of Elementary and Secondary Education. *School and District Profiles,* 2005. Available at: http://profiles.doe.mass.edu/help/data.aspx

4. Donovan, S., and Cross, C. *Minority Students in Special and Gifted Education.* Washington, DC: National Academy Press, 2002.

5. The standard for disproportionality is 20 percentage points difference between the overall population of students of a particular race in the school and the population of students with disabilities in the school in that same race. Oswald, Donald P., Coutinho, Martha J., and Best, Al M. Predictors of Overrepresentation of Minority Children in Special Education. In D. Losen and G. Orfield (eds.), *Racial Inequity in Special Education.* Cambridge, MA: The Civil Rights Project and the Harvard Education Press, 2002.

6. The percentage of enrolled students who received one or more out-of-school suspensions (Massachusetts Department of Elementary and Secondary Education).

7. Ibid.

8. Two of the leaders whom we call principals were technically called headmasters. As this title held no different responsibilities than the title of principal, for the

sake of simplicity and consistency, we use only the term *principal*. In addition, the two principals at BAA were co-principals.

9. Wilkens, Christian, and Hehir, Thomas. *The Samuel W. Mason Elementary School, Part II.* Harvard Graduate School of Education, Programs in Professional Education. Cambridge, MA: President and Fellows of Harvard College, 2007.

10. Yin, Robert K. *Case Study Research: Design and Methods,* 3rd ed. Thousand Oaks, CA: Sage, 1994.

11. Bolman, L. G., and Deal, T. E. *Reframing Organizations: Artistry, Choice and Leadership,* 3rd ed. San Francisco: Jossey-Bass, 2003.

12. Skrtic, T. M. The Special Education Paradox: Equity as the Way to Excellence. In T. Hehir and T. Latus (eds.), *Special Education at the Century's End: Evolution of Theory and Practice Since 1970* (pp. 203–372). Cambridge, MA: Harvard Education Press, 1992. (Originally published in *Harvard Educational Review,* 1991, 61(2), 148–206)

13. Skrtic, in Hehir and Latus, *Special Education at the Century's End,* p. 207.

14. Ibid.

15. Ibid., p. 238.

16. Ibid.

17. Elmore, Richard F. *School Reform from the Inside Out: Policy, Practice and Performance.* Cambridge, MA: Harvard Education Press, 2004, p. 3.

18. Abelmann, Charles, Elmore, Richard, Even, Johanne, and Kenyon, Susan. When Accountability Knocks, Will Anyone Answer? Philadelphia: CPRE Publications, 1999. (ERIC: ED428463)

19. Wagner, R. B. *Accountability in Education: A Philosophical Inquiry.* New York: Routledge, 1989.

20. Abelmann, Charles, Elmore, Richard, Even, Johanne, and Kenyon, Susan. *When Accountability Knocks, Will Anyone Answer?* Philadelphia: CPRE Publication, 1999, p. 3. (ERIC: ED428463).

21. Abelmann, Elmore, et al., *When Accountability Knocks, Will Anyone Answer?,* p. 3.

22. Ibid.

23. Abelmann, Elmore, et al., *When Accountability Knocks, Will Anyone Answer?*

24. Ibid., p. 140.

INDEX

A

Abelism, ix–xiv

Abelmann, Charles, 88, 219–222

Accountability, 88–97; and accountability mechanisms, 89; collective, 93–94; external, 95–97; and individual responsibility, 92–93; internal, 94–95

Adequate yearly progress (AYP; NCLB), 161, 166, 173, 182, 186, 189, 191

Administrators: and collaborative culture, 119–120; role of, in universally designed schools, 119–122

African American community, 93

African American students, 33, 73, 106, 144, 165–166, 182, 212–214; at BAA, 16; at Mason, 14, 27, 28; and NCLB, 165–166; at O'Hearn, 8

Alice (teacher, O'Hearn), 49

Allen v. *McDonough,* 164, 198

Alvin Ailey American Dance Theatre, 16

American Recovery and Reinvestment Act, 187

American Sign Language, 29, 70, 92, 146, 154

Americans with Disabilities Act, 101

Andrews, Seth, 195

Angelique (student, Tucker), 108, 109

Annenberg Foundation, 176

Anthony (Henderson), ix, x, xiii

Asche, Adrienne, xiii, 146, 150, 151

Asian students, 213, 214; at BAA, 16; at Hunter, 73; at O'Hearn, 8; at Tucker, 106

Australia, 33

Autism, ix, xx, 6, 8, 14, 66, 92, 102, 115, 142, 146, 168, 194, 195, 199, 203, 209, 212

AYP. *See* Adequate yearly progress (AYP)

B

BAA. *See* Boston Arts Academy

Behavioral disabilities, xii, 12, 66, 112, 114, 116, 122, 136, 145, 146

Bev (O'Hearn), 81, 83, 85, 116, 118

Bilingual education programs, 102

Blair (visual arts teacher, BAA), 45, 52–53, 57, 80, 83, 85, 113, 115

Blindness, xiii, 11, 33, 92, 144, 146, 150–154, 195

Board of Education, Brown v., 164

Board of Education of the Borough of Clementon School District, Oberti v., 196

Congress, 141, 142

Corrective action, 96

"Cosby Show" (television series), 202

Courageous Conversations About Race: A Field Guide for Achieving Equity in Schools (Singleton and Linton), 49

D

Dare to Dream: Sharing African American History Through Storytelling (student performance; O'Hearn), 5

Deaf students, xx, 16, 35, 36, 44, 64, 71, 86, 92, 101, 106, 135, 144, 146, 147, 153, 154, 195, 209, 212

Deal, Terrence, 31–32, 53

Dedicated time, 121–122

"Default culture," 39

Default culture (Elmore), 39, 91

Delphine (O'Hearn), 48, 49, 51, 105

Democracy Prep Charter School (Harlem, New York City), 195

Developmental Disability Act, 197

Dilemma of difference (Minow), 154

Direct assistance to children and families, 162

Disability equity, 93, 177

Distributed leadership, 132–133

District leadership, five lessons for: and creating specialized inclusive schools in large urban districts, 144–147; and holding harmless resources, 148–149; and selectively supporting entrepreneurial principals, 147–148; and supporting efforts to extend time, 148; and supporting inclusive education, 143–144

Dorchester, Massachusetts, 8

Down Syndrome, 5, 8, 10, 201, 202

"Drill and kill" remedial approaches, 80

Driscoll, Dave, 176

Dyslexic students, xii, 69, 71, 92, 102, 134, 172, 188

E

Early Periodic Screening and Testing Program (EPSDT), 170

Echelson, Drew, 107–110

Education of All Handicapped Children Act (IDEA Part B; 1975), 164

Education policy: federal, 163–171; how, affects our schools, 161–178; importance of support from school superintendent in, 176; local, 174–177; policy mechanisms for, 162; state, 171–174

Education Reform Act (Massachusetts; 1993), 171

"Egg crate" structures, 37, 46–47, 64

Elementary and Secondary Education Act (ESEA; 1964), 163–167; specific policy recommendations for, 186–196. *See also* No Child Left Behind (NCLB)

Elmore, Richard, 39, 80, 88–92, 94, 95, 138, 185, 218–223

Emotional disabilities, 212

English language learners (ELL), 86, 165

Entrepreneurial activities, 38–40

Entrepreneurial opportunities, 133

ETFs. *See* Evaluation team facilitators (ETFs)

Evaluation team facilitators (ETFs), 41

Even, Johanne, 88, 219–222

External accountability, 95–97

IEP. *See* Individualized education plan (IEP)

ILT. *See* Instructional leadership team (ILT)

Improving America's School Act (IASA), 165

Inclusion: as benefit to all kids, 9–10; as central mission, 19–22; differing from norm in, xx–xxii; identifying successful schools in, xx; promising news on, xviii–xix

Inclusion cacophony, 129–131

Inclusive mission: centrality of, 19–22; and mission-driven leaders, 20–22; teacher support for, 19–20

Inclusive vision, 132

Individualized education plan (IEP), 42, 62, 108, 111, 118, 140, 141, 168, 217

Individuals with Disabilities Education Act (IDEA), 62, 63, 96, 97, 108, 109, 123, 134, 141, 142, 149, 161, 182, 217; amendments to (1997), 168; in federal education policy, 167–168; and future direction of special education, 196–199; Least Restrictive Environment (LRE) provisions, 63, 167; Part B: Education of All Handicapped Children Act (1975), 164; Part D (discretionary programs), 169, 199

Instructional leadership team (ILT), 12, 13, 52

Internal accountability, 94–95

J

John (teacher, BAA), 82

Jones, Quincy, 16

K

Karen (teacher, Mason), 20, 49, 51, 52, 84, 85, 104–105, 112, 113, 118

Katzman, Lauren, 216

Kennedy administration, 164

Kenyon, Susan, 88, 219–222

Kipp Tech Valley (Albany, New York), 195

Kozol, J., 49

Kurzweil, Ray, 39

Kurzweil technology (text-to-speech software), 9, 39, 69–70

L

Lampron, Trish, 136–137

Latin America, 33

Leaders, 25–53; and each school taking own path to inclusion, 34–36; and emergence of inclusive network, 44; and entrepreneurial activities strengthening structures, 38–40; and how they led their schools, 31–53; and human resource frame, 46–53; and political frame, 40–41; and politics of district office, 41–44; and power of teacher, 44–46; and professional development defined, 48–49; and structural frame, 37–38; and symbolic actions large and small, 36; and symbolic frame, 32–34

Learning disabilities, 212

Least Restrictive Environment provisions (IDEA), 63, 167, 182–183, 197, 198, 217

Leigh (special education supervisor, Mason), 42, 120

Linton, C., 49

Professional bureaucracies, 60–61

Professional development: activities chosen dependent upon teacher collaboration, 51–53; activities chosen with teacher input, 51; definition of, 48–49; role of, in universally designed schools, 118; teachers' commitment to, 50; teachers' relationships supporting, 50–51

Protection and Advocacy Centers, 197

Q

Questions for discussion, 205–208

R

Race to the Top, 174, 187, 193

Rachel Holland, Sacramento City Unified School District v., 196

Rauscher, Laura, x

Readers and Writers Workshops (Annenberg Foundation), 176, 184

Reading First Program (NCLB), 176–177, 192

Reframing Organizations (Bolman and Deal), 31–32

Regulations, 162

Rehabilitation Act (1973), 163; Section 504, 163, 164

Relationships, 80–82; as supporting mission, 82–83

Research study: Bolman and Deal framework for, 215–216; data collection and analysis in, 214–215; and demographics, 212–213; and school academic data, 210–212; and school demographics (percentages), 213; and selection of schools, 209; theoretical

frameworks and analysis for, 215–222; and Thomas Skrtic, 216–218

Response to intervention (RTI), xxi, 102, 106–112, 207

Responsibility, individual, 92–93

Riley, Richard, 170

Rose, David, 103, 104, 139

Rousso, Marylyn, 150-151

Roxbury section, Boston, Massachusetts, 13

RTI. *See* Response to intervention (RTI)

S

Sacramento City Unified School District v. *Rachel Holland,* 196

Samantha (special education teacher, O'Hearn), 47, 84, 92, 113

Samantha (teacher, O'Hearn), 19

Samuel W. Mason Elementary School (Mason), xx, xxi, 5, 21, 33, 38, 39; approach to improving literacy instruction, 71; as counter-cultural, 46; evaluation team facilitator (ETF) at, 42; as gem among warehouses, 11–15; Janet Palmer Owens as leader at, 27–28; mission statement, 19; selection criteria for, 209–210

San Diego, California, 194–195

San Juan, Puerto Rico, 28

School culture: collaboration and coherence in, 83–88; evolvement of coherent effective, 86–88

School leaders, seven lessons for, 131–138; and establishing inclusive vision, 132; and establishing strong relationships with parents and community, 134; and establishing structures that

Tucker Elementary school (Milton, Massachusetts), xxi, 149; funding for, 111–112; moving toward instructional leadership at, 107–108; new principal at, 107; Reader and Writers Workshop, 109, 110; response to intervention (RTI) at, 109–110, 122; results at, 112; and RTI in action, 110–111; special education at, 108–109; as suburban RTI success, 106–112

Turtle Haven school, 90–91, 222

Tyack, D., 61

U

UDL. *See* Universal design for learning (UDL)

Universal design for learning (UDL), 101–118, 131, 132, 135, 137, 139, 183–185, 192–193, 207

Universally Designed Classroom (Rose and Meyers), 139

Universally designed schools, 101–123; and intensive supports for some students, 116–117; role of administrators in, 119–120; role of professional development in, 118; and teachers working together to improve student behavior, 117–118; and universal design and schooling, 102–104; and universal design for living (UDL), 101–118; and universally designed instruction, 104–112; and universally designed positive behavior supports, 112–116

U.S. Department of Education, 163, 170, 184

U.S. Supreme Court, 163, 164

W

Wagner, R. B., 88–89, 219

Washington D.C., 198

Wellesley College, 150

"When Accountability Knocks, Will Anyone Answer?" (Abelman, Elmore, Even, and Kenyon), 88, 219

Why Anansi Has Eight Legs (African folk tale), 6

Wilkens, Christian, 195

Will, Madeline, 132

William T. Henderson Elementary Inclusion School (formerly Patrick O'Hearn Elementary School), ix, x, xiii, xx, xxi, 5, 74, 106, 173, 201

Y

YouTube, 5, 106

CPSIA information can be obtained at www.ICGtesting.com
Printed in the USA
BVOW02n0526240614

356949BV00007B/14/P